Art and Sex

in
Greenwich Village

Art and Sex
in
Greenwich Village

Gay Literary Life After Stonewall

FELICE PICANO

CARROLL & GRAF PUBLISHERS
NEW YORK

ART AND SEX IN GREENWICH VILLAGE
Gay Literary Life After Stonewall

Carroll & Graf Publishers
An Imprint of Avalon Publishing Group, Inc.
245 West 17th Street, 11th Floor
New York, NY 10011

AVALON
publishing group incorporated

Copyright © 2007 by Felice Picano

First Carroll & Graf edition 2007

This memoir is a product of the author's recollections and is thus rendered as a subjective accounting of events that occurred in his/her life.

All photographs are taken from the author's personal collection.

ISBN-13: 978-0-78671-813-9
ISBN-10: 0-7867-1813-7

9 8 7 6 5 4 3 2 1

Book design by Bettina Wilhelm

Printed in the United States of America
Distributed by Publishers Group West

Preface

Over the past five or six years, I've found myself in the unusual position of historian. I've written features articles for *The Gay and Lesbian Review,* and in *Advocate* interviews and articles for *Out,* I've explained or corrected younger writers' often wildly erroneous views on what our life was like a mere twenty or thirty years ago. Errors do tend to creep in and through the Internet, errors are instantly perpetuated unchanged forever and all over the e-verse. So this is a real problem.

I'm a man in my early sixties now, and more importantly, I'm a survivor, not just of AIDS, but of the sixties and seventies drug and dance scene, the Vietnam War era, of poverty, and of depression. So this new role is sort of to be expected.

But it's a role I never prepared for. In the parlance of the counterculture, I was supposed to live hard, die young, and leave a beautiful corpse, as so many men of my time actually did—men smarter, more talented, better looking, and just plain better than me. In a way I'm an anachronism; I sometimes feel I don't belong here, and I keep thinking there's this enormous party going on filled with all the cool people I used to know who are now dead and wondering where I am.

Beyond chicly late is where.

A book like this is filled with those dead: gay men and lesbians, mostly, who accomplished enough to be famous years after they are gone, many who were well-known then and are not known at all now, or only a little known—and some never appreciated in their time. In some ways this text is a corrective to a great many academic texts, web sites, and online info centers that distort—knowingly or not—what really happened, what was important to us, what counted at the time.

Of course, witnesses are notoriously unreliable and often out of whack with reality. Except that in my case I've got two firm supports. The prime one is the now close to thirty volumes of journals I've been keeping since 1968, writing one entry every physically healthy day of my life, that I've used to check for the information here. (The earliest twenty-odd volumes are, along with many of my papers, are now housed in Yale University's Beinecke Rare Book & Manuscript Library). If I write dialogue herein, it's generally taken directly from the journals; if not, it was called up to my memory by reading a particular entry in my journals.

Because my second support is my memory, which is—pleasure or curse—amazingly good, what is now called eidetic and used to be called a photographic memory, I've since trained to be as precise as I could make it. I can take down directions off MapQuest, look at them once, leave them home and still easily find what I'm looking for. I used to drive my partners nuts when we would argue as I not only repeated their words back to them verbatim but told them what was cooking at the time and what music was playing in the background. Many, many memories are etched indelibly in my mind; I'm not sure whether I want them to remain or wish they would go, since they range from the precise sounds of a loved one's death rattle to a night at the Ice Palace in the summer of 1974 when my shirtless partner Don Eike and I slid, dancing, through the tightly packed crowd on our perspiration, from one end of the long place to another, while humidity covered every possible mirrored or hard surface with mist.

I'd like to emphasize some things before you read this book. First, yes, we did know what we were doing in pioneering gay literature, gay publishing, and a gay arts scene; what we didn't know was that it would end up being *the* scene, and thus of historical importance. Like all young people with too much talent, energy, and frustration with the status quo we did aim to change things. But it's a surprising product of our achievement that we changed things so completely that most GLBT people alive today are unaware that pretty much most of their "establishment" was created within such a short time by so few people and so recently; it all seems so very entrenched.

I recall a very young photographer, Don Herron, visiting from Texas in the early 1980s. For his degree, he was shooting people in bathtubs. He couldn't do that back in modest, fundamentalist Texas, but he had no trouble finding subjects willing to bare all or most in Manhattan. As a result, his photo-thesis turns out to entail an entire, unparalleled age of the New York bohemian scene—shots of people from Divine and Cookie Mueller to Robert Mapplethorpe, from designer Halston's boyfriend Victor Hugo to footballer Dave Kopay to of course, yours truly. In a way that happened because that really might have been the last time that an entire bohemian art scene existed in one place and at one time.

This book was started several years ago when I began exhibiting the art, photos, books, manuscripts, letters, papers, and other pieces that comprise the historical art exhibit Early Gay Presses of New York. The lectures I gave, which got longer and more complex, and the little tours I led only brought more questions, far more than I could handle in person.

At first I thought it would be another memoir, like the three I had already published. But then I found myself having to explain in detail certain things, almost from the beginning: why did I begin my press, SeaHorse, with a poetry book, and not fiction, for example? How was the literary minimalist movement (now just a footnote) crucial to short story writing and to Gay Presses of New York? What happened to the explosion of lesbian and gay theater we helped engender and witnessed? Where is it now?

Also, the more I wrote, the more I wanted to find out what happened to those many authors whose careers my partners and I at SeaHorse, Calamus, JH Press, and GPNy helped launch: Harvey Fierstein, Jane Chambers, Dennis Cooper, Brad Gooch, and Robert Glück, just to name a few. I'd been too busy to look into it over the years.

So this book is a hybrid: a memoir, yet a history, too.

I know that this book is as "true" as I could make it. I hope that it is also entertaining, accurate, and above all, a useful text now and later on. GLBT history is short but full, and there are still huge gaps to be filled. We still need a history of leather clubs, of women's coffee shops and the music and poetry they brought into being, of gay bars and discos of the 1970s, of tough dyke clubs in the 1950s and 1960s. People are still alive who know about all these subjects and many are willing to impart their knowledge. All we need are more people willing to ask them. I also think it is significant, even if I'm not sure how, exactly, that although I applied for a more than a half dozen grants over the four years of research and composition for this book, from a variety of places supposedly devoted to supporting this kind of work, that not one such entity saw fit to aid me.

—*Felice Picano*

1

Key West and a Sea Horse

The idea for starting a gay publishing company came to me one afternoon while bathing in the surf of one of the rocky little limestone beaches of Key West, Florida, in the winter of 1976. In truth, the idea only began to solidify then. I'd been interested in opening my own publishing house for some years before that—if only to be able to publish my own, supposedly unpublishable, although not gay-themed work. And of course in all those years before, I'd never had the money to do so.

The sea horse as the originating motif and then as the name of my new press came a few days after I arrived in the Conch Republic when one afternoon at the beach I noticed the very nicely muscled biceps of a sexy Italian-American young man, a man who stood out both because of his slickly beautiful body and because of the really nice artwork of the tattoo. After a few hours of staring at him and getting little or nothing in the way of a response, I at last conquered my natural shyness, went over to him as he was coming out of the water again and wiping himself down with his towel, and asked why he was sporting a tattoo of the small marine animal.

Relieved, I guess, that it wasn't an attempted pickup, or if so, at least a pickup with an interesting opening line, he explained that the sea horse is one of the few animals in nature where the male parent actually bears the young and gives birth. As he was a male artist, the sea horse had become a sort of totem to him of the single, creative male in nature. Like myself, he was in Key West for a few months that winter, but he was trying to get paintings done for an upcoming two-man show in, I believe, Boston, where he lived.

I don't remember his name and I subsequently saw little of him in Key West—once or twice on a bicycle, coming or going from the daily spectacle of "sunset" at Mallory Pier, but never at any bar, restaurant, or tea dance, and never again once I'd left Key West. If he's still among us, he may remember meeting me and that, I'm sure, awkward and inept conversation. I'd be happy to give him credit for naming what would become a path-breaking and prestigious little venture that surprisingly turned out to be significant to modern gay literature and even gay culture.

By early February 1976, one of my novels *had* been published: the second one I'd written (the first remains unpublished to this day), the psychological thriller *Smart as the Devil*. Furthermore, it had been nominated for the Ernest Hemingway Award, newly instituted that year to honor first published fiction writers. Although my book had earned me a typically meager first-novel advance from Arbor House—my boss at Rizzoli Books, where I was still working at the time, mocked me, and the amount I received, when I told him I was quitting work to become an author. The book went on to sell paperback rights to Dell, was taken by the Literary Guild Book Club, and had since sold British and German rights: a total which *had* allowed me to leave Rizzoli.

My next mainstream novel, another thriller about relationships on the singles scene, *Eyes*, had sold to Arbor House at three times the amount of the first book, and it, too, was picked up by Dell, the book club, and even more foreign publishers—in Portugal and Japan! *Eyes* was written in 1975, mostly at Fire Island, finished in September in Manhattan, and published exactly a year later in hardcover.

I'd already long had a concept for my third novel, and I'd written that entire novel, completed it on December 29, just before the new year of 1976. My advance for that book, *The Mesmerist*, a psychological novel set at the turn of the twentieth century in Nebraska Territory, and the fee from Dell Books, were substantially higher than anything I'd received before. For the first time since I'd worked as an editor for a graphic arts magazine seven years before, I was on financially solid ground.

By the time my visit to Key West was over, and thanks to a bicycle accident, I had a splint on my arm. On the jet from Miami to New York, I met an extremely cute Canadian air steward who took one look at me struggling down the aisle with my arm splint and one tiny carry-on bag and insisted on helping me, putting me in the last empty row of seats right next to his station in the back of the plane. As a result of our conversation, we became quite friendly during the three-hour flight and I dated him the next night in Manhattan and saw him on and off about a year afterward.

One of the things I talked about with my newfound friend were my future plans for the SeaHorse Press. And as the airplane was landing at Kennedy Airport, I remember thinking, *How exciting. Now I'm going to begin a gay publishing company and publish my book of poetry.*

This was almost immediately followed by a thought of equal intensity— and absolute terror. Because the truth was, although I'd now had several books of my own published, I didn't know the first thing about *how* to publish, or, truthfully, even how to put a book together. And I was going to have to learn fast.

———

The SeaHorse Press would be the first East Coast gay publishing company, the first consciously-begun gay male literary press, and the second gay publishing company in the world. By the time I began it, in the spring of 1977, no one else had the concept of a company like SeaHorse, which would put out nothing but gay-themed poetry, short stories, plays, fiction, and nonfiction: work that was, in the words of SeaHorse's premiere announcement, both "fine and accessible literature."

The very first publisher to do openly gay male books as gay books, and not as some kind of once-in-a-while avocation, was Winston Leyland's Gay Sunshine Press in San Francisco—not long before, and almost as an afterthought. Gay Sunshine had started up as a quarterly magazine in a folio newspaper format in the latter days of the peace-love-drugs era, with typically hippie-style graphics and formats.

Leyland's had been one of the first, and one of the very few magazines to publish openly gay poetry, which was how I came to know of it. When I finally collected my poems in my 1978 volume, a half dozen had previously appeared in *Gay Sunshine* magazine.

But Gay Sunshine's first books were less original concepts than compilations of already existing material: an anthology of poetry culled from the magazine, another of translations Leyland himself had done of some Central American homoerotic literature. They also published a pamphlet-length interview between my friend, gay activist Allen Young, with Allen Ginsberg, who'd gone to Castro's Cuba and discovered how appallingly gay Cubanos were being treated. I believe this was Gay Sunshine's biggest seller in its early period and for many years thereafter.

The only other periodical that regularly published my—and other writers'—gay poetry before I collected it in a single volume was *Mouth of the Dragon,* a handsome, slender quarterly put out by a handsome, slender New Yorker named Andrew Bifrost. Some of the poets from those early magazines and volumes were Paul Mariah, Harold Norse, Ian Young, Allen Ginsberg, John Giorno, Kirby Congdon, James Broughton, Antler, and Maurice Kinney, an Englishman who published a controversial poem about Jesus Christ being gay. Notably *not* to be found in those few gay magazines or early gay anthologies of the time was work by poets including James Merrill, Richard Howard, John Ashbery, or even Thom Gunn, all of whom were still professionally closeted. Their friend and colleague, Greenwich Village bohemian Edward Field, however, had already put out some of the best gay poetry around in a collection called *Variety Photoplays,* which stood up even decades later. Distinguished poet James Schuyler, who was in and out of Payne Whitney Psychiatric Clinic in those years, would also come out soon enough in his work and life.

The short-lived New York–based newspaper *Gaysweek* also published gay poetry, including one of my poems. My first published gay short story, "The Interrupted Recital," (later to appear in my collections *Slashed to Ribbons in Defense of Love* and *The New York Years*) also came out in *Gaysweek*'s "Arts & Letters" section in March 1978, almost the same time that my poetry book was published.

Lesbian literature and publishing had fared a lot better than men's work in terms of output, partly because the early 1970s saw the rise of feminism as a political movement. The formation of the National Organization for Women (NOW), and its many famous spokeswomen with an eventual goal of the passage of the Equal Rights Amendment (ERA) to the U.S. Constitution, was extremely newsworthy at a time when gay rights was still considered freakish and far-out by the media. For many women, the philosophy could be summed up in the message soon seen on bumper stickers: "Feminism is the philosophy. Lesbianism is the practice." Untrue as that would later actually prove to be, politically speaking, lesbians interested in furthering their culture in the early 1970s received all kinds of support from feminists in a way rare for openly gay men.

Among the early women's presses that either put out lesbian books or were open to them were Women's Press Collective (*Lesbians Speak Out*), Diana Press, poet Alta's Shameless Hussy Press, Daughters Inc., Persephone, Seal Press, and the longest-lived of them all, Naiad Press. Begun by life-partners Barbara Grier and Donna K. McBride in 1974, Naiad started slowly but then consistently published books for women, and especially for gay women: novels, romances, poetry, nonfiction, sci-fi, and when author Katherine V. Forrest came along, a slew of mysteries.

Meanwhile, books like Rita Mae Brown's *Rubyfruit Jungle,* put out by a Daughters Inc. in 1973, did so well that Bantam, a major paperback house, picked it up in 1977. Still, for every *Rubyfruit* or *Sexual Politics* or *Sappho Was a Right-On Woman,* both by Kate Millet, there were a score of other women's books, such as *Our Bodies, Our Selves,* Marilyn French's *The Woman's Room,* and Erica Jong's *Fear of Flying,* feminist titles that ignored or quickly passed over any lesbian issues.

The feminist bookstores that arose in this period included Labyris, Charis, I.C.I., A Woman's Place, and Sisterhood Bookstore in L.A. Only A Woman's Place in Madison, Wisconsin, and Charis are today still in business.

Meanwhile lesbian magazines had been around since the fifties, thanks to Barbara Gittings and the Daughters of Bilitis's official organ, *The Ladder.* Other magazines featuring lesbian literature, such as *The Furies* (1972–73), *The Amazon Quarterly* (1972–75), and *Lesbian Tide* (1971–77) were short-lived, often fraught by monetary woes and political division. One of the best known, *Off Our Backs,* became so politically constricting that several lesbian authors of great talent who were interested in going beyond the accepted feminist code of topics were blatantly excluded. So, for example, Dorothy Allison first came to readers' attention when she published poems and stories in *Christopher Street* and the *New York Native,* a magazine and newspaper more associated with gay males than women.

Other lesbian authors found they were unable to make the leap from small to larger presses. Diana published Judy Grahn's *Common Woman* as early as 1969, and Woman's Press Collective of Oakland put out her *Edward the Dyke* in 1971, but it was only when the title poem of the latter volume crossed into the gay male magazines some years later that Grahn began getting the attention that would lead to her writing important nonfiction for mainstream publishers. Aside from Naiad, which was in the forefront, it really wouldn't be until the mid-1980s that lesbian literature could shake itself free of its earlier feminist connections and concentrate on being literature for gay women. Companies like Firebrand, Cleis, and Seal Press made their marks at that time. By then the ERA had failed to pass and NOW was no longer a burgeoning organization, but one in stasis, or even in decline.

As for bisexual or transgender literature, if there was any literature about those subjects being written, it wasn't being published anywhere this writer is aware of.

What about those famous gay male novels of the sixties and seventies? There were a few—not many—and they have to be divided into two camps: the literary and the pulps.

Christopher Isherwood's first book dealing openly with the subject of homosexuality, *The World in the Evening*, came out in 1954, and according to editors Jim Berg and Chris Freeman in *The Isherwood Century*, was either misunderstood, denounced, or ignored. His next novel, *A Single Man*, his first completely out novel and for many his masterpiece, was published a decade later. Some six months earlier, a pretty much unknown writer who still hustled Los Angeles's downtown Pershing Square published his masterpiece, *City of Night*. Put out several months apart in time, set in the same city less than eight miles distant from each other, these two important novels by Isherwood and John Rechy seem to have been written about two utterly different countries, nations, cultures—dimensions even—they are so very different.

In 1978, when the seven gay writers who would form the Violet Quill Club began to meet and discuss how to make gay life into literature, we kept coming back to these two novels, and to a few other books published around that time: Burt Blechman's *Stations* and Sandford Friedman's *Totem Pole*, Gore Vidal's *The City and the Pillar* and Tennessee Williams's short stories. While we admired all of these works to one degree or another, we also agreed that they were "homosexual" fiction. They reflected *not* the post-Stonewall gay world that all seven of us lived in daily and had lived in for years even before the riots, but instead an earlier era, an earlier mindset—one in which the Stonewall Rebellion and gay politics were not only never anticipated, but also a complete improbability.

Of those five very good writers, only John Rechy really ever made the leap into a post-Stonewall mentality, partly because he was substantially younger than the others, and he did so without losing a scintilla of his own unique style and obsessions. His *Rushes* (1979) is a text of its time, completely contemporaneous with Andrew Holleran's *Dancer from the Dance* and my own first published gay novel, *The Lure*. Tennessee Williams, in his novel *Moise and the World of Reason,* uses as his setting the West Village's crumbling docks, where gay men had group sex nightly in the seventies, yet the book's characters inhabit a softer, more romantic universe than what Arthur Tress's many contemporaneous photos of those docks/sex hangouts would showcase. And Isherwood's outed characters in *Christopher and His Kind,* a rewriting of *Down There on a Visit,* inhabit a novel that deals with homosexual life in the 1920s and 1930s. Gore Vidal would deny that he was gay or wrote gay novels, and even denied there was such a thing as a gay literature. Only Truman Capote of their generation would come out as fully as John Rechy, outing himself on the *Johnny Carson Show* on TV. His last two books, *Music For Chameleons* and *Answered Prayers,* are narrated by a quite gay Capote himself.

Two other novels we Quillians admired, for different reasons, seemed to be what the British call "sports," that is, aberrations, one-offs. These were James Purdy's remarkable (even among his own oeuvre) *Eustache Chisolm and the Works* (1967) and Terry Andrews's *The Story of Harold* (1974). Both dealt with the specialized arena of S/M sexuality foreign to most gay men of the day, and, so like the above-noted novels, they, too, inhabited their own unique universes, not the daily gay one we and most American gay men in Dallas, Los Angeles, San Francisco, New Orleans, Boston, Atlanta, and Washington, D.C., increasingly lived in.

Opposite the literary books were the pulps. These were the gay books you could see every day on wire paperback racks in a few places where gay men lived or hung out: in New York's Times Square or Greenwich Village's Village Cigars, for example, although they weren't for sale a hundred feet across the street at the Sheridan Square Bookstore—a legitimate bookseller. The pulps had titles like *The Boys of Muscle Beach, The Gay Haunt, Whisper His Sin, Mister Madam, Prison Femme,* and my own favorite title, with its sixties futurist thrust, *Keypunch Queen,* about a gay computer operator who trades computer files for sexual service. Very few of these books were read or discussed by the writers I encountered who went on to create a bona fide gay literature, despite Michael Bronski's contention in *Pulp Friction,* his study of these books, that they constituted a "golden age" of gay male literature that lies "outside the canon."

Also outside the canon was popular author Gordon Merrick, who moved in the late 1970s from screenplays and mainstream novels to gay male romances set among the upper crust. Merrick had a huge hit with *The Lord Won't Mind* and then went on to develop a fifteen-year career out of very similar books while living on an Aegean island. But perhaps only one title among the hundreds of pulps published every year, *Song of the Loon,* captured the imaginations of younger gays of the time, probably because it was a sexy, fey western—and most of us actually preferred the satire on it, *Fruit of the Loon,* that wasn't long in arriving. I used to tease my arty friends by telling them that I'd written a pulp and sold it for payment of five hundred dollars and a blow job—the supposed going rate in the late 1960s—under the name Irving Feydreit titled *Elevator Boys in Bondage.*

What the pulps offered readers and the rare if more literary novels either couldn't or didn't seem interested in offering was a sense of gay people pervading regular society on a day-by-day basis. According to the pulps, gay men and lesbians could be found everywhere: in business, in prison, ranching, piloting submarines, drill instructing in the army, on oil rigs, anywhere you looked. And the portraits of gay men and lesbians they offered— although virtually always leading to suicide, institutionalization or (assumed) celibacy in the priesthood—were fairly accurate to what we expected from gay-themed books.

So there we were in what was for me the fateful winter of 1976–77, almost a decade after the 1969 Stonewall Rebellion that had set off the gay liberation political movement, without an authentic literature that reflected this reality. But that was no surprise because what, besides the Gay Activists Alliance, did we have to show for all our rebelling and marching? Certainly no legislative changes. That wouldn't come until later.

We did have gay pride festivals, especially the mid-June Sunday annual marches, which had begun in 1970 and had very slowly grown to include more people watching—and heckling—from the sidelines than people marching in them.

There were also private dance clubs, which, when allied to gay summer resorts, would take on a very special meaning and become an important nexus of gay culture. At first there was the Tenth Floor. It was begun around 1972 by three gay men named Michael in a sixty-by-one-hundred-foot artists' loft on the tenth floor of an otherwise (by day) completely straight commercial building on Twenty-eighth Street between Seventh and Eighth Avenues in Manhattan. The Tenth Floor only held from fifty to a hundred people, and on its busiest night (usually New Year's Eve) the club hosted no more than two hundred people.

Which two hundred people (mostly men) it held, however, was the key to the Tenth Floor's success. Not the rich, not the famous, but the cute. The cute, the sexy, the hip, the mostly out, and of course, those who went to Fire Island for the summer: them, and naturally all the guys they wanted to sleep with or who wanted to sleep with them. The R. Crumb–like cartoon of a totally zonked-out guy that read "No Drugs" on the front door of the Tenth Floor was meant for anyone *but* its members. Inside there was no booze—no liquor license meant no cops harassing them—but instead huge bowls of punch and huge salvers of assorted fruit for snacking on between dancing. The disc jockey of the Tenth Floor was Ray Yates, a pal of mine through artist Jay Weiss, and by the last months of the place Ray's handsome German boyfriend Horst was working the lighting system, which had become significantly more complex.

The 1970s would end up being an age of great dance music and also great DJs. I'm thinking of Howard Merrit and Roy Thode, of Bobby DJ at the Ice Palace, Richie Rivera at Flamingo, and Junior at the Paradise Garage. But among them Ray Yates was first and he was prince. For one thing, Ray *lived* recorded music. He spent hours of every day in record stores—vinyl LPs at the time—all over the New York City metropolitan area, including Far Rockaway, Queens. His tastes were broad, and they were sophisticated. Within months of premiering at the Tenth Floor, Ray had begun to DJ for live fashion runway shows by haute couture designers Halston and Yves Saint Laurent in Europe and the U.S. jazz, salsa, conga, soul, rock, pop, and of course disco all received equal attention from Ray, especially the latter, for this was the age of disco and not since the jitterbug era after World War II had so much dancing overtaken American youth and captured its civilization.

The Loft, south of Houston Street, opened during the last year of the Tenth Floor in a much larger space, on two floors with a balcony. What made it different besides its size was that the Loft depended upon a much more ethnically mixed crowd: African American, Latino, and women members as well as men. Meanwhile, in another artists' loft off Duane Street, much farther downtown in Manhattan and only a few blocks from City Hall, actor and Broadway theater gypsy Michael Fesco opened his place for weekend dancing. Named after the celebrated Havana nightspot that had all but defined pre–Castro era Cuban nightlife, Flamingo was as much the product of Fesco's Cubano-Miami immigrant friends and lovers as of his own artistic imagination. When, in 1975, it moved a half block away from the Loft into a huge space above a bank with an entrance on lower Broadway, it assured itself of instant and total success. At the end of that first season, buses went directly from Flamingo's closing party to the Sayville Ferry Dock leading to Fire Island Pines, and that success was compounded and solidified.

To people outside, on the fringes of gay New York in the 1970s, Studio 54, Ian Schrager and Steve Rubell's semiprivate club in its Sixth Avenue former television studio setting (*The Ed Sullivan Show* had aired there for a decade), appeared to be the *ne plus ultra* night club. But the two owners made sure they'd obtained copies of Flamingo's membership list and sent to all of us on that list free, plastic "Sundays at Studio" membership cards. These turned out to be good for *any* night, and we would exit taxi cabs, glide right past the dressy heterosexual throngs amassed at the front door who were begging to be let in, held in place by various doormen, including in Studio's earliest days, and before he'd made it as an actor, doorman Alec Baldwin.

The various doormen and Rubell confirmed for me in private conversations Studio 54's unspoken yet official policy that "the party inside doesn't begin until the place is half gay." And one very rocking Saturday night, when I left my thrilled out-of-town guests on the dance floor there and went for vodka, I sat next to Rubell and congratulated him on Studio's apparent and very public success. Steve moped, brooded, and in melancholic despair he finally lamented, "Big deal! All the hot guys in New York are at Flamingo tonight."

As for other recognizable signs of a gay culture, well, there were some hopeful newcomers, including *Christopher Street* magazine, begun in September 1976. At first, it was a glossy black-and-white magazine put together on a shoestring budget by writers Charles Ortleb, Thom Steele, and St. Martin's Press book editor Michael Denneny. The latter, when asked exactly what *Christopher Street* was supposed to be, reportedly explained, "A gay *New Yorker*," to which Gore Vidal reportedly quipped, "I thought the *New Yorker was* gay."

It wasn't, of course, although it sure had a lot of gay men—and a few lesbians, too—working for it, and writing for it. The *New Yorker,* in fact, was a case in point about how hidden gays in literature were in this period. One of its top fiction editors, William Maxwell, was gay, and although he'd published a half dozen books by then—*They Came Like Swallows, Ancestors, The Folded Leaf, The Chateau*—it wouldn't be until 1980 that Maxwell allowed the publication of his semigay autobiographical novella, *So Long, See You Tomorrow.* He was in his mid-seventies by then and many of the big, mainstream gay books had been already published.

The New Yorker's poetry editor of the era was Howard Moss, a smart and lovely man. A minor yet quite good poet who discovered and published just about everyone who went on to be anyone in poetry for the next twenty-five years. Moss's greatest coup, however, was getting W. H. Auden under a stipend to the *New Yorker*. This meant that in return for a fixed monthly income until his death, Auden gave Moss any and all of his new poetry, which Howard would then publish. I personally knew Auden around this time, and I remember him crowing about it over dinner at the home of his amanuensis, Orlan Fox, in 1969. But this hardly constituted gay poetry. Auden never 'fessed up to writing the infamous poem, "A Day for a Lay"— though he made sure I got a copy—and when in an ultra-pro-gay mood I cornered him one day and asked Wystan why he never wrote about being gay, he weaseled out of it, saying, "Mother no longer remembers what gay sex is—it was all so long ago."

I happened to meet Howard Moss "socially" around the same time. I use quotation marks around that word because while it's true I encountered Howard at a small party in an apartment on West Twelfth Street in Manhattan once occupied by playwrights Edward Albee and Terrence McNally, the place was by then inhabited by four other gay men who had given the place not a facelift but a name change, to "Oz—where anything can happen and usually does," as well as a rather severe attitude change.

I'd met one of the apartment's occupants, Marty Brennan, at Julius, the legendary Village gay bar, where we'd become friends a few years before. He'd also become part of "The Jane Street Girls" crowd I found myself in when I returned to New York from my stays in Rome and London. Brennan had rented the Albee-McNally place along with Harlan Crandall, who would become known as the Fire Maiden—as in Marty's description of his roomie to strangers, "The Fire Maiden has sex with boys while reciting T. S. Eliot's *Four Quartets*." Tenant number three was Charles Sheffield, soon known as Miss Chuck, and a fourth was a tall, slender man in his forties with a prodigious male member and an international history of directing plays and opera whom I only knew as Miss Kitty. (Chuck being butch around newcomers to Oz would spit out: "Show them your dick, Kitty!") Naturally, the high-spirited and imaginative Marty would become the focus of this drug-, alcohol-, and sex-drenched ménage, and as their LSD-induced fantasies grew bolder, li'l ol' Clark Kentish Marty at last evolved into the fantasy "Tess America Superstar."

How their mild-mannered neighbor Howard Moss entered these madcap gates I'm not sure, although it may have been through an AWOL marine known as the Christmas Child (since that's when he arrived in our midst), whom they all mutually befriended. However, one Sunday afternoon, they did perform a semistaged reading of one of Moss's plays at Oz, in which the Caucasian Marty played the protagonist, a twelve-year-old African-American piano prodigy known as the Black Debussy.

Having learned on one less-than-usually-hallucination-saturated evening exactly who Moss was, came the day of the play I told him I wrote poetry, including some that had been published. "Send it to me at the magazine," Howard said.

"It's gay," I replied, "You'll never publish it."

To which Moss replied, "Probably not, but I'd like to see it anyway." He told me that he kept a dozen of my poems in his desk at the *New Yorker,* including "The Deformity Lover," and I was later told he recommended my book of poems when it was published. But of course, he would *never* publish any of it.

Another gay magazine of the time with an interest in the arts was *Mandate,* a black-and-white photo magazine which purported to be a show business rag under the leadership of its ever-arch editor John Devere, thus allowing it to publish rather spectacular photos of (tastefully) seminude and nude men: actors, dancers, and ballet boys shot by the gay photo wiz of the day, Kenn Duncan. Those photos—and a few others by Jim French, Roy Dean, Old Reliable, and Bob Mizer's semi-camp America Model Guild (AMG) Studio near-nudes holding spears and lariats, pretty much constituted whatever gay visual art was around in 1976. This despite the fact that many of the acclaimed new artists of the 1960s were either bisexual or gay, Andy Warhol and Robert Indiana among them.

What about gay theater, film, and TV? There *was* gay theater. Some. Thanks to Doric Wilson, really, whose new theater company, TOSOS, pretty much said it all. The acronym stood for The Other Side of Silence—pretty definitive. TOSOS's first gay play—Wilson's *Now She Dances,* was first produced in 1975; while *The West Street Gang,* which made Wilson's name in gay (rather than theatrical) circles, was only produced in 1977 and in a gay bar, Spike, on West Twenty-second Street in Manhattan, eight years after Stonewall.

Wilson, along with Robert Patrick, Bill Hoffman (*As Is*), Tom Eyen (*Women Behind Bars*), and Harry Koutoukas, had come out of—I almost wrote *had survived to write about*—that madcap 1960s theatrical breeding ground in Greenwich Village known as Cafe Cino. The place was Joe Cino's wacky brainchild (read Patrick's hysterical novel *Temple Slave* for a prejudiced yet by no means inaccurate view of the place and people). Pulitzer Prize winner Sam Shepherd also began his stellar career in this festering dramaturgical embryo factory—a place that my own younger brother, Jerry Picano, who was on the scene at the time due to his daily drug sharing with some of the more removed Warhol Factory denizens, often referred to as the Cardboard Cafe, as in his own abortive, now lost play of the time, *Johnny Escarole and the Cardboard Café.*

Although playwright Robert Patrick would have his greatest success with a generational, mainstream play, *Kennedy's Children,* in 1973, like Wilson, he had early on penned and had produced gay-themed plays like *The Haunted Host* (1964), *Ludwig and Wagner* (1972), and *Mercy Drop* (1973). But again it was the production of *T-Shirts* in 1978, first at the Out & About Theater in Minneapolis, then later on in New York and San Francisco, that solidified his reputation as a well-known gay playwright.

John Vaccaro and Ronnie Tavel's Playhouse of the Ridiculous was another breeding ground—although by no means at all officially gay—during the late sixties and early seventies. It was at one of their productions, *Conquest of the Universe,* staged at the company's Manhattan theater, that I got my first taste of the collapsing "Fourth Wall" of theater which Richard Foreman and Maria Fornes made so much of philosophically: drawing the audience directly into the action.

Another, this time much more official, Warhol pal, the actor Ondine (star of Warhol's film *The Chelsea Girls*), dropped by my Jane Street apartment to shoot up amphetamine as he and other Factory inhabitants periodically did. But instead of sticking around to sip tea, play Maria Callas records, and chat, as usual, Ondine told me to get "dressed"; we were going out.

A taxi left us at the Seventeenth Street Playhouse of the Ridiculous Theater, and we just made it in before the doors were closed. Our seats were in the third row, middle, and as we sat down and the play began, Ondine began speaking in much more than a stage whisper: "That's *my* part. I was fired last week. That bitch up there sucked John's dick. *That's* how she got the role." With increasing loudness and vituperation, Ondine continued, so that even while I was amused, I was squirming—and looking for a way out. Forget people shushing Ondine. They got an earful back.

Finally Ron Ricard, playing a role onstage, stopped, looked at Ondine in the audience, and said, "Bitch! Face it. You were *too old* for the part." Ondine jumped up and began verbally lashing out. In minutes, Ondine had crawled over seats and people between and was onstage. At which point, I realized he'd been a plant, and I'd been had. Ondine was in the play.

The brilliant Charles Ludlum had worked for and learned a great deal at John Vaccaro and Ronnie Tavel's feet. Ludlum's own Theater of the Ridiculous in the seventies and eighties—always a theatrical must-see during the great age of off-off-Broadway, with plays that combined satire, camp, and often moving drama—would be a direct outgrowth of all the madness Vaccaro and Tavel first toyed with, including, by the way, the ability to improvise. Several years later, at the beginning of his play *Caprice,* a take-off on Molière's *Would-Be Gentleman,* Charles came onstage, act one, scene one, wearing a supposedly supertrendy "Armachi" suit tailored from that plastic green stuff that grocers lay out to display persimmons and tangerines upon. In the front row, Andrew

Holleran and I burst into gales of laughter. For our pleasure, Ludlum stopped the action, stepped forward and modeled the suit for us, including the inner pockets and "label." This of course brought the house down.

I later discovered that *Conquest of the Universe* was the very production that had ended Ludlam's connection to Vaccaro. Rising star Ludlam had had artistic differences with founder John, whom many people who knew both of them agreed had become increasingly wild by then, veering away from the written script for any reason at all. Ludlam left, taking his great company of actors, including Lola Pashalinski, Black-Eyed Susan, Everett Quinton, and Bill Vehr with him. Stuck with an announced opening night of a new play, Vaccaro had gone crying to Warhol, who'd suggested members of his own Factory "company." That's how Ricard, Ultra Violet, Mary Woronov, Taylor Mead, and of course Ondine had gotten hired. They—and especially the happily chaotic Ondine—pleased Vaccaro by using the play's text as more or less as "a series of suggestions."

Later on in the seventies and eighties, Ludlam would much more carefully craft a brilliant if still wacky and definitely more gay theater, writing plays such as *Camille: A Tearjerker, Stage Blood,* and *The Mystery of Irma Vep.* But while he would spend mornings writing and evenings rehearsing and acting, Ludlam spent many, many afternoons on his knees in the back booths of the Christopher Street Bookshop, where he claimed to orally receive most of his "inspiration." There, I'd invariably see and wave to him bimonthly, while I was delivering the more louche Gay Presses of New York titles for the shop's small book shelf.

Meanwhile we did have gay film—well, Paul Morrisey's idea of gay film, anyway. Around 1969, Marty Brennan got a job as a waiter in the back "Red Room" of Max's Kansas City, a block or so from Union Square and Warhol's second Factory, and probably the hippest bar and place to eat—and perform— in Manhattan at the time. One late night, I found myself back there, being served by Marty, who also brought poppers hidden in red napkins for me to sample. In the same room that evening were the usual music stars: Janis

Joplin, Jim Morrison, Jefferson Airplane's Jorma Kaukonen, John Sebastian, and many of the Warhol hangers-on, including my brother Jerry and his amphetamine crowd—Rotten Rita, the Wonton, and so on. And at another end of the room was my older brother Bob, who was at the time dating Nico, the Swedish-born "singing star" of Warhol's rock group, The Velvet Underground. Nico's group would give a show upstairs at Max's later on, and at Sunday dinner in Queens a few weeks afterward she would argue with my Italian-American father, who would shout back at her his conclusive assessment of her—and his three sons'—entire lifestyle: "*Avant-garde? A van' cul!* Up your ass!"

High on poppers that night, I went around Max's Red Room saying hi to my sibs and their various pals. I also made a play for a tall, handsome redhead whom Andy had introduced as his latest movie star. While I was flirting, Andy said, "You're cute! Come up to the Factory and I'll screen-test you." I did go up to the Factory the next day looking for the cutie, Eric Emerson, and I was duly screen-tested. (Dozens of these "screen-tests" were played at Los Angeles's Museum of Contemporary Arts' gigantic Warhol retrospective in 2003, but mine wasn't among them.)

But the big surprise was learning that night at Max's and having it confirmed the next day at Warhol's studio that the dorky Paul Morrisey, who'd worked one unit away from me in a big, former elementary school at the East End Welfare Center in Spanish Harlem from 1964 to 1966, before I went to Europe, was now Warhol's main filmmaker, building upon Warhol and the Factory's reputation for classic, sixteen-millimeter multi-reelers like *Empire* and *Blow Job* (the latter flick, Ondine later assured me, featuring his own hard-working, bobbing head).

Paul and Andy had broken through with their multiscreen, multinarrative viewpoint film *Chelsea Girls* and were now getting financing to make "real" movies. Morrisey's *Flesh* (1968) was a day in the life of the handsome junkie hustler, Joe D'Allesandro ("Little Joe"). *Trash* (1970) featured Holly Wood-lawn as a transvestite hooker on welfare in contention with a case worker (a role Paul knew well, naturally) and with her sometime boyfriend, Little Joe. *Heat* (1972) followed fabulously over-the-hill actress Sylvia Miles as she tried to recapture her youth. Of them all, *Trash* was the most explosive, and as utterly gay a film as anyone had made or seen up till then. And although Paul and Andy would follow it with others films, *Trash* continues to embody the basic, totally transgressive elements that truly defined gay life of its time, and that in fact, make today's gay male filmmaking so vanilla they're often painful to watch. But it wouldn't be for another decade that films like *Parting Glances* and *Longtime Companion* came along, now-classic movies that defined gay life in the 1970s and 1980s.

But there I was, and there we all were, in the winter of 1976 and 1977, with so little actual explicitly gay culture that I could just recount for you what it all was. Evidently something had to change. I knew it. Everybody gay around me knew it. And furthermore, we all knew that if we didn't do something about it ourselves, no one else would. It was up to us.

2

Seahorse Press Begins;
or, How to Make a Book

It will probably come as an enormous shock to the reader that my first gay publishing company came about as a result of poetry. Today, hardly anyone but poets read poetry, so a little explanation of this is in order.

Pretty much anyone who went to college in the U.S. from the fifties through the seventies—and took more than the single required English or literature course—became aware of I. A. Richard's book *Practical Criticism*. Or if not the book, then at least its message: you didn't need to know anything about the poet, the poet's nationality, upbringing, or ideas, to not only thoroughly understand a poem, but through careful analysis, to understand the literary, cultural, even the religious, political, and social layers within a poem.

The great example, of course, was modernist T. S. Eliot, whose 1922 poem, "The Wasteland," with its many footnotes, was a twisted knot just waiting for interpretation from any one of a score of points of view. Academics and poets alike, such as Robert Penn Warren, Cleanth Brooks, and others, followed in Richard's footsteps with their own books on how to unspool poetry, and the result was that both reading and writing poetry in that era was, as odd as it sounds, downright exciting.

I had loads of fun in college writing papers on Rainer Maria Rilke's *Duino Elegies* and Hart Crane's "The Bridge." My first professional publication was an extended version of the term paper on Rilke I'd done for a class, and it appeared in one of those slender, handsome scores of quarterlies that dotted people's bookshelves and coffee tables during the period—and are now pretty much a thing of the past.

Poets of the time were reviewed in the front pages of the *New York Times Book Review*, in the *Atlantic Monthly*, and in the *New Republic*. New titles by Robert Lowell, Richard Wilbur, W. S. Merwin, James Merrill, Theodore Roethke, John Berryman, Elizabeth Bishop, Anne Sexton, Pablo Neruda, and Sylvia Plath made them gods to writers in a way that may be difficult to understand today. It seemed then that every new poetry book published opened yet another level of consciousness, of revelation, of character, and of story not available in fiction of the era, except from a few writers like John Fowles, John Barth, and Ken Kesey. For the most part, novelists and short story writers were well over being modernist—especially given how large James Joyce, Virginia Woolf, Marcel Proust, and Thomas Mann loomed—but few had discovered ways of being postmodern; that wouldn't take shape until the 1990s.

Among living poets, W. H. Auden reigned supreme, with Ezra Pound, T. S. Eliot, and Wallace Stevens presiding from Beyond as the Holy Trinity. New poetry books sold in the tens of thousands and appeared on major bestseller lists. And there were—there have always been—popular poets, too, among them Leonard Cohen and Rod McKuen, whose books—along with John Lennon's and Bob Dylan's lyrics—were relevant to the time and sold in the scores of thousands, making poetry for a brief time almost equal to rock music in terms of its cultural influence.

So what happened, that forty years later poetry has fallen into such utter irrelevance even to the dwindling group of serious readers? The answer, quite simply, is that academia got hold of poetry, and academia turned out to be the kiss of death. Today, aside from two or three popular poets (that we back then might have considered inconsequential) like Billy Collins, no one reads poetry but other poets. And it's pretty much true that poets teach poetry at universities, poets edit and publish the poetry magazines and the quarterlies, poets write reviews of other poets, poets chair university committees that hire other poets into academia, and poets select works for university presses that publish poetry books. Academic poets are also the people who nominate and judge most poetry prizes, and so they decide what poetry is. The net result is that most contemporary poetry is drab and insular, safe and uninteresting. And aside from the poet noted above, if a poetry book sells three thousand copies today, that's a major best seller—meaning most publishers won't earn money off poetry and so aren't interested in putting it out.

Compare this to the not-so-distant past—SeaHorse Press published poetry books from 1977 through 1985: *The Deformity Lover,* three printings, 6,500 copies sold; Dennis Cooper's *Idols,* three printings, 5,800 copies sold; Gavin Dillard's *Notes From a Marriage,* four printings, almost 7,200 copies! This from a tiny gay publishing house—staff of one—with no mainstream reviews and virtually no distributors. Most sales were direct to customers by mail order and via bookstores. Even our later poets like Mark Ameen and Rudy Kikel, who were almost unknown and putting out their first books, sold over 3,000 copies. And it was true for the other Gay Presses of New York: poetry sold if it was even half good.

A glimpse into the table of contents of Winston Leyland's second anthology of poetry, *Orgasms of Light* (1977), lists the following poets: Constantine Cavafy, Emilio Cernuda, Kirby Congdon, Dennis Cooper, Gavin Dillard, Kelmward Elmslie, Sergei Essenin, Charles Henri Ford, John Giorno, Robert Glück, Will Inman, Maurice Kenny, James Kirkup, Mikhail Kuzmin, Federico García Lorca, Harold Norse, Pier Paolo Pasolini, Robert Peters, myself, Edouard Roditi, Frederick Rolfe (Baron Corvo), Aaron Shurin, Jack Spicer, Mutsuo Takahashi, Gennady Trifonov, John Wieners, and Jonathan Williams. The book remains one of my favorites, but I find I can return to numerous collections and anthologies published between 1975 and 1985, since they remain relevant and well done.

This might explain why, when I decided to begin the SeaHorse Press, a collection of poems would be its first book.

My second decision was the author I selected to start the press: me. By then I'd published two novels and was about to publish a third. The first had been a critical success; the second had been a mass-market paperback best-seller; the third would unite critical acclaim and sales. I assumed I had a market of readers (albeit a fraction of the readers of my novels), who might venture to pick up a collection of my verse.

To begin with, I could count on those who read poetry, a sizable group at the time. Those who already knew me as a poet would also buy my book. A few years before I'd begun to attend—and read at—various group poetry events, where I was told my poetry was both good and easily understood. These poetry readings were admittedly few and far between in the time and were generally an outgrowth of another, earlier movement that had enshrined a certain kind of writing that we now know as the Beats. Coming along in the fifties and lasting about a quarter century, William Burroughs, Allen Ginsberg, Jack Kerouac, and their later and less well-known pals and colleagues had set up a kind of model of what a subversive writer was or should be. Ginsberg was the best known, with his proto-hippie clothing, his Buddhist chanting and drumming, his open drug use, and his very open homosexuality.

How open? Well, while others read their work at the tony Sara Delano Roosevelt House, a small event organized by a gay film club connected to Hunter College, Ginsberg quietly, insistently, propositioned twenty-eight-year-old me by explaining that if he blew me (which he said he hoped to do), it would continue an unbroken line of blow jobs going all the way back to Walt Whitman—mentioning among the connections "Bosie," naturally, and Edward Carpenter.

I demurred, however. And much as I appreciated the Beats and what they'd done, I was more than a little chary of them, believing that most of those still alive had allowed themselves to become caricatures of writers, and that their personalities had overwhelmed their work. I wasn't clear how or why that had happened. Back then, the media's capacity to distortedly recreate a person's character was not as much of a thorough onslaught as it can be today, but it did exist, and it could be effectively harnessed, as writers like Truman Capote and Kurt Vonnegut realized—and attempted. All I knew was that if I succeeded as a writer I didn't ever want the same thing to happen to me.

One other advantage of being SeaHorse Press's first author was that the book would require no advance to be paid out, although I did print up and sign a contract with my company and issue royalty statements and checks regularly thereafter until the book went out of print. (It was, after all, a free-standing business.) Add to that the fact that by publishing myself, I wouldn't have another artistic ego to deal with immediately, and it was clearly a good thing. But while this cut down on start-up costs somewhat, I'd later discover—and authors take note—that for the most part what gets paid to most writers is but a fraction, one of the smallest wedges, in the pie chart of any book's total expenses.

Keep in mind that I only vaguely grasped what I was doing by beginning SeaHorse Press, thereby spending from my sudden excess of money earned from my novels. What I did discern quite clearly, however, was that there was a great big gay and lesbian community out there and it was not remotely being served by publishers. Even when, a decade later, mainstream publishers had actually jumped on the bandwagon and began publishing gay books, the need for lesbian and gay small presses remained, because what was being published turned out to be highly commercial, usually but always "safer" in terms of material and story lines, and usually fiction—predominantly novels.

Glaringly missing was poetry, drama, and short stories. Also missing was experimental writing, like the San Francisco–based new narrative writing, also known as language writing, of Sam D'Allesandro and Robert Glück, which mixed up times, places, and even character sequences. Forget about working-class stuff, authors from the middle of the country, Southern writing, and gay writing by Asians, African Americans, or Latinos! Nor was there a place for satire, humor, history, memoir, or autobiography.

No surprise, since there were only two openly gay editors in the New York publishing world of 1977—Michael Denneny at St. Martin's Press and Bill Whitehead at Dutton—and they could only do so much. In later years both men told me they'd rejected many works that should have been published and never were. Other editors were sympathetic, or interested, and they ended up putting out as many gay books as that out duo. But that totaled five to ten books per year tops until the 1990s, when gay lit became a genre—like children's books, or self-help, or cookbooks.

So I knew that SeaHorse Press would have little trouble filling in such glaring gaps. There was no problem finding books to publish. At first slowly, then more rapidly, manuscripts came pouring in. Within three years of starting the press, I always had a large backlog of submitted work to read and of good books to publish.

But my early decision was almost immediately followed by a problem of greater size and intensity, leading to a state of absolute terror, because the truth was although I'd now had several books of my own published, I didn't know the first thing about *how* to publish, or, truthfully, even how a book was put together. And if I was to become a publisher, I was going to have to learn fast.

———

How do you make a book? I don't mean philosophically, I mean physically. Pretty much any halfway intelligent person can tell you how. Print words on pages. Bind the pages together. Wrap them inside printed covers, and voilà— you've got a book. It sounds so simple. Until, of course, you begin to get into the details.

For my first SeaHorse Press book, I hired an art director from my Fire Island Pines–Flamingo–Studio 54 social set. Dino Di Giorlando was recommended by my cover artist, George Stavrinos, and several other people. We met, settled on a fee, and he quickly unfolded the many complexities for making a book.

Here's an example of what I mean: 99 percent of all books are black type on white paper. What could be simpler? Well, I soon discovered the contrary. Printing inks seldom come in black. There's actually no such thing as pure black. Printing inks are blue black, charcoal-gray black, green black, brown black, even purple black. A book left exposed in the sun too long almost always burns off the blackest part of the ink used, revealing the melded color beneath. That's why faded type looks sepia or grass green.

So what color did I want my *Deformity Lover* to be set in?

I knew a little about typefaces. That is, I *thought* I did, until Dino showed me a book of about a thousand typefaces. After several hours of us looking and discussing, I settled on an elegant Palatino. And while typefaces come in all sizes, in printed books they generally come in very few—eleven to fourteen point—because it is the easiest for most people to read. I ended up choosing thirteen point. So I now had the type down.

The next meeting concerned paper color. No, all book paper is not white. Dino also had books of swatches of supposedly "white" papers that varied from buttery yellow to ice blue, from pale ecru to dove gray. Having selected our ink color, we of course now had to match it to the appropriate paper, because the bluer the paper, the "cooler" it would come off. The tanner the paper, the "warmer" it would read. Grayish white would convey an official, catalog-like feel, while yellower white would imply luxury, but only if the paper's weave, thickness, and finish were just right—otherwise it could look faded and cheap. Mind you these would all be unconscious or barely conscious reactions on the part of the reader. But they were strong enough unconscious reactions that we found ourselves spending a long time on each aspect. We ended up choosing a charcoal-gray black, thirteen-point Palatino on creamy white.

Next came books of paper *textures* for me to select from. This would be the setting for the print, the way a dining room wall is the setting for a favorite painting you hang. Dino and I picked a soft but durable paper with a slightly horizontal weave pattern and a high rag content—meaning it would look great. This would be for the first printing; after that, I would use less expensive weaves and papers, both for the internal pages and for the cover. But this was to be a terrific looking first edition, with a colophon in the back pages listing its many attributes.

The covers of the *Deformity Lover* required another entire set of aesthetic decisions. We already had artwork—George Stavrinos's lovely drawing of a man's torso and head. We needed a typeface, size, ink color, and paper weight, color, and weave for the book covers, that complemented both the art *and* the interior pages.

Another thickish paper with a high rag content but a less subtly horizontal weave was selected. The book cover's ink would be a greener black because that color would hold the details of the George's pen-drawing lines with greater accuracy than the grayer ink we'd chosen for inside. Somewhere in the midst of all this, while I was looking at cover type, I decided to reverse one of the letters—the *f* in the word *deformity*. A drawing of a perfectly gorgeous man, then the lettering all fouled up: it would stop readers in their tracks. The cover would make a statement about the contradictions explored in the poem and by the collection as a whole.

Next came the meeting with Dino, the typesetter, and me. In 1977, there was no such thing as desktop publishing. Type had to be set onto a roll of photographically-treated paper that then had to be cut and laid out on preplanned boards. All of those boards were then photographed again, and the negatives were used for printing. That meant that each page had to be keyboarded into a typesetting machine that would then print out sheets of pages.

Patrick Merla, an acquaintance who worked as a typesetter and copyeditor for *Christopher Street* magazine at the time, was also a friend and copyist for author Edmund White, and came with excellent references. He did a great job, and also offered recommendations for our design. For later Sea-Horse Press titles we used Patrick on several occasions, and also Joseph Arsenault and John Reed.

But once again, merely typesetting a single page of text—a four-line poem—required a score of decisions I had never previously thought would be needed: how wide would the *vertical* spacing be between lines of poetry? How wide would the poem be *horizontally* on the page? How much (really narrow) width would there be between every letter in a word? Between every word in a line? It seemed endlessly detailed. At last, however, all the many little decisions had been made for *Deformity Lover,* and I could sit back and wait for the result.

What I also did at this time was continue to gaze through various books of typefaces, ink colors, paper weaves, and paper colors, trying to get to know them or at least familiarize myself with them enough so that in the future I would be able to much more creatively make decisions. So when SeaHorse was printing its fourth title, Brad Gooch's short story collection *Jail Bait and Other Stories,* I decided I wanted to use as typeface on the book cover the very same type used by the U.S. Treasury Department and Mint on ten- and twenty-dollar bills. It would subtly convey the sense of money changing hands. While on the fifth title, Clark Henley's *The Butch Manual (or The New Drag and How to Do It),* I used the very same cover type found on the cover of the classic *Boy Scout Manual* of our youth—a snippiness very few people picked up on, unfortunately.

This kind of technical, almost infra dig knowledge would also provide me with a vocabulary for dealing with future printers, typesetters, and other publishing tradespeople. By the time I'd finished the first book, I felt confident enough to become SeaHorse Press's art director, and thereafter I art directed all of SeaHorse's books and later on almost half of Gay Presses of New York's books. Meaning that I actually laid out the cover art, the type, the front and back covers, the title pages, and all of the interior pages of any volume I was behind—an often arduous but always exciting way to be deeply involved in every book I'd brought in and published.

———

I have mentioned *Christopher Street* magazine and the Violet Quill Club. Both need further explanation, as they were important elements in my life as a writer, editor, and publisher in this period. They were also crucial to the growth of gay literature, and so are necessarily part of the story of Gay Presses of New York and their role in creating contemporary gay culture.

Poet and critic David Bergman, in the introduction to his anthology *The Violet Quill Reader* (1994), points to my own journals, excerpted in his book as "Rough Cuts from a Journal," as setting up the date parameters in which as he writes, "seven gay male writers, joined by friendship, ambition, and concern for their art, got together—eight times, in fact—to read to one another from their works in progress."

The truth is, as usual, a bit more complex: we were a great deal more and less than "friends": some of us were at the time or had previously been each others' lovers. Also, we didn't merely read our work. We discussed what we were writing, hoped and dared ourselves to write, and what others we knew were writing and planning to publish—Vito Russo, author of *The Celluloid Closet,* came to one of our meetings.

We talked about what we were doing might eventually mean, and what other writers—Edmund White's mostly closeted writer pals, for example—thought of what we were writing. (Not much. They told him to write something else, *anything* else.) We questioned and debated what gay literature should be, what it ought to include, what—if anything—it should exclude. We knew it had to include, and if not explicate then at least implicate, sex, since sex was the main element by which we differed from other writers, and also because there were thousands of years of mainstream writing about love and sex, and not much about same-gender love and sex. We also met to discuss what each of us could individually do in our attempt to form what we'd later call a "beneficent conspiracy" to put gay literature on the map by forcing the mainstream to recognize our writing—our main goal.

September through May of 1979 were the key months in which we seven came together as a group, although the group's official readings didn't begin until March 31, 1980, and lasted little more than a year and a half thereafter.

Seven writers in New York: not so unusual for the time. But Andrew Holleran had been born and raised on the Caribbean isle of Aruba, gone to school in New England, and lived part-time in northern Florida. Edmund White came from Cincinnati, Ohio, in what he would satirize in his book, *Fanny: A Fiction,* as the smug, cold, stupid Midwestern heart of the U.S. George Whitmore came from the West, from Colorado, while Christopher Cox was from southern Alabama, and his single published book would be about another southern place, Key West, the country's southernmost city. Like White, Michael Grumley was another Midwesterner, from Davenport, Iowa, one of the Quad Cities on the Mississippi River. I had grown up chiefly in Long Island and southern New England. Robert Ferro was from Brooklyn, and then horsey, suburban New Jersey. And so, in a real geopolitical sense, although of course not racially, through our origins and early experiences, we represented distinctly varied versions of what it had been like to grow up and become gay men across the U.S. in our generation.

We'd come together rather unexpectedly. Andrew Holleran had gone to the Iowa Writers' Workshop in the mid-1960s and found Robert Ferro and Michael Grumley in his class—along with John Irving, Mary Gordon, and Gail Godwin. Ferro and Grumley soon became lovers, and then life partners until their deaths three months apart in 1988. Those three remained in touch throughout the intervening decades. Meanwhile, I'd met Edmund White in 1974 in Fire Island Pines when I visited the house where he was staying because a Greenwich Village neighbor of mine was also visiting there. George Whitmore met Edmund in 1975, and they dated a while. I met George in 1978, and then we began dating and would do so on and off for another year, splitting up in the summer of 1979.

Ed met Christopher Cox in early 1978, and by the end of the year they were living together. I was introduced to Holleran by my friend Hal Seidman in September 1978 at a Fire Island Pines house party. Later in 1978, Holleran,

Robert, and Michael were among those attending a preview screening of a television film on gay life to which I'd also been invited, and that was when Holleran introduced me to the couple. I remained friends with Robert till his death, and with Michael almost until his death. I connected Holleran with Edmund in the early summer of 1979 in a carefully orchestrated dinner at a mutual friend's place—the Last House on the Ocean—in the Pines. We seven all first came together at George Whitmore's sublet just off Washington Square in the fall of 1979 at a Sunday brunch to discuss our futures.

Robert and George were the social glue of the group, and (with Chris Cox) the least published of us when we began. So they have felt that they had more at stake in forming the group and in keeping it going. It's therefore not really surprising that Robert and George's falling out was responsible for the Violet Quill no longer meeting. Bergman, in his study of the group, *The Violet Hour* (2004), claims the breakup occurred as a result of George Whitmore reading his story "Getting Rid of Robert." According to Bergman, Robert and Michael thought the story was aimed at them, while it was really more about Edmund and Chris's break up, which was happening around that time. As I was host that evening, busily preparing our dessert and coffee, I didn't hear the end of the story and so was blithely unaware of the contretemps. Holleran did hear it, and I had to pull him out from under my sofa where he'd retreated during the reading.

In the future, that particular evening would be seen by us as yet another example of Whitmore's acting out. He'd done so before at previous VQ meetings, annoying first Holleran when he'd written and read aloud a story titled "Last Dance," which poached from Holleran's novel (and used a detail picked up at his beach house that Andrew had wittily mentioned to the group). George had flustered and embarrassed me a few months before that when he'd gone ahead and written "The Black Widow"—which he'd then nervily published in the anthology *Aphrodisiac: Fiction from Christopher Street*. I also published a story about the Black Widow—a former housemate, fuck buddy, and friend of mine named Frank Diaz. "Perfection of the Man, Or . . ."

appeared online a few years ago. However, Diaz was someone George had *never* met; his entire story had been constructed out of the beach-blanket gossip of my acquaintances that George had picked up while staying at my Pines rental.

In retrospect, George was undergoing pretty dynamic psychotherapy during which he was acting out all that time—with or without his therapist's encouragement or sanction I never knew. He and I broke up romantically when he arrived for a long and, on my part at least, eagerly awaited weekend of *l'amour* at my Pines house. Once there, he immediately announced that he'd reached a moment in his therapy when he could no longer have sex, and on top of that, he had just quit smoking that very day. No stranger to acting out myself, I went into the next room and returned saying I'd just taken two hits of LSD, and now *he* would have to cope with *me*. George fled my house and I later found out he left Fire Island by the next ferry. High, I called pals and partied for the next forty-eight hours. Years later, reading his novel *Nebraska*, it became evident to me that George had been dealing with the demons of preadolescent sexual molestation.

So that night of the last VQ meeting, it was in no way surprising that Whitmore had once more abused someone he knew and was supposedly friendly with. Except that by reading that particular story aloud, George had managed a mini-coup: offending four people at once. And so he had now officially trashed the *entire* Violet Quill Club, in effect ending our group's cohesion. Years later, George berated me and Holleran for not supporting him against Ferro and White. But by then Holleran had retreated to Florida as he often did, I was busy with the SeaHorse Press and Gay Presses of New York, and all of us were over the Violet Quill Club and couldn't see why George would still care.

We seven Quillians brought to all our subsequent meetings a rather mixed history of writing and publishing. Robert and Michael had published first among us: a nonfiction travel book, with a somewhat occult, definitely specialized subject. Their *Atlantis: The Story of a Search* (1970) was about how the two, while living in Rome, had decided after reading Edgar Cayce (the so-called "sleeping prophet") exactly where to search for the fabled antediluvian continent; how they organized and fitted out the trip to do so; and what they ended up discovering in the area of the Bimini Islands. The only thing gay about their book was the very sexy photos of the two young authors in bathing suits on the inside back cover.

Michael would go on to write three more volumes of not particularly gay nonfiction: *There Are Giants in the Earth* (1974), about extraordinary, seldom-seen hominids such as yetis and Sasquatches; *Hard Corps* (1977), about S/M leather life; and *After Midnight* (1978), a well-reviewed series of literary portraits of people who live and work when most of us are sleeping. The only other book his partner, Robert Ferro, published in the next decade was the enigmatic symbolist novella, *The Others* (1977).

Edmund, the VQ's elder, was the third of us to publish: the novel *Forgetting Elena* in 1973, which got a wonderful write up in *The New York Times Book Review* and a recommendation from Vladimir Nabokov. But it would be Ed's second and third books, *The Joy of Gay Sex* (with Dr. Charles Silverstein) in 1977, and *Nocturnes for the King of Naples* (1978) that for us represented his commitment to this strange, new burgeoning entity that we and people our age—but no one else, really—were calling gay literature. Nonetheless, Ed continued to make his living not from the sales of the few thousand copies of his novels, but by laboring in the great unsigned fields of American Grub Street, anonymously writing volumes of Time Life Books' many series of that era, on various subjects from music and geology to witchcraft and mysticism.

I was the fourth published in the group with *Smart as the Devil* (1975), *Eyes* (1976), *The Mesmerist* (1977), and finally, *The Lure* (1979). The first book of my coeval, Andrew Holleran, was the popular and well-received *Dancer From the Dance* (1978), remarkably well written yet utterly campy, with individual yet recognizable gay characters. But he would only publish four more books over the next twenty-five years, two of them in the 1980s.

Whitmore's first book was a self-published poetry collection, *Getting Gay in New York* (1977), which I'd read and which had kind of oiled my first meeting with him—we began having coffee to talk about it and ended up having sex. That was George's only book in the 1970s, and he would only publish three more titles in the 1980s before his untimely death: the novels *The Confessions of Danny Slocum* in 1989, and *Nebraska* in 1989, and the nonfiction *Someone Was Here: Profiles in the AIDS Epidemic* in 1988.

Chris Cox published only *Key West: A Companion* in 1983. But Chris was always more of an editor—working full-time for Dutton and New American Library, and then for Ballantine and Random House, publishing a wide list of trade paperbacks that included an occasional gay book, but more often non-gay books by gay authors, like *The Tales of Patrick Merla*, an intriguing collection of modern *märchen*.

About us seven writers Bergman's introduction to *The Violet Quill Reader* goes on to say, "Not much to mythologize. Except that several of these writers became the most important gay authors of the 1980s, setting a standard for gay fiction against which the present boom in gay writing is always compared. . . . Collectively they produced a vision of gay life that haunts us still—a vision of beauty, privilege, friendship, sexuality, loss, and lyricism."

I suppose it's true that Holleran's *Dancer* and *Nights in Aruba*, Whitmore's *Danny Slocum*, White's *A Boy's Own Story* and *The Beautiful Room Is Empty*, Ferro's *Family of Max Desir*, *The Blue Star*, and *Second Son*, and my own *The Lure*, *Late in the Season*, and *Ambidextrous* are chief among the score of gay titles that formed the first and second vital periods of modern gay fiction that occurred from 1975 to 1990 and that solidified gay writing as a critically viable new literary genre—and also as a profitable publishing phenomenon. What set this work apart from the extremely few other gay-themed books coming out of major publishers of the time was our positive take on gay life and gay men, our seriousness of purpose as writers as reflected in the themes and stories, the depth of characterization and description of the world we portrayed, and the literary yet remarkably honest sexuality we insisted upon depicting. No wonder several of those titles remain among the most reprinted, most translated, and most widely read gay male books even today. Bergman concludes, "Together [the writers of the Violet Quill Club] left their mark on how we will come to view American literature and American culture."

———

Almost contemporaneous with the publications of the writers of the Violet Quill Club, *Christopher Street* magazine was launched in July 1976. The premiere issue had a cover by David Edward Byrd illustrating an open closet door, its unused hangers still jangling from being flung open. The magazine was founded by poet Charles Ortleb, writer Thom Steele, and book editor Michael Denneny. Its function, according to the jacket copy on *Aphrodisiac: Fiction from Christopher Street,* put out by Coward, McCann in 1980, was to be a "forum for gay consciousness, exploring every aspect of the diverse gay world through provocative articles, interviews, and cartoons," as well as "poetry and stories by well-known writers and promising new ones."

Four Violet Quill Club members appeared in that *Christopher Street* anthology: Holleran, White, Whitmore, and me—along with stories by Tennessee Williams, Kate Millet, Jane Rule, and Christopher Bram, among others. Eventually all seven of us would have work published either in the magazine or in the *New York Native,* (1981–94) *Christopher Street*'s offshoot newspaper, which surpassed it in sales, popularity, and even, some thought, in prestige. During the year and a half that I edited the *Native*'s quarterly "Books Supplement," all the other Quillians were naturally invited to offer reviews and essays and did so. Because I was fortunate enough to get to ask other writers to write for it, the supplement ended up being a who's who of New York gay and lesbian writing of the time, including the work of Susan Sontag, Richard Sennett, Richard Howard, Bertha Harris, Dorothy Allison, and Richard Hall, to name only a handful

It would seem that we seven writers in the group and the magazine (and later, the newspaper) were what my Rhode Island grandmother would call "hand in fist." Well, yes and no.

Definitely Edmund White and later Andrew Holleran were early on asked into the magazine. *CS* published an excerpt from *Dancer* before it came out, and Holleran ended up writing a monthly column titled "New York Notebook" for almost five years, containing some of his most trenchant, insightful, and funniest writing. (About a quarter of those essays were later collected in the volume *Ground Zero* in 1988.) One other story of his, "Someone Is Crying in the Chateau de Berne," was also published in *Christopher Street*.

White previewed his novels *Nocturnes for the King of Naples* and *A Boy's Own Story* in the magazine and published several excerpts from his travel book and sociology text *States of Desire: Travels in Gay America*. But his next novel, *Caracole*, wasn't gay themed, and today White isn't sure why *The Beautiful Room is Empty*, in 1985, wasn't premiered there. Perhaps because those were the end days of both the magazine and the newspaper. There never was any falling out that he can recall to explain it.

George Whitmore published several stories and a few poems in *CS*, as well as an excerpt from *Danny Slocum*. Robert Ferro published one novel excerpt. My own first piece published in the magazine came about, I believe, only after Michael Denneny exerted pressure on the other editors. In 1980 Ortleb accepted for publication my short story, "Slashed to Ribbons in Defense of Love," which then appeared in both the magazine and the fiction anthology—with an unauthorized truncated ending. I did two lengthy interviews for the magazine: one in 1980 with playwright Lanford Wilson, who'd just won the Pulitzer Prize, and another with my friend Vito Russo, who was about to publish his groundbreaking study of homosexuality in cinema, *The Celluloid Closet*; both, I believe, arranged via Denneny. Neither Ortleb nor Steele ever approached me—or Ferro or Grumley—for work, and I sometimes wondered if I was eventually published there only because of the popularity and acclaim of my novel *The Lure* at the time made it impossible to totally ignore me. In future years, *CS* did publish some of my best new poems, including—with a photograph I'd taken—the quartet of "Window Elegies" which later on became a separate chapbook.

Working with Brett Averill, editor of the *Native* (1980–88), turned out to be a different kind of experience. First, unlike Ortleb and Steele, Brett was always available at the office, an editor who took and returned people's phone calls and notes and who actively sought writers, feature articles, and reviews. Averill and I got along well, and he solicited a great deal of my participation. As a result, I became a book, film, and theater reviewer for the paper. Doing at least a dozen good-size essays on Auden, Mann, Genet, Wilde, and Mozart, I soon discovered that important people in the arts— James Merrill, Ned Rorem, and Lennie Bernstein among them—were reading and were eager to talk to me about my reviews whenever we might meet. I met Bernstein, for example, when he was dating Thom Steele. He took me aside at a party to thank me for taking Peter Shaffer apart in my review of his play, *Amadeus*. I'd been reading Mozart's letters, and the composer seemed utterly unlike the imbecile of the playwright's imagination. Bernstein agreed with me, finding Shaffer's play awful and a "disservice to music."

Michael Grumley was also connected with the *Native*. Early on he began a column titled "Uptown" that ran for years and that detailed what was going on in upper Manhattan, meaning Harlem and Spanish Harlem—he and Robert Ferro lived for years in a flat on West Ninety-fifth Street in palmier, low-rent times when Ninety-sixth Street demarcated the color line between whites and Latinos to the south and blacks to the north on New York City's West Side. Michael also sometimes illustrated his columns with his characteristic light-line drawings. Several years later, Haitian-born poet Assotto Saint told me he had read Michael's column faithfully and that it was so informative and so ear-to-the-ground that he'd been convinced (wrongly) that Grumley was African American.

Andrew Holleran wrote several feature stories for the *Native*, among them pieces ranging from the lighthearted ("The Mister Blueboy Contest") to the political (gay congressman Barney Frank's scandalous connection to a male hustler) and the tragic (the Ronald Crumpley shootings of men outside New York gay bars). George Whitmore published twenty-nine episodes of his serial novel *Deep Dish* over a year and a half in the biweekly newspaper.

There was a reason for these connections and all this activity besides the obvious: at the time there weren't that many other gay magazines around, so we in the Violet Quill club published wherever we could. There was *After Dark* and *Mandate*. But the most famous of all gay publications was David Goodstein's pioneering *Advocate,* considered the first national gay periodical. Starting in the late 1970s and up to his illness in the mid-1980s, the *Advocate* was edited by the brilliant, temperamental, erratic Robert McQueen, and during his tenure that journal became important among lesbians and gays in a way it never had been before. I made it my job to ensure that gay books, plays, and poetry got as much coverage in that much-read national biweekly as their regular, necessary "news and reviews."

I first met McQueen on my book tour for *The Lure* after some well-publicized appearances in San Francisco, where the magazine was then located, and during my visit to the Bay Area, McQueen courted me like a potential lover. After several meals, parties, and a night in his penthouse rooftop hot tub, Robert at last persuaded me to write several personal essays for the magazine. The first was about New York City—titled "I'll Take Manhattan"—in 1981. Later that year, I penned another, "Why Bother Having a Lover?" The last, my favorite, came out in 1985, and was titled "An Essay On Vanity," as though Alexander Pope had written it. These pieces allowed us to exploit each other successfully; McQueen played off my reputation by getting me to write personal essays on topics people were interested in; I used the *Advocate* to write work for a national readership that I think still stands up today. In between, and for several years after, I wrote book reviews for the *Advocate*'s long lasting, influential cultural editor, Mark Thompson. George Whitmore also wrote articles for Mark, but his history with the magazine was longer than mine, and much more checkered. Earlier, he had famously quit as a news reporter over Goodstein "going capitalist" when he editorialized that gay men should go out of their way to become rich and powerful.

Later on, under other editors, both Holleran and I would be repeatedly invited to write what were supposed to be significant feature articles for the *Advocate* only to find that everything we wrote had to fit some undisclosed new "objective news style." Our pieces were handed in, seemingly ignored, then without any consultation with us, pared down to a few, almost nonsensical paragraphs and published. Holleran shrugged it off. But I'd been asked to drop everything to do mine and had signed an agreement specifying length, payment, everything but style—and so I called in my agent, my attorney, and the Authors Guild, demanding full reimbursement. These experiences ended both of our connections with the paper—his for good and mine until quite recently.

Meanwhile, *Christopher Street*'s editors never explicated their all but incomprehensible criteria for publishing fiction. This meant that many of us writing gay short stories had to look afield more often than not if we wanted to see our work in print. There were few enough other magazines at the time that would even consider publishing a gay story or poem (certainly none of the literary quarterlies, and not the *New Yorker*). Whitmore and I, and several other writers we knew, decided to publish wherever we could—if only to get the work out there, read, and discussed. As a result, any connection any of us might make was acted upon and shared with each other. That meant for a short time, we even submitted to the nudie magazines of the day. Four of the stories later printed in my critically acclaimed SeaHorse Press collection *Slashed To Ribbons in Defense of Love* (1983) first appeared in *Blueboy:* "Mr. World Buns" and "Teddy the Hook," but also the more serious "Xmas in the Apple" and "Expertise." "Spinning" first came out in *Stallion,* and the much anthologized "Hunter" was first published in, of all places, *Drummer,* a leather magazine. Whitmore published his short fiction in a similar fashion, including in Honcho, even though none of our stories was more than somewhat erotic and not even remotely pornographic. It was just another avenue by which the Violet Quill Club members hoped to get good gay literature out to a public—any gay public.

To the extent that our books sold and were reviewed, we succeeded. But it wasn't merely about our writing, or the work of our friends. All lesbian and gay literature also fell within our purview. We routinely ganged up and wrote letters to the editor of *The New York Times* and other book review sections chastising them, deriding the (usual and expected) knee-jerk negative reviews of GLBT books they published. One example of how we directed our criticism: virtually all gay-themed books were reviewed in tandem, as though it required two gay novels to equal one non-gay novel. We made phone calls demanding reviews of what we felt were important gay works, which they routinely disregarded.

It wasn't only the larger or the more conservative papers we had to be on the lookout for, either. In December 1981, I was approached at a friend's book party by the books editor of the *Village Voice,* a significant counterculture institution. She had read some of my reviews in other papers—the short-lived *Seven Days* and somewhat longer-lived *SoHo Weekly News*—and asked me to write for the *Voice.* I said fine and a few months later phoned her with a suggested review for what I thought was a terrific new title I'd just read in galleys. After I described the book to her, her response was a bored, "Well, we're not really interested in lesbian negritude." The book was Alice Walker's Pulitzer Prize–winning best seller *The Color Purple,* never reviewed, nor to my knowledge even mentioned, in the *Voice.* I published my review in the *Native Book Supplement,* and never again contacted that editor.

I am happy to be able to write, however, that what we members of the Violet Quill wrote individually and as a group between 1977 and 1988 was useful in what I've since called the "beneficent conspiracy" for gay literature.

———

SeaHorse Press's second and third books followed *The Deformity Lover* fairly quickly, partly because that book was successful. It was reviewed in the gay press of the time, and it sold enough to go into a second printing, then a third, in each new year. It would later turn out that my poetry book also sold well through ads in *Christopher Street* and the *Advocate*—in fact, I was still getting mail orders containing cut-out ads when I decided to close down the presses in 1994.

The second title I published was *Two Plays by Doric Wilson,* containing *A Perfect Relationship* and *The West Street Gang.* Choosing the plays represented my ongoing interest and commitment to theater, especially to gay theater.

Looking at my carefully compiled catalogue of my writing from 1966 to 2002, I can't help but notice that after an early, immature (now lost) short story written when I was twenty-two, the next two pieces are two short plays, written one after the other in the summer of 1968. Very short plays, in fact. It would be another sixteen years before I wrote another, this time hour-long, play, *One O'clock Jump.* But shortly thereafter I wrote the adaptation of my novella, *An Asian Minor,* for the Meridian Gay Theatre, retitling it *Immortal,* and the following year the first act of my third play, *The Bombay Trunk,* which was eventually finished, and like the others, produced, although not until 2002.

Nor was I the only one of the Violet Quill Club members who wrote plays. Two of Edmund White's were produced. *Blue Boy in Black* (1963) had won a Hopwood Award while White was still in college. A Broadway agent picked up the play, it was produced at the Masque Theater in Manhattan, and it received major reviews, including one in the *New York Times.* A second play, *Trios,* actually written in Whitmore's apartment, which White used as an office for a period of time, was produced in London's West End in the 1980s.

Neither of those plays had gay content. But like my own, George Whitmore's plays did. George had been a drama major at Bennington (best friends there with gay playwright Victor Bumbalo, whose plays GPNy would later

publish under the title *Niagara Falls*), and two of George's plays were produced in New York during the 1970s. Andrew Holleran also wrote plays,
although to my knowledge, none were ever produced.

Doric Wilson, born in Oregon in 1941, had come to New York knowing
he wanted to be a playwright early enough in his life to become involved while
he was still in his twenties in Joe Cino's Café Cino, that breeding ground of so
many good playwrights. Doric's plays got produced, worked well on stage
(and, in the case of *West Street Gang,* in situ), and got audiences, reviews, and
notices. In 1977, when I met him, Doric was one of the very few successful,
openly gay playwrights around, one I very much wanted to get out to the
public via SeaHorse Press. Beyond his apparent knowledge and reverent use of
theatrical traditions and his solid dramatic structures, Doric's writing had an
immediacy and urgency; Doric himself had a perfect ear for the dialogue of
his gay "street" characters, unmatched by any of the (admittedly very few)
other openly gay playwrights of the time.

I had no real idea of how well his plays would sell. I printed about three
thousand copies, and slowly but surely they sold over the next five or six years.
He rewrote *A Perfect Relationship* and after that was restaged, I reprinted it as
a separate volume. Even so, for years after the first book came out, theater
companies across the country (across the world, really) wrote to Seahorse
Press to obtain performance rights for the plays. Meaning they'd gotten the
book first, or heard about the plays and read the book—that's how they knew
the plays. So, it was doubly beneficial for Doric.

Two Play's black-and-white cover used a drawing by my then boyfriend,
artist Scott Façon. Instead of using an expensive art director—start-up costs
on *The Deformity Lover* would be recouped only after the second printing
was half sold—I farmed out the printed pages to a friend. Delightful writer
and all-around cool guy Stan Leventhal was working as an editor at *Playguy*
and *Honcho* under George Mavety, the grossly overweight, Canadian-born
heterosexual who for several decades ran the largest gay porn magazine
empire in the Northern Hemisphere. They ended up putting together a less

beautiful, more functional, but quite salable, and more importantly, a less expensive second SeaHorse book.

That volume was scarcely out in stores when I was already art directing a third SeaHorse title, another poetry book, this one by young Californian Dennis Cooper. His *Idols* was a collation of several chapbooks he'd put out over the previous decade, beginning when he was sixteen years old in private school—including the chap books *Tiger Beat* and *My Mark*, which Cooper added to and amended considerably. I'd read Dennis's poems in *Gay Sunshine* and a few anthologies, but it was Violet Quill Club member Chris Cox who truly brought Cooper's work to my attention. When I was out in Los Angeles on a book tour for *The Lure* in the fall of 1979, I met and liked Dennis.

Unlike his later novels, Cooper's early poetry was fresh and hip; never naive, it was nonetheless dewy and admiring. It was undeniably drawn from his privileged adolescent life, yet it proved to be universal in its depiction of gay yearning. At the same time, it was sophisticated in how it dealt with prickly issues like love, sex, obsession, and drugs, with an almost throwaway casualness. Cooper in the eighties was like a young Rimbaud, and for me, nothing in his later work has recaptured that perfect soft, steady glow.

Chris Cox's connection with many younger gay writers grew as his connection with the other five Quillians eroded following his romantic breakup with Edmund. I ended up being virtually the only one of us Cox remained in contact with, and I was around him a great deal when he was dying of pancreatic cancer, merely the latest opportunistic disease of his short life, in St. Vincent's Hospital, in 1989. Chris was one of the most extraordinarily social literary people I'd ever met. I recall bumping into him on the street in early 1980; he asked if I had a half hour free for a cup of coffee. I said sure, thinking we'd go to a local diner. But he walked us a block to the infamous Chelsea Hotel, on Twenty-third Street and Seventh Avenue. After an elevator ride and a walk through a very long corridor, we ended up knocking at the door of a little tower apartment high up and partly over the avenue. At last, a rotund elderly man with a hatchet of a nose and a thick Southern accent answered, and was introduced to me as the composer and writer Virgil Thomson.

Virgil and Chris gossiped nonstop for the next hour while I attempted to cut through the increasingly ornate verbiage and intensifying Deep South accents. Thomson was more than eighty at the time and he moved quite slowly; he was partly deaf, partly blind, and more or less mumbled about this flat he'd lived in for a quarter century, getting around it half by place memory. I'll never forget how he boiled water for the ancient French-press coffeemaker he used in the tiny, messy kitchen area. While busily dishing to filth some composer I'd never heard of, Thomson thrust one of the stove's gas burners on full blast, went in search of a safety match, at last found one, struck it, and tossed it in the general direction of the stove (whumpf!). It's a wonder he died of natural causes at the age of ninety-two.

Chris Cox invited me to various readings and parties in New York and California, and he would end up recommending a slew of intriguing writers, including Joe Brainard, Tim Dlugos, David Trinidad, Robert Glück, Kevin Killian, and Brad Gooch. My friend, illustrator David Martin, provided the striking cover art for Dennis Cooper's *Idols*—a gorgeous male nude statue on a plinth crumbling from below. *Idols* went into a second printing (like the first two titles) and launched Dennis's career, which he noted in the copy he signed to me. I would publish two more of his books, his narrative prose *Safe* and *Closer,* but our relationship ended badly, almost inexplicably, some years after that: a rarity for me among the authors I worked with.

Meanwhile, I'd become even more ambitious and had come up with the idea of putting together an anthology. By 1979, several gay anthologies had either come out or were in the works. Besides Winston Leyland's two books, the best known collection of the day—because it was from a mainstream press— was *Different* (1974), edited by Stephen Wright and released as a Bantam mass-market paperback. It as followed by another trade paperback, collated by gay academic Seymour Kleinberg, curiously titled *The Other Persuasion: An Anthology of Short Fiction about Gay and Lesbian Men and Women* (1977).

The immediate problem with both collections for me and many of my contemporaries was that unlike several practical, informative, nonfiction anthologies of the time also available as mass-market paperbacks—such as *After You're Out* (1974), *Lavender Culture* (1977), and *The Gay Report* (1977), all edited by Allen Young and Karla Jay—the fiction collections weren't gay, but instead homosexual: about a life and lifestyle quite different from that which my friends and I were living. Some of the pieces included went back to the nineteenth century and were by heterosexuals or by writers perceived as such, including Guy de Maupassant, Henry James, D. H. Lawrence, Sherwood Anderson, Stanley Kaufman, William Faulkner, and that macho homophobe, Ernest Hemingway. While there was a smattering of work by known homosexual writers like Gore Vidal, Christopher Isherwood, Joseph Hansen, Alfred Chester, and Samuel Steward (writing as Phil Andros), they didn't provide any cohesive view of lesbian and gay life at the three-quarter mark of the twentieth century. Rather, they provided a rather wobbly, lopsided view of how a variety of writers had looked at the subject. As such, these books were interesting, but by no means trenchant, relevant, or in any way comprehensive.

(Incidentally, I finally met Phil Andros in 1981 at San Francisco's first gay bookstore, the Walt Whitman Bookshop. He was in his seventies, still handsome if frail, and a dandy in his dress. He was introduced to me after my reading and told me he was about to publish his memoir of his friendship with Gertrude Stein and Alice B. Toklas. I congratulated him and asked him to show me his famous tattoo. He said he would if I could tell him what the tattoo was. I said I'd heard he had a foot-long ruler tattooed on his arm so he could measure men's erections. He unbuttoned his left shirt cuff and rolled it up—and sure enough there was the ruler!)

My own anthology, *A True Likeness: Lesbian and Gay Writing Today,* was in stark contrast to these others. My transparent aim was to show the truth about gay life as contemporary gay men and lesbians wrote about it. The work would be written by and for both men and women. It wouldn't be limited to just poetry or just short stories—it would contain some of each, but also short plays and excerpts from novels. And it would be by both known and new writers, providing a much wider view.

A True Likeness came about partly because I felt that something like it was needed—I once told an interviewer of the time that I wrote the books I did because if I didn't write them, no one else would. That went double for the anthology I edited. I published it partly to showcase the work of the many talented writers I'd become aware of in a very short few years. All of the other Violet Quill Club members were asked (sometimes asked repeatedly) to contribute; and all but Cox ended up doing so. Chris kept on rewriting one short story again and again, never feeling that he'd quite gotten it right. Despite many warnings, he missed the deadline—by over a decade! In fact, his short story only saw the light of day five years after his death in 1994, when he was no longer around to hold onto it and revise it yet one more time, appearing in David Bergman's *Violet Quill Reader*. And even then, the editor found he had to choose from a half dozen versions and as many titles. (David finally settled on "Aunt Persia and the Jesus Man.")

For my book, Holleran provided his *Christopher Street* story "Someone is Crying in the Chateau de Berne." Ed handed in the second chapter of *A Boy's Own Story,* which he'd begun writing a few months earlier. As a result, I ended up nervously editing Edmund's work, which he—professional that he is—claimed to appreciate. Robert Ferro sold me a chapter from what would be his breakout book, *The Family of Max Desir.* Michael Grumley got me the first chapter of what would remain one of his several unfinished (and to this day unpublished) novels, *A World of Men.* Whitmore sent the text of a new play, *Legacy.* Other authors in the book included my friends Richard Umans, Robert Herron, and Joseph Mathewson, the latter with a one act play; short fiction by men and women including Jane Rule, Jane DeLynn, Emily Sisley, Nancy Stockwell, Beau Riley, Richard Hall, and Philip Kravitz, and poetry by Joan Larkin, James Schuyler, Joe Cady, Judy Grahn, Aaron Shurin, John Iozia, Bink Noll, Jon Bracker, Ian Young, Rudy Kikel, Kerrick Harvey, the irrepressible Walta Borawski, and *CS* editor Chuck Ortleb—who was a pretty good poet.

The writers' voices and their subject matter was wildly divergent. Iozia wrote about the gay club scene, slyly, from an insider's point of view. Ortleb wrote angrily about gay politics. Schuyler was sweetly in love. Grahn described the life of butch working-class dykes, while Stockwell's story was about the women's golf circuit. Borawski wrote about street—and sometimes about drag queens; Emily Sisley, about lesbianism in academia.

Unlike just about every other writer or editor before or since, I stuck with the introduction as my only contribution to the anthology. I wrote about gay and lesbian writing as the literature of a homegrown social dissent movement, similar in several ways to the samizdat literature being secretly circulated at that time in Leonid Brezhnev's repressed USSR (and being made much of by the *New York Times*). What made our literature important, I pointed out, was that while it was not heavily oppressed, as was that of Anna Akhmatova and Aleksandr Solzhenitsyn, it was instead *ignored,* as though it—and we—did not exist, did not count at all. It was a passionately argued essay, and reading it today is a sobering indication of how relatively little time—twenty-six years—lay between the anthology's urgent need to exist and to matter, and today's openness, and concomitant blasé attitude about gay life and writing. Who was it who said any successful revolution eats its young? Nowadays it seems to be far worse: it just neglects those who made the revolution.

As any editor or publisher will confirm, putting an anthology together is not the easiest nor the most gratifying task. Those not included in it bitched and whined at the time, feeling insulted and snubbed, and cut me for years, some for decades afterward. Those who were included needed to change "just one line" (i.e., every other comma) every other week. Some of the writers took far too long proofreading their galleys, until I had to blow the whistle and say I was printing whatever I had on hand at a certain date.

As to what to use as cover art—lesbian and gay male visual representation had become an issue so fraught with couched meaning, implication, and sexual politics by then that I began receiving phone calls and letters on the subject from half the contributors before the collection was even fully done. So I ended up deciding to use no art at all. Instead, the cover was composed of type. The top half of both front and back covers consisted of the book's title and the names of all the writers inside in black type against a blue background. The bottom half consisted of the same title and names, but upside down, in white type against the same blue background. ("Oh, I get it," one design-challenged person commented, after pondering the anthology cover for an inordinately long time: "It's like . . . reflected!")

The book was long—356 pages—and that meant it would need a far sturdier binding than previous titles. I insisted upon 99 percent acid free paper for all SeaHorse books, and finding a grade I could use that would bind tightly, be affordable, and take print well wasn't the simplest process. For the first time I didn't use any of our many local, underground, or counterculture printers or binders—the only ones who usually would print gay books—because I didn't fully trust any of them for the job. Instead, I ended up with a large printing house in the northern wilds of Michigan. When calling printers around the country to get estimates for the job, I insisted that that they be gay or feminist: after all, the money I was spending was gay money, and I wanted the manufacturers to know it from the beginning. The first printer I phoned, who'd been sending us flyers for months, asked if the book was porn, so I hung up. The second printer told me she would handle the book entirely herself: although she wasn't gay, she'd been looking for just such an opportunity.

The typesetting took three times longer than anything earlier and was thus three times as costly as any book I'd published previously. It also required far closer scrutiny—even so a few typos crept in. As a result, the final book had to be twice as expensive as any previous title of SeaHorse Press: $11.95. Would it *ever* break even? (Never mind make a profit.) I wasn't at all sure. And frankly, by the time the finished copies of *A True Likeness* arrived, I almost no longer cared.

Six months later, I was interviewed on Pacifica Radio in Berkeley, California, by a guy I'd have to describe as a perfectly West Coast, soft-spoken, wild-haired, bearded hippie. Asked what it was like publishing such a large and complicated volume as *A True Likeness,* I replied, "Well, it was like fist-fucking. You have to do it once—for the experience." He almost fell off his chair, clutching his chest as though experiencing a coronary, silently mouthing the words "We're live!" while the two guys in the control room stood up in extreme agitation and spun completely around, getting their headphone wires all twisted up. I laughed.

A True Likeness was shipped in late February. By then, thanks to solid sales of several thousand copies each of the first three titles and to new business agreements SeaHorse Press had made, hundreds of copies were shipped directly from the printer to BookPeople and Small Press Traffic. These were good-size distributors of small press titles in Berkeley, California, and West Haven, Connecticut, with which GPNy would end up doing a lot of business with.

I'd talked about and even shown an early copy of the book to Jill Dunbar and Jenny Feder, two of the three owners of Three Lives & Company, a new bookstore that had opened in New York City's West Village. Although they and their partner, Helene Webb, were lesbians, as was most (if not all) of their staff, their avowed intention was not to give neighboring Oscar Wilde Memorial Bookshop competition (as Craig Rodwell, its owner, repeatedly, paranoically declared), but to be more of a neighborhood bookstore, which, given their location, also meant being somewhat literary. The women had opened the store at the corner of Seventh Avenue South and West Tenth Street in the early fall of 1978, and in the year or so since had sold gay titles in some quantity, including my own *The Lure.* But while they were frank about being gay, they'd not done really anything specifically public about it, and continued to sell a wide variety of both gay and non-gay authors.

I don't recall which of us came up with the idea—probably I suggested something like having some of the authors from the new anthology come into the shop and sign copies, since after all they lived in the area and most of them shopped there. At a later visit, one of the three owners pointed out that Three Lives & Company had an unused second floor, facing lower Seventh Avenue South, originally intended for offices and for overstock, but so far still unused. Should we have the signing there, away from the quite limited bookstore floor space?

Good idea, but what would attract people to go up those stairs?

We decided to have two readings in mid-March: one Saturday and one Sunday afternoon. It would be the first declaration by the owners of their open support of gay literature, and it would be the first event at the bookstore. Signs were made up and put in the window for two weeks beforehand, and many of the people who saw them said they would come. Even so, none of us had any idea what to expect.

The two upstairs rooms were almost all windows on three sides and linked by a wide, open doorway. There were clean wooden floors, newly painted plaster walls, and not one thing else. The day of the first reading was very chilly, with snow predicted. One chair for the readers and a standing lamp were brought up to the larger room, and at 4 PM sharp I showed up with four readers from the anthology who'd gathered at my apartment: Emily Sisley, who drove up from the D.C. area, and Manhattanites Jane DeLynn, John Iozia, and Michael Grumley. We walked the five blocks to the shop. It seemed a mite busier than usual, but I really wondered if the event was a miss, not a hit, until Jenny came downstairs smiling and said, "It's packed!"

Seated on the floor in the cold, bare little rooms were maybe twenty people including Edmund White, Chris Cox (and their new boyfriends) and Andrew Holleran. I spoke a little about the book and what it represented, and then announced each reader; Jenny announced that this was kicking off what would be a regular series of reading at Three Lives.

In 1981, shared body heat and the excitement of hearing poets and fiction writers reading their work and telling us stories about our lesbian and gay lives—for most listeners for the very first time in a public space in 1981—seemed to completely warm us up. Two read, we broke to smoke cigarettes and buy books, and then reassembled and two more read.

The next day, poets Dan Diamond and Chuck Ortleb and VQers Robert Ferro and George Whitmore read, some from work not in the anthology. Word had gotten out the night before, so it was standing room only again—perhaps thirty of us crowded together. As George, the last reader of the session, read, the sun set and snow began to silently fall outside. By the time he was done it was night, and the windows were swagged with ice, frosted white. Chris Cox had alerted a photographer pal of his from the *SoHo Weekly News* who came both nights and took photos of all of us for the paper. Chris then wrote a short article for the *SWN* on the reading.

The anthology was launched at those readings, as were several careers, among them most noticeably Whitmore's and Ferro's, who had read wonderfully and had been warmly applauded for their soon-to-be-published novels, *The Confessions of Danny Slocum* and *The Family of Max Desir*. And the reading series at Three Lives & Company became an important literary institution. In the following years writers such as Saul Bellow and Eudora Welty would read there. (The store eventually moved to its present location at the corner of West Tenth Street and Waverly Place, and in 2001, Jill Dunbar and Jenny Feder sold it to Toby Cox, who still runs it.)

At those two readings, the new movement of GLBT literature, which had been quietly happening for some five or six years already, somehow seemed to be officially and quite publicly launched. When asked, the other members of the Violet Quill were all pleased about this, although we didn't know at the time how important this particular public act of expression would be. Bookstore readings, for some reason nearly nonexistent for decades in New York City would soon become commonplace, first for gay and lesbian writers and feminists, then people perceived to have a social agenda, and ultimately, for all writers. Eventually, readings would move beyond commonplace and become a required practice.

For years afterward, I would hear about those readings at Three Lives (which couldn't have accommodated more than fifty people at once) from so many different people that the two chilly afternoons took on a kind of mythic resonance. You simply *had* to have been there, whether you actually were or not.

Several months later, during the summertime, I was having lunch directly across the street from the bookstore at an open-air café with Greg Kolovakos, an acquaintance who worked for the New York State Council on the Arts (NYSCA), and who later became a cofounder of the Gay and Lesbian Alliance Against Defamation. He told me he'd also been present (he *had?*) and that "those readings were the most important thing that's happened to me as a gay man and a writer!" I wasn't so sure about that. But Greg had brought papers with him to our lunch: an application for a NYSCA grant for SeaHorse Press. Together, while laughing and eating, we filled them out. Some months later, to my astonishment, the press received a grant of $3,000; the first and last literary grant I ever saw.

That windfall made me decide to do two more books. I launched the next two SeaHorse Press titles together: Dennis Cooper's first published prose fiction, *Safe,* and Brad Gooch's short stories, *Jail Bait.*

If the anthology had put SeaHorse on the map in the New York literary world, those two titles by promising young writers of the day would turn my little press into the place where new gay writers of the 1980s yearned to be published. Our next event would be huge: cocktails at a new dance club, with scores of people from other publishing houses present. And soon enough some people were speaking of SeaHorse Press with the same respect in their voices that my friends and I had spoken in college days and in the 1960s of publishers like City Lights Books, New Directions, and the Grove Press. While a few years earlier I'd had to explain what SeaHorse Press was and why I'd begun it, by late 1981, people would already know the name of the press, some people would know one or another SeaHorse author. Some guys, trying to be hip, would say right to my face (and to my great amusement), "I think I know an editor there."

But in between I would meet Larry Mitchell and Terry Helbing, and apparently not having enough to do (living a full romantic and sexual life, writing a book a year, plus articles, essays, poems and plays, running Sea-Horse Press, going out dancing every weekend with the appropriate recreational drug use), and so I would help launch a second and even more successful publishing house.

3

Calamus & JH Press Begin

If poetry was the key to the beginnings of SeaHorse Press, then theater, and especially gay theater, was without question the way JH Press and eventually the Gay Presses of New York got together. No surprise then that 75 percent of JH Press's total output as well as GPNy's single biggest hit were plays, and that all four little companies published over thirty dramas and comedies. This may sound improbable today, when vital theater is about as rare as crucial poetry (and about as popular), but it was true then.

Calamus Press, with its unmistakable allusion to Walt Whitman's homo-erotic poetry, grew out of a more basic need: to get the author's own second title—which he believed was an important book—published, period.

Obviously, in the years and then in the months leading up to my trying to launch SeaHorse Press, the two men who would become my partners in Gay Presses of New York some five years later were already busy with their own very creative gay lives. When we finally came together, it was like three vectors that had been moving in the same direction from three different starting positions finally, if unexpectedly, approaching simultaneous apogees.

———

Larry Mitchell was born in Muncie, Indiana, a town so utterly middle class, so inexorably Midwestern American, that Robert Staught Lynd used it as the basis of his path-breaking sociological investigation, *Middletown: A Study in Modern American Culture* (1959), required reading when I was going to college.

Born in 1942, Mitchell was the only child of older parents, and his first real break from "Middletown" was going away to Colby College in Maine. In many senses, Larry never went home again. But Lynd seemed to somehow predetermine him intellectually for many years longer, since Larry ended up majoring in sociology so seriously that he later attended Columbia University's graduate program where he received a PhD degree in the field.

The long-term upshot was that Mitchell would himself teach sociology for the next thirty years, first at Cornell, then, and for a much longer time, at the College of Staten Island, where he'd be close to the forefront of many of the political and social movements of the second half of the twentieth century: racial integration, counterculturalism, feminism, and gay rights.

The most immediate result, however, was that Mitchell moved to Manhattan just at that time when New York City was becoming an acknowledged world center of both the arts and of political rebellion. Although he would spend periods of time in San Francisco, upstate New York, and Cape Cod, Mitchell early on became a New Yorker and still lives there part of the year.

Like many of us in lower Manhattan in the sixties, Mitchell became part of the counterculture, and like many of us, the second part of that term was of equal importance to the first. Contradictorily, and like many apparently urban dwellers, Mitchell joined the back to the land movement, and bought a farm in Ithaca, New York, that became an important focus for him, but that he now admits he "hardly lived on."

Despite that fact, in 1978, he and his colleagues began editing and publishing *R.F.D. Magazine: A Country Journal for Queer Folk Everywhere*, a homoerotic magazine of poetry and prose written by, for, and about gay men living in rural areas of the country. The magazine was taken over after

Mitchell and his cohorts by the handsome and nurturing Paul Mariah, under whose hand it—and many poets personally and professionally—flourished for several decades. Remarkably, *R.F.D.* is still published today, out of North Carolina.

Mitchell's first book, *Great Gay in the Morning!*, was another product of the counterculture. Published by Times Change Press in 1972, it was all about living in a gay commune in San Francisco. Like many cultural products of the time, the book was allegedly authored by the collective, although Larry now says he did all the writing.

While that book could be considered only a somewhat slight slant on a familiar theme of the era—other books with similar topics included Ray Mungo's *Total Loss Farm* (1970) and Steve Diamond's *What The Trees Said* (1972)—four years later, Mitchell came up with the concept for another book, one far more original, which he says came to him entire and in detail in a single afternoon "while I was on quaaludes."

The result would be one of his best-known books, quickly adopted as a defining text by Harry Hay and the Radical Faerie movement. *The Faggots and Their Friends Between Revolutions* (1977), Mitchell's book of stories and anecdotes, exuded lots of gay charm, with just the right amount of "let's get real, kids" attitude mixed in to send it into five good-size printings over the following few years. This was a distinct coup for a new press, as it had been repeatedly turned down by major publishers, and yet another indication that commercial publishers seldom know what they are overlooking. *The Faggots and Their Friends* would define Mitchell's singular writing style without calcifying it: in his next four books, published in the following fifteen years, his writing developed into an instrument capable of entertaining storytelling, social and relationship critique, humorous eroticism, political and social satire, even fantasy.

Before that could happen, of course, Mitchell had to find a publisher for *The Faggots and Their Friends*, and with the counterculture a suddenly defunct fad in the often trend-driven publishing world, that turned out to be impossible. After "too long trying," Mitchell, like myself, Helbing, and too many others to mention, decided that maybe Karl Marx was right after all when he'd written that the workers themselves ought to possess their own means of production and of capital gains. Around the same time I was learning to become a small press publisher (but for utterly different reasons), so was Larry, on the other side of lower Manhattan—and with similarly successful results.

The outcome was the Calamus Press, the name shamelessly taken from the great poet Walt Whitman's erotic section of his massive compendium *Leaves of Grass.* Larry funded the press and his book himself from his earnings as a teacher and from family money. He had no intention of printing any other books, but quickly found himself pressured into doing so by his peers, as well as by the growing necessity he soon recognized for providing an outlet for fresh and important gay voices to reach their public.

This has to be understood as part of Mitchell's activist continuum. Only a few months after putting out *The Faggots and Their Friends,* Larry and several of *his* friends formed a group calling itself the Pink Satin Bomber Collective—a joke on the typical 1978 gay male clone outerwear: gray green silk U.S. Air Force jackets (I had one and loved it!). At Ithaca, New York, the Pink Satin Bombers put on an in-your-face event titled *An Evening of Faggot Theater in Three Parts,* which had run at Manhattan's very avant-garde Performing Garage in what would later become SoHo and was then still "very downtown." Mitchell soon wrote another play for the group, *Get It While You Can,* performed at Theater for a New City on First Avenue between Eighth and Ninth Streets—the Lower East Side, which was by no means the gentrified East Village of today, but instead a filthy, roach- and rat-infested, indiscriminate motley of bohemians, welfare mothers, motorcycle clubs like the Hell's Angels, artists needing cheap space, and second generation Russian immigrants too timorous to cross the East and Hudson Rivers.

Looking at a copy of *The Faggots and Their Friends* today, with its "soft" cover design and sweet illustrations by Ned Asta, so different than SeaHorse

Press's own first offering and yet published within a few months' of it, I can't help but note the welcome diversity that Larry brought to the Gay Presses of New York once he got going. During the 1980s, Mitchell's links with the East Village and its denizens coalesced further. Visual artists Bill Rice and David Wojnarowicz, photographer Peter Hujar, playwright Jeff Weiss, performance artists Bette Bourne and "her" ensemble Bloolips, and younger writers like Gary Indiana and Ray Dobbins (who might be thought of as part of the East Village punk scene)—all made contributions to American culture.

The financial success of Mitchell's first book allowed Calamus to publish other writers, among them Boston poet Ron Schreiber's *False Clues* (1977) and *Tomorrow Will Really Be Sunday* (1984) and Richard Ronan's *Flowers* (1978), as well as playwright Robert Patrick's collection *Mercy Drop and Other Plays* (1980), which included the well known gay plays *T-Shirts* and *The Haunted Host*. Mitchell also put out fiction: Alabama Birdstone's 1981 sci-fi novel of gay concentration camps, *Queer Free,* Dobbins's working-class short stories *Don the Burp* (1990), and Indiana's first—and I still think best work of fiction, *Scar Tissue* (1987).

But it was Mitchell's own books that kept the Calamus Press in the black and that eventually boosted both GPNy's reputation and helped solidify his own name. *The Terminal Bar* of 1982 was a thinly disguised roman à clef about the denizens of the infamous Phebe's Tavern off Cooper Place, hangout of so many East Side artists, druggies, and wannabes. *In Heat* (1985) was a romantic comedy about a group of mostly gay friends dealing with sexual liberation and the necessity of having to keep up being avant-garde.

Both novels won him a wider audience and Larry didn't disappoint. His fifth book, *My Life as a Mole and Other Stories* (1989), illustrated by Bill Rice, was extraordinary in its depth and reach, so much so that it received a brilliant review in—of all places—that most mainstream of gay publications, the *Advocate*. There, John Preston wrote that the title novella, *My Life as a Mole,* "is a spare, unsparing meditation on the fate of pleasure in the ugly world that AIDS has foisted on the human menagerie. By turns acerbic and inconsolable, this trenchant and eerily graceful book conjures up a landscape of loss and regret peopled by ghosts and their sometimes grudging custodians." The book went on to win the Lambda Literary Foundation's Small Press Book of the Year Award.

Mitchell's eyesight had begun failing by then—macular degeneration had set in—and it would be several more years before he completed and then published his last novel, *Acid Snow* (1992). A bleak, almost desperately cheerless look at how the Lower East Side had been exploited, co-opted, and ravished by outsiders while its most steadfast population was left to deal with continued poverty and squalor, this was perhaps Mitchell's most important work—and his last.

By 1994, Larry's increasing blindness led him to retire from teaching as well as from publishing—and unfortunately also from writing. It had even begun to limit his going out at night. "People think I'm blind drunk," he once quipped, when he explained why he got a white-tipped walking cane, "instead of just blind." When asked why he'd stopped writing, Mitchell said that for him, "writing has to be something I can see right in front of myself. I can't do it any other way."

His substantial accomplishments as a writer, dramaturge, friend, mentor, and sociology professor, and his contributions to gay culture, should be ample for any single lifetime. When interviewing Mitchell for this book, I asked how he viewed his work and his time as a gay publisher, both at Calamus and with GPNy. With typical self-deprecation, humor, and yet also with complete earnestness, Larry said, "Well, I once had this naive image that as a publisher I'd be having all these intellectual, stimulating lunches with authors, and that would be so Algonquin Hotel, so worthwhile. But the truth is that most of the authors were pains in the neck. And what I recall most is me ending up taking their whining phone calls, typing up endless invoices, and lugging their books all around New York City. Under those conditions, who even wanted to eat? Never mind have lunch."

———

Like Larry, Terry Helbing was a Midwesterner. Terry was born on May 21, 1951, in East Dubuque, Illinois. Like Larry and me, his family background was about as bourgeois as they come. Terry's father was a prosperous banker. There was a previous child, Doris, almost two decades Terry's senior, who was seldom a factor in his life. Unlike our families, however, Terry's had a peculiarly middle-class dysfunction: both his parents became alcoholics, and once he was in New York, Terry would become a determining factor in organizing one of the first local chapters of friends and relatives of alcoholics, Al-Anon. Despite his railing on about his many problems with his parents when he was young, substance abuse would haunt his life, and end up proving to be the key to Terry's own undoing long after his parents were dead.

Unlike the rest of his family, theater was Terry's obsession from an early age until his last days on earth. And so, oddly enough, was amateur bowling. As a twelve-year-old, Helbing was already a league bowler and champion in Illinois. Once he was settled in New York, Terry took up bowling once again, often taking long subway and bus rides to the far-flung reaches of New York's outer boroughs and suburbs every weekend he was not onstage because that was where the bowling alleys and best players were. In 1987 Terry, Ken Hale, and Tim Contini, along with thirty-seven other bowlers, founded the Gotham Open Tournament, which became a significant link in the International Gay Bowling Organization. According to web site content from that club, "Terry Helbing, along with Hale and Contini, was a crucial ingredient from the very beginning." The first Gotham Open Tournament held at the Thirty-fourth Avenue Bowl in Long Island City, Queens, and was composed of ten local teams; the first team winners were Terry Helbing, Dan Romer, Scott Sullivan, and Malcolm Navias. Their team name? Lies 'Em In Alley.

There were other advantages to bowling besides the merely recreational and social ones. Terry's regular bowling was immediately apparent in his usually excellent physical condition; he was tall and fit, but neither slender nor lightweight. And this was especially apparent in his arms and legs. Often, just as we would be making an entrance—at a party, the theater, a bar—Terry would roll up his sleeves so his muscled forearms showed, and he had dozens of very short sleeved shirts that he wore out, even in the dead of winter, to showcase his biceps—which he sheepishly admitted facilitated sexual hookups.

Like Larry Mitchell, Terry had also left the Midwest for New England, going to Emerson College in downtown Boston, then as now one of the few four-year colleges specializing in communications and performing arts. When he arrived in New York several years after graduation, he intended a career as an actor, an aspiration he cherished and worked toward for the rest of his life. However, he ended up earning a living at *The Drama Review* under its second editor, Michael Kirby.

A little of the magazine's history will be instructive, as it both parallels and reflects the huge upheaval going on in the field of drama at that time, and that ended up making drama such an important an art form. Begun as the *Carleton Drama Review* in 1955, it was taken over at Tulane University in New Orleans when prodigy Richard Schechner joined the graduate faculty. There it became the *Tulane Drama Review* and prospered tremendously by following Schechner's dictum that it "challenge prevailing ideas about theater, what it is, how it should be presented, and the rituals and ideals behind it." When Schechner began to encounter increasingly conservative political and community pressure against his ideas in New Orleans, he and the six other Tulane professors quit the school's graduate program in protest en masse and moved to New York University, in effect eliminating completely Tulane's theater department without any professors and throwing the graduate program into disarray for years. He brought the magazine along with them to NYU and renamed it *The Drama Review,* thus retaining its well-known three-letter logo. In New York, Schechner's talents were better appreciated. He quickly formed the Performance Group, which made its mark with his play *Dionysius in 69,* which infamously broke the fourth wall by actively including the audience in the action, and sometimes even "kidnapping" people off the nearby streets to participate.

Schechner left *TDR* in 1969, and after a brief stint by Erika Munk, Michael Kirby took over as editor, gradually altering the magazine to make it less an organ of social and political rebellion and returning its focus to theater. Terry Helbing began as Kirby's managing editor in 1974, and eventually became associate editor, and he remained until 1986, when Schechner regained control.

While there, Helbing himself edited several special issues: one on Jewish theater that was widely praised, and another groundbreaking issue titled "Sex and Performance" in 1981 that for the first time brought GLBT theatrical works into a prominent academic context. Despite no longer being at *TDR*, Schechner's influence on Helbing's view of theater was immediately apparent to anyone (including me) who had worked with him onstage. And it was indisputable in the name Terry chose for his long-running theater column, "The Fourth Wall."

His influential *Drama Review* position would give Terry stature in his chosen field and prove to be an important launching pad for him as a reviewer, columnist, editor, publisher, and even to some extent as a theater producer—but if he ever wrote a play, or even a dramatic sketch, none of his friends or colleagues heard of or read it. Later on, it would be me, a fledgling playwright at the time, not the experienced dramalog Terry, who would end up editing Harvey Fierstein's *Torch Song Trilogy* for publication.

Before working for *TDR*, Terry had already begun his acting career, even his gay theater career, appearing in the 1973 Boston and New England touring company of Jonathan Ned Katz's gay pride play *Coming Out!* Terry got more acting parts, including that of a policeman in the original TOSOS production of Doric Wilson's *West Street Gang*, a play about the Stonewall Riots performed at the Mineshaft, the infamous sex club. That's where I first encountered Terry.

Helbing's acting career would go on to include starring roles in Terry Miller's *Pines '79*, which he also produced for the Glines. He also starred in *The Demolition of Harry Fay* by Sidney Morris and appeared in *Franny, the*

Queen of Provincetown, an adaptation of John Preston's popular 1983 novel about an effeminate man's travails in a gay male clone community. In 1991, Terry's last onstage performance was in *Cocktails at the Red Rooster,* a benefit for Joseph's Surgical, an AIDS organization. When the Meridian Theater reproduced it, Terry also appeared in Doric Wilson's *Street Theater.* And according to Doric, in his last two years of life, Terry worked hard and traveled much after his accident to regain his voice, eyesight, and motor skills, primarily because he was intent on reviving his acting career.

Helbing's competence, coolness under duress, and growing experience also led him to take on nonacting work in the gay theater scene, first as general manager for the Sixth Anniversary Repertory for the Glines, but more importantly as a producer himself.

While many gay people focus on a single art, Terry Helbing, like Larry Mitchell, me, and many other writers of the post-Stonewall era, worked in a variety of capacities and in many media. In many senses, we had to: there was so much to be done and so few people who were out, talented, and also willing to work. Edmund White once drew a portrait of the sophisticated gay man of the 1970s. He had a successful career, a great personal life, a good sex life, lots of community connections, and also belonged to a gym, knew all the latest pop music, could cook gourmet meals, and knowledgably discuss Montserrat Caballé's tessitura. It was funny but true, and undeniably hard work—compared to today, when many younger gay men are proud of themselves if they can use the Internet and still have nice abs.

Terry cofounded the Gay Theatre Alliance, an organization dedicated to the growth of gay theater, and he served as its president. He would soon collate and edit the *Gay Theatre Alliance Directory of Gay Plays,* the first complete listing of GLBT theater works, which he published through JH Press in 1980. Helbing cofounded the Meridian Gay Theatre Production Company in 1983 with writer Terry Miller to produce plays and musicals with gay and lesbian themes. The Meridian became the only continuously operating gay theater with a home base on the East Coast, as considerable a venue as Minneapolis's concurrent Out And About Theater and San Francisco's Theater Rhinoceros. Helbing became Meridian's artistic director and together, Helbing and Miller initiated a playwrights and directors series that featured staged readings of new plays and also sponsored a national gay playwriting contest every year until 1987.

During the late 1970s and throughout the 1980s, GLBT theater was a small but extremely active and vital force, both in the GLBT community and in the theater world. Gay plays ran the gamut from angry social protest to lighthearted comedies, from psychological portraits of GLBT characters in crisis to wildly campy rewritings of previous genres, stealing from Dumas tragedies, thirties movies, and fifties television. Few shows that were put on failed to find audiences, and while these were not large audiences—a typical GLBT theater had sixty to ninety-nine seats—some plays, like Doric Wilson's *Street Theater,* Jane Chamber's *My Blue Heaven,* and my own *Immortal,* ran months at a stretch. Actors moved back and forth from Broadway to off-Broadway and into GLBT theater, and from those into movies and television. Many straight actors of that era got their first breaks with substantial parts in gay plays—Jean Smart and Brad Davis come to mind.

Helbing had already begun writing articles on theater, books, video, and music for the *Advocate, Christopher Street, SoHo Weekly News, Seven Days, Genre, Theater Week,* and many other publications. As if that wasn't enough, Terry began his weekly theater column, "The Fourth Wall," in the *New York Native,* and became theater editor of the paper. His column included reviews of shows, theatrical compact discs, insider news, and information about upcoming shows of all types.

And, as a sideline, Terry still had time and a consuming interest in what was the largest private collection I've ever encountered of sixties girl-group singers. The living room walls of his tiny West Village apartment on Charles Street were devoted to stacks of 45s of probably every R&B singer or assemblage of the era. He also had, naturally enough, several pink plastic and Naugahyde portable record players from that era, useful and valuable—if somewhat campy—collectibles. (They sported poodle skirt motifs and the florid, embroidered signatures of Pat Boone, Peggy Lee, and Diana Ross.) The little free time Helbing had in his ridiculously busy career and his bowling club schedule was spent cataloging and taping the Shirelles, the Chiffons, Martha and the Vandellas, Little Eva, the Angels, et al. Their bluesy, lovelorn complaints and bubbly enticements to dance formed the background music to our GPNy meetings at his flat, especially the annual royalty statement get-togethers that Terry and I had in his small kitchen, four floors above Greenwich Street, where we'd compile and discuss book sales, returns, and check amounts for Gay Presses of New York titles, and, since it was easier for two to do it (and get it right) than for one, for our own presses, too. There, on his faux-wood 1955 metal table, amid his usual vast aggregate of soda, chips, and Chinese and Indian restaurant takeout (Helbing was a vegetarian all his adult life) we'd happily enumerate, chat, and slowly get to know each other better.

Terry had begun JH Press in 1981, only a few months before he, Larry, and I had our first lunch together to discuss beginning a new composite publishing company. A windfall inheritance from his unmarried paternal uncle, Joseph Helbing, after whom the press—JH—was named, facilitated the process. Terry's belief that his uncle was a closeted gay man did the rest. But it was mostly based on his experience as an actor, stage manager, director, and producer that he'd encountered so much excellent talent in GLBT theater that he felt it was time to do something about it, to in Terry's own words, "put his money where his mouth was." The Gay Theatre Alliance and the Meridian Gay Theater would be two of the most important manifestations of his enthusiasm. *The Gay Theatre Alliance Directory of Plays,* one of the first books out of JH Press, would be one of his most lasting contributions, along with his anthology for Heinemann, *Gay Plays Today* (1988) a compendium still used in many academic courses.

Among the most uniquely talented of those Terry had encountered when I first met him was his own personal favorite writer, Jane Chambers. Born in

Columbia, South Carolina, in 1937, Jane's life and career can stand as a sad if eventually triumphant paradigm of what it meant to be a woman playwright, and especially a lesbian playwright, during the twentieth century. She entered Rollins College at seventeen, but found that she could only get into the play-writing or directing courses there if there were empty slots after the men had already enrolled. Frustrated, she went to California's Pasadena Playhouse from 1956 to 1957, then briefly to New York City, ending up in Poland Springs, Maine, the next year, where she worked for a decade in the fledgling field of local television, an area hungry for talent and unafraid of intelligent, competent women. Twelve years later, Jane finally got her degree from Goddard College in Vermont, where she met Beth Allen, who would become her manager and life partner. In 1971, Jane won the Connecticut educational television award for her play *Christ in a Tree House.* The following year Jane secured an important Eugene O'Neill fellowship for playwriting and worked on new plays that were produced at the O'Neill Theatre Foundation in New Haven.

This led Chambers back to New York, although unfortunately not to the theater, but instead to television where—tellingly—she went to work as a writer for a soap opera, *Search For Tomorrow,* winning A Writer's Guild of America award for her writing for the show in 1973. At the same time she helped organize the Women's Interarts Center, where she began a theater program.

Chambers was thirty-seven years old in 1974 when Playwrights Horizon's produced *A Late Snow,* her first off-Broadway production and one of the first openly lesbian and gay-positive plays. Other dramatic doors remained slow to open. Only in 1980 did the Glines produce what has come to be known as Jane's signature work, *Last Summer At Bluefish Cove,* with a superb cast, starring Jean Smart, who would go on to major parts in film, television series, and on Broadway. The story of a group of women at a summer colony, one of whom discovers—and carefully reveals to the others—that she is dying of cancer, the play was a critical and financial success. It was followed at the

Glines by her comedy, *My Blue Heaven,* in 1982, but also, and alas with terrible irony, by Chambers's own diagnosis of brain cancer. The last of her plays performed in her lifetime was *The Quintessential Image,* at the Women's Theater Conference in Minneapolis in 1982.

Jane Chambers died early in 1983, in Greenport, Long Island. A modest, cheerful, gracious, and loving person, she is now considered one of the most important women playwrights in American theater. Critic Beth A. Kattelman writes: "Chambers was one of the first playwrights to create openly lesbian characters who were comfortable with their own homosexuality. She believed that this would help eliminate homophobia. As Chambers told the *New York Times,* 'As we become more comfortable with ourselves, the rest of the world will become comfortable with us.' She opened the door for other playwrights who wished to write affirming plays about lesbians." Even so, in Jane's own lifetime she experienced only a few short years of dramatic accomplishment and acclaim.

Terry Helbing had grown close to Jane and Beth when they all worked together at the Glines, and they remained close right up to first Jane's and then Terry's end. Helbing made it a primary directive of JH Press that Jane Chambers's genius, so long kept down, denied, and then cheated by an early death, would flourish and become more widely known. From 1982 on, Terry published all of her gay-themed plays, as well as putting out her book of poetry, *Warrior at Rest* and her sci-fi novel, *Chasin' Jason.* He even reprinted her 1974 lesbian-themed gothic novel, *Burning,* previously published in a Jove mass-market edition.

Helbing also worked along with Beth Allen as manager and agent of Chambers's plays, and in the decade after Jane's death, productions proliferated around the country. His own Meridian Gay Theater did several in excellent productions. Terry considered it a real coup when, in 1987, he was at last able to gain publishing rights to what he considered Jane's best play, *Last Summer at Bluefish Cove.* He put out the usual gay play script series trade paperback but in addition, he published a signed, limited edition hardcover, with an introduction that Jane had written long before in preparation for the volume. Helbing's personal feelings found an echo in those around him. Chambers's books consistently proved to be the best selling of all JH Press titles. And when he put together the anthology *Gay Plays Today,* he included Chambers's *Eye of the Gull.*

Clearly those who had attended Chambers's plays helped sales. But since GLBT theater barely existed outside of a half dozen already named places, it must have been more mainstream play audiences (as well as GLBT readers) who were helping to boost the sales of hers and other gay playwrights' work during this period—perhaps because there was so little gay literature being published at all.

Terry was also close to other colleagues he published. Terry Miller, in whose *Pines '69* he had acted and which he published in 1982, was a lifelong friend. Helbing also enjoyed Arch Brown, whose comedy, *Newsboy,* he put out in 1983. Terry produced Robert Chesley's *Stray Dog Story: An Adventure in Ten Scenes* at Meridian and published it in 1984, the same year he published C. D. Arnold's *Dinosaur Plays.* Named the JH Press Gay Play Script Series, this was going to be only one part of a much larger venture—the publication of all minority theater of value. In addition, Doric Wilson confirmed in a recent conversation that Terry planned to put out a black play script series and a women's play script series. When Francine Trevens took over JH Press's line following Helbing's death, she followed his wishes by expanding TNT's gay script series and by adding many more women playwrights.

One of Doric Wilson's best-known plays had initiated the original JH Press series: *Forever After: A Vivisection of Gay Male Love without Interruption* (1980), while *Street Theater: The 27th of June, 1969* (i.e., the eve of the Stonewall Riots) came out seven years later. Doric and Terry remained friends, associates, and at times quite vocal brawlers throughout Helbing's life.

Aside from Chambers, perhaps the most unusual of Helbing's working friendships was with playwright Sidney Morris. JH Press would include two of Morris's plays in its gay scripts series: *If This Isn't Love* in 1982, and *The*

Demolition of Harry Fay (which Terry had starred in earlier) in 1986. For those in literary academia who may be thinking that Morris's name sounds awfully familiar, it might well be. Morris was known as one of the foremost authorities on medieval English verse, and he compiled several anthologies still in print and used today, including *Carmina Latina,* an olio of bawdy texts in that dead language similar to those used by Carl Orff in his choral masterpiece, *Carmina Burana.*

The Terry Helbing papers, fifteen feet of records and personal papers from the 1960s through the 1990s, are now available at the New York City GLBT Center's collection.

———

In the winter of 1979–80, the link among Larry Mitchell, Terry Helbing, and me was Larry's boyfriend, Bill Castleman. Bill was an actor who'd played a featured role in *The West Street Gang* along with Terry and had begun working as stage manager at the Shandol Theater, which would become the Chelsea, the Manhattan home of Helbing's Meridian Gay Theater. Bill would later be wonderful in the part of the dog turned young man in Chesley's *Stray Dog Story.* I had already met Terry several times at the offices of the *New York Native* farther downtown, and somehow the fact that Larry and I were both doing small press publishing of GLBT books, which Terry had just begun doing, came up in conversation between Terry and Bill. Castleman suggested we three all get together. I'd just published Doric Wilson through SeaHorse Press, and I'd heard of Larry and his book, *The Faggots and Their Friends Between Revolutions.* Both Larry and Terry knew about me because I'd just completed the first national book tour of an openly gay novelist for my book, *The Lure,* and publicity about me in the city, as well as across the country, in both the gay and mainstream press, was inescapable. There were so many preexisting connections, we three almost *had* to connect.

As Terry and I lived around the corner from each other, Larry taxied over from the East Side and we met for lunch at a French provincial restaurant on the corner of Greenwich and Eleventh streets called the Black Sheep. Anyone watching and listening to us that afternoon wouldn't have noticed anything special going on—never mind anything momentous about our coming together. We certainly didn't act or look as though we were about to supercharge gay literature and lift it to new levels of artistry and popularity. We were mature men by then. At thirty years old, Terry was the baby; I was thirty-seven, and Larry, thirty-nine. We'd all been around gay life, books, and theater at least a decade and there were very few stars left in our eyes. Our plans were modest in scale, our goals equally small, and above all, we hoped, practical: to publish among the three of us, and in addition to what our little companies were already putting out, at least one more GLBT book per year that none of the bigger publishers would touch. We tossed around names of people we knew in common, and we discussed some writers, shows, and films we each enjoyed; but so would many gay men having lunch. Unlike most gay men however, Larry and I talked about our little bit of small press publishing experience: how much work it required, how generally drab it was. There wasn't a great deal of excitement. It was all pretty lackluster. Despite that, by the time it was time to split the bill, we had decided to start the Gay Presses of New York. It would be months until we solidified the idea, but in essence, we'd decided upon all of the basics of the venture in those first few hours together.

Aside from GPNy, I never worked with Larry Mitchell, although we became friends. But I did end up having a completely independent and by no means insignificant work relationship with Terry Helbing—as playwright to his theatrical producer. But that was still several years in the future.

4

Torch Song Trilogy

In interviews and conversations over the years, and in fact whenever people have asked, I've said yes, Gay Presses of New York did indeed have a business philosophy, a credo by which we lived and operated the company. It was this: "Don't be greedy and stupid at the same time."

A joke, of course. But that really was our motto on several occasions, formulated by Larry Mitchell and me during one phone conversation about some piece of good fortune and good business having to do with our first publication.

If any of us three mentioned our motto, another would invariably add, "And try to have some fun."

From the very beginning, we never thought we'd make a lot of money or influence anyone, never mind become the overnight publishing success we became.

By the time Gay Presses of New York was formed and officially incorporated, all three of our separate presses were already in place: mine for four years, Larry's for three and a half, and Terry's for six months. So none of us was in the least bit starry-eyed about what we were facing, and what we expected to accomplish. Our immediate goal, simply stated, was to be able to publish one more good gay book per year through this new publishing entity we were forming together. We each knew how much work it was and how much it would cost us in time, energy, and cash to publish just one title. We also knew how much we could expect back from that one book.

Strangely, luckily, each one of us had launched our individual presses with successful first books:

Define "successful"?

Okay: books that had sold well enough to go into a second printing, earned enough to pay for that second printing, and left something with which to run the company and sign a second book.

We were modest. Realistic.

Which was why, during one of our conversations before the company was officially formed, we asked ourselves and each other what kind of book we wanted to publish to launch the new line. SeaHorse had already done gay male poetry, plays, and short fiction; JH Press had put out a lesbian play, a romantic comedy; Calamus had published short fiction, poetry, and plays. We were open to any of these genres as long as we felt the writing was good, the author had a future, and—most importantly—we liked it.

As for what we expected from GPNy, that was even more simple minded and basic. We expected the company to pay for itself in two to three years, so that the new publications could be paid for entirely out of earnings from earlier books. We expected GPNy to pay our medical insurance. As a corporation, we could obtain group rates. This would affect Larry and me less than Terry; Larry was still teaching courses at Staten Island Community College and had health coverage through his job, while I belonged off and on to the Authors Guild and the Writers Guild of America, East, each of which provided some health coverage. We also expected the new company to provide a sales and distribution umbrella for all four companies. While we'd each continue our own publishing companies, GPNy would issue a yearly catalogue containing all the books, disbursing whatever it netted to our separate lines and perhaps also become a cover organization once we got much wider distribution, a dream we believed could take us up to a decade to achieve. And we expected GPNy to buy us a Christmas dinner at the end of each year—and a business-free dinner at that.

It was Bob Lowe, by then an attorney at Rosenstock & Losey, who suggested the "financial instrument" we eventually chose to describe the company and, given what happened to us, we profusely thanked him for his prescience and good sense later on. We'd already seen and would continue to see other small press publishers, book clubs, and bookstores collapse and go under for lack of a proper fiscal structure. Some of the causalities that died or went dormant in the 1980s included the Gay Book Club, publishers like Persephone, Women's Collective, and Daughters Inc., and many shops, including I.C.I. Bob discussed various financial plans with us but urged us to choose the form of a partnership corporation. This would provide us with legal protection against potential lawsuits: if someone sued us and won, only GPNy's assets, and not any of our own individual assets, would be at risk. The partnership corporation also operated a bit like a tontine, in that each of us held one-third share responsibility and received one-third of any profits. If one of us could not, by reason of mental or physical incapacity, work for GPNy, he would continue to collect profits but would be superseded as operating officer by the remaining two partners. If one of us died, the other two would inherit his share of the company. It was simple, and it eliminated inheritance problems, probate, and other possible obstructions upon which other firms would later totter, founder, and then fall.

The three of us met at my Greenwich Village duplex on West Eleventh Street on the afternoon of Halloween of 1981 and took the corporation papers Bob Lowe had prepared for us up to a notary public on Fourteenth Street and Eighth Avenue. It was a short walk away, located inside a Spanish-speaking travel agency directly across the street from a funeral home we would all sadly become much too familiar with in the coming decade. There, we signed the papers and had them notarized.

We stopped off at the Greenwich Savings Bank two doors away and opened our bank account, each of us putting in a check for $100. We then returned to my apartment, cracked open a bottle of good wine I'd been saving, and while drinking discussed what to publish as our first title.

Terry had seen a play a few weeks before at Ellen Stewart's La Mama Theatre, one leading light for emerging theatrical talent and experimental work in New York City since the sixties. He'd liked it so much he'd given it a starred review in some of the magazines he wrote for, including *The Drama Review*, which Terry still coedited out of an office at New York University. He was about to see the play again and thought he could get us tickets. Larry already had tickets for the play, and he'd heard wonderful things about its young star, who was also its playwright. We agreed that all three of us would see (or resee) the play in a few days and talk the following week.

That done, we discussed the GPNy logo that an East Village pal of Larry's had already sketched out for us. Joseph Modica, who would end up art directing dozens of Calamus and GPNy titles, had taken a photo of the Empire State Building at a sharply angled perspective seen from below and then polarized it so it was totally stylized. He'd then blanked out the flat facade and put in place instead large, Superman-cartoon-like letters *GP* at the top and *NY* at the bottom. From just the sketch alone we knew we liked the design: it was cheeky, it was phallic, it was dynamic, and it was Manhattan-centric. With one look, anyone would know that it meant New York. Of course the logo, like many other things concerning the press, would undergo many subtle changes. But like the press, it retained its very strong, basic concept.

We'd already had to do divvy up responsibilities in order for the incorporation papers to be made out. Citing his and his father's long experience in banking, Terry suggested that he be the treasurer. The financial aspects of the company were of the very smallest interest to us, and Larry and I ceded this position to him instantly. I'd already said I'd like to be editor in chief, and so I was. Larry became publisher and president; Terry and I, vice presidents. And we really weren't planning on having any full-time employees unless GPNy expanded much faster and further than we had any intention of it doing.

But what about acquiring new work? How should that be done? It was decided that each of us would bring in an author, play, or manuscript and present it to the others. If one of the two others was interested, he would read it. Two OKs would be all that was needed to get a book published. Whoever brought it in, however, would see the book he'd acquired through the process of getting it edited, typeset, art directed, printed, bound, and shipped. In general that was how it worked, although naturally we all pitched in, and in some cases worked way beyond our stated jobs on particularly gnarly projects.

As both Terry and Larry had followed SeaHorse's precept of adding at least one "announcement" advertisement to any title's budget for their individual presses, we continued that principle for GPNy's books. In addition, royalties would be rendered once a year and, like SeaHorse Press's statements, would be paid only on those books actually sold and paid for, although how many copies were actually shipped in that period would also would be notated for the authors or their agents to see. This was done to avoid the complex, sometimes embarrassing, often inexplicable system of publisher's "returns."

All other matters that came up would be decided by agreement. If there was any contention, two votes out of three would win the motion. By the way, in the ensuing years of GPNy, we discovered that we were in agreement on all points; not once was one of us upset over a decision by the other two. GPNy began, went on, and remained a remarkably agreeable situation throughout its life.

A week after that meeting, we met once again at my apartment. As mine was the largest and airiest place, it soon was deemed the handiest place to meet, and in fact it became GPNy's official office, where we met with authors, bookstore owners, printers' and binders' representatives, art directors, illustrators, photographers, and accountants. We did use Terry's smaller place on Charles Street whenever we were mailing out flyers or catalogs, and whenever he and I did the annual royalty reports. Until, that is, he was no longer able to, at which point I would bike over to Larry's apartment on East Fourth Street, and we'd do them in his kitchen.

By our third meeting in my floor-through duplex living room, we had a mock-up of the final GPNy logo, company checkbooks, stationery, our municipal business papers, and even a likely first book.

Each of us had by then seen the play we had first discussed as a possible initial project, Harvey Fierstein's *International Stud*, and all three of us liked it—although I liked it a bit less than the others. Moreover, Terry had interviewed its writer-star for a gay paper and he said he'd written a second play, connected to the first one, called *Fugue in a Nursery*, using the same main character from the first play but moving him deeper into life with a gay boyfriend and a bisexual married lover. Terry had read the second play, and gave us copies of it to read ourselves. He said that the more or less unknown author was in the midst of writing a third play, taking the same characters even deeper into life, with the main character's mother and even an adopted son; it would be titled *Women and Children First*. The play was to be a trilogy. In fact, the playwright was calling it *Torch Song Trilogy*. Maybe we ought to wait until all three were done and produced?

Larry and I read the second play and we agreed it was both continuous and yet a definite step forward in artistry and depth. If the third play were as good or even better . . . All we could do was wait for him to finish it and hope.

Terry had already met him; it Larry's and my turn to meet Harvey in person. This would prove to be an unusual encounter, not in the least because it occurred in what I considered the depths of Brooklyn.

————

Although I'd grown up in New York and had lived there most of my life except for a year or so in Europe in the '60s, by 1981 I barely knew Brooklyn or the Bronx, mostly because of the successful efforts of a city planner named Robert Moses. During the fifties and sixties, Moses had built a chain of highways girdling four of the five outer boroughs, and in fact called the Belt Parkway. As a result of this early freeway system, one could move by car from the depths of Queens and Nassau county, where I grew up, to Manhattan and at the same time seldom if ever actually set foot in any other New York neighborhood. Since I only got around by car or subway, what I knew of Brooklyn was, like most gay men of my time who lived and worked in Manhattan, limited to Brooklyn Heights, with side trips to Boerum Hill, where Bob Lowe and my friend Jon Peterson lived.

Thus I was kind of surprised to come out of a G train subway station one summer morning and find myself in Carroll Gardens, which was terra incognita to me, a prime Little Italy located in the darkest heart of Kings County—Brooklyn to you. Four- and five-story tenements like those I knew in Greenwich Village dominated, but they were located on streets nearly void of cars, certainly strangers to taxicabs, but instead filled with gardens rife with staked and regulated beefsteak tomatoes, oversized eggplants, and fat bell peppers peeking over the wrought iron fences of neatly tended front gardens.

Two obviously Italian-American grandmothers greeted Larry and me on the concrete front stoop at the address I had marked down, and when we asked for Fierstein, they pointed to a painted black doorway beneath the little balcony where they sat eating Stella D'Oro cookies and drinking Aranciatas.

We were surprised by Harvey's size: he was over six feet tall with square shoulders, and he was, well . . . bulky. We'd seen him on stage in *International Stud* wearing men's and women's clothing and he'd seemed utterly normal in size. In this narrow corridor leading to a low-ceilinged subterranean, fairly cramped railroad flat, he was gargantuan!

And sweet. We sat in the minuscule living room, the brightest part of the tiny place because it had small windows on either side of a door, flung wide open to the June afternoon air, and a back garden bursting with flowers and naturally enough scads of the trademark vegetables and herbs of Carroll Gardens. Harvey served tea out of Woolworth's most basic china. The flat was close, overfilled with furniture and other objects that I recognized from my own first years living on my own in New York as hand-me-downs, throw-outs, and salvaged-from-the-sidewalk. But his apartment was also neater and cleaner than most I'd lived in.

How can one separate Harvey from his brand-name hoarse voice? Today, it's a perfect way to know he's arrived at a packed party: his signature across floors and rooms. But back then it was only the second time I'd heard his voice, and I kept wondering how and where he'd gotten it. He gave some kind of quasi-fantastic, semi-medical reason for his odd voice. But with absolutely characteristic modesty, Harvey told us that whatever the reason for it, his voice had served him very well in his life, because it got him work in clubs when he was still far too young to even *be* inside a club where liquor was served. His voice and his size. And, of course, although he never mentioned it, his talent.

Our job was simple: to tell him about Gay Presses of New York and of our hope to become his publisher. As all three of us—Larry, Terry, and I—had already published plays by dramatists whose work Harvey already knew well: Doric Wilson, Robert Patrick, and Jane Chambers, he knew who we were and he was thrilled—he used the word several times, "sincerely *thrilled*"—to be connected with us and our new venture.

He was still writing the third play, titled *Women and Children First,* and even though Ellen Stewart had offered to put it on at Café La Mama, Harvey had demurred: he wanted the play to be seen as the last part of the trilogy, one of an evening of all three plays. He was talking to John Glines and his lover, Larry—people we three GPNyers knew well—about putting on the trilogy that coming fall at their theater in the American Thread Company Building on Avenue of the Americas in SoHo, a place where Terry had produced shows and Larry and I had done benefit readings. So we were already almost connected already.

In less than an hour, Harvey Fierstein told us about his life, and illustrated it with photos, occasional playbills from shows he'd been involved with, and finally with costumes.

He had a large closet filled with women's clothing. In truth, he had far more women's clothing than men's clothing. No surprise really, when he told us that he'd been dressing in drag and doing his own makeup since he was fifteen years old. He'd been earning his own living since then, because that's when he'd left home. His mother—who I would later recognize in Anne Bancroft when *Torch Song* was filmed—was a Jewish mother par excellence, Harvey said, which meant she was interfering to the point of insanity. It was Harvey who told me this joke: "What's the difference between a pit bull and a Jewish mother? The pit bull lets go when you're dead!" Yet he loved her and they were "talking again—for the moment," and so Harvey spoke to her by phone several times a week.

On his own for half his life already, Harvey had been taken in and essentially been raised to adulthood by various groups of drag queens and theater troupes. He'd worked in drag most of his life, and the scene in *International Stud* when he makes up onstage and transforms himself into a woman in front of the audience was a transformation he'd been doing for years, almost daily. I'd later discover that he'd had his stage debut "as a boy" in Robert Patrick's seminal gay play, *The Haunted Host,* which I had seen, and which Larry Mitchell was planning to publish.

Harvey told us about drag queen house mothers and how they raised their drag daughters. He told us about working at a big successful cabaret like Manhattan's East Village Club 82, where he'd reached the pinnacle of drag fame. He told us about the mostly straight male patrons at the place, and how most of the romantic relationships he'd had so far in life had been with these questionable patrons, as well as how disastrous those relationships had been. The way Harvey told it, he'd been beaten and robbed too many times to count, and that was still fewer times than he'd had his heart broken.

He told us of adventure upon adventure working, from stints as far north as Provincetown and as far south as Atlantic City. For a city boy like Harvey, these were great distances and faraway places. He illustrated each play, each act, each relationship for us by pulling out the gown, heels, feather boa, and headdress he wore then, modeling them against his black T-shirt and denims. He sang snatches of songs, both real and with somewhat risqué, doctored lyrics that he'd sung either onstage or off, but while wearing that outfit. He described in detail the sets and the lighting of each show he'd done. In front of us, Harvey metamorphosed from an angry and brash teenager into a sophisticated woman of the world, and from there into a screaming harridan, and from there again into a forlorn lover abandoned by yet another guy who'd wronged him—"and you know I should have known better, trusting and stupid as I was."

Harvey transmuted a tiny, cramped apartment filled with second-hand furniture into a theater before our eyes. We sat there, drinking it all in, amazed, amused, entertained, bemused, uncertain whether all or indeed any of it was true or not, because it was, after all, *the theater, darling*—and who cared if it was true or not?

When we finally left—and we were hardly able to tear ourselves away—we kissed each others cheeks, continental style, and we knew with a burning certainty that we would somehow publish his plays no matter how good the third one was and no matter if our other partner disagreed. Because if GPNy didn't publish them, I promised myself that SeaHorse Press would.

———

My partners agreed: we offered Harvey, as an advance against royalties, the royal sum of what was in GPNy's bank account, placed by us, recall, that first day of incorporation—a scintillating $300. And he accepted.

Working with his theatrical agent of the time, the aged Helen Harvey, was a bit more problematic. Some years before, I'd actually been represented briefly by someone working for Helen, but he had never sold my first novel. I had slumped back into authorial obscurity for another five years. If Helen recognized my name or me at all, she gave a wonderful impression to the contrary. Helen had been around so long and had been alternately useful and interfering in so many playwright's lives in the New York theater world that it's doubtless churlish of me to introduce her as she really was, given our blessedly short acquaintance. Even so, to say that Helen was physically unprepossessing is to say that an ant is small. Helen was ghastly to look upon. She looked like a witch who'd been dipped in a cauldron of boiling oil and her personality might be said to lie in temperament somewhere between that of a recalcitrant cud cow and an enraged hornet. Words like *termagant, harridan,* and *virago* are ordinarily overused in writing. All of them would apply to her. During the brief conversation Harvey, Helen, and I had in her office somewhere in the depths of the Brill Building, she managed to insult Harvey, his play, our company, gay theater, and just about anyone or anything she managed to alight upon. She asked irrelevant, meaningless questions. She raised issues so out of the question that in a court of law, she would have been declared non compos mentis. And finally if she was less of a pain in the ass that day with us than I understood she usually was, it was because she doubtless believed at the time—as did we all at the time—that no one would much care what happened to this queer play or its equally queer book version. Certainly her behavior once the play proved to be a hit revealed venality and immorality, along with a blithe disregard for ethics, that I found breathtaking.

Nevertheless, the contracts were signed. Harvey received a check. It was a done deal.

Helen had been possible disaster number one—just narrowly averted. Possible disaster number two would arrive soon and be a bit knottier to deal with: the cover artwork for *Torch Song Trilogy,* the book.

Harvey had been using as a theater placard something he'd himself drawn or painted (it was unclear which, even when I had the original actually in hand) while he'd been writing the play. It featured his face at the top, much stylized but evidently feminine, with a black veil or scarf pulled across it so only the top half showed. Below was the considerable blank space needed for the type required for the title, playwright's name, theater, actors, and dates. It could have been adapted as a book cover, and we even found a typeface from the fat display type book a printer's rep had sent me that looked enough like

Harvey's hand-lettered printing. But even so, the art was crude, and it wasn't that attractive—even if it had been effective.

At least it had been for the first play. For the second one, Ellen Stewart had used a color photo from the play rehearsal of the four characters—Harvey, his boyfriend, his bisexual lover, and the lover's girlfriend—all in one bed. Harvey insisted we use the first artwork, for *The International Stud,* for the complete trilogy book.

Part of what had made SeaHorse Press successful and an easy press to continually publicize via the emerging new gay print media was the excellent, provocative, and visually compelling art I selected for book covers. By 1981, they consisted of drawings by artists (and sometime fuck buddies) George Stavrinos and David Martin, and by my boyfriend of the time Scott Façon, as well as by photographers Jack White (for Dennis Cooper), and Robert Mapplethorpe (for Brad Gooch). In their own ways, both Calamus Press and JH Press had distinctive—if different—visual styles for their own book covers. Given our terrific artists and designs, gay newspapers and magazines often reprinted our artwork in their own pages. As a result, our books got lots of publicity.

All three of us were very much aware that gay men (and lesbians, too) were graphics and design savvy, yet that in other ways they were pushovers. There were so few GLBT books in those days that people would buy them even with atrociously unattractive covers. But Harvey's art didn't look like anything the three of us had used as cover art before. On the other hand, it was a new company. Maybe it should have a distinctive look.

My own problem was different. Trained as an artist, I hated how poorly finished the artwork itself was. This was OK for a theater placard, which is seen from a distance, but not for a book, which is, after all, usually an intimate object inside the home, held for long periods of time fairly close to one's face. After some phone discussion, Harvey saw my point and allowed me to photocopy his artwork and to experimentally give it a finer finish by filling in white spaces, straightening out drawn lines, evening out the size of the eyes. All of it was really minor, but the end result worked far better. I was somewhat mollified and Harvey claimed he didn't see any difference—bless him. Later placards and book covers—including the theater book club edition—would utilize even greater stylizations of this artwork, based on my example.

Through his connections with impresario Ellen Stewart, Terry managed to obtain copies of black-and-white photos from the staged productions of the first two plays, and Harvey a few snapshots from an unstaged version of the third play. These went into our book. Each printed play also had its own cast list, with the unstaged version filling in for the third play once again. As editor in chief of the minuscule new company, I was given the text of Harvey's plays to edit. This consisted of little at first, until I wondered how Harvey would react to a real, albeit light-handed, editing, and called to ask him.

"Do it. Send it over. I'll look," he replied while loudly trying not to burn French toast. A week later he called me back. "It's fabulous. You did a fabulous job. It's sensitive yet absolutely necessary. I've taken all but two of your editorial suggestions."

He then told what the two were he'd not taken, and over the phone, while he finished cooking and eating yet another afternoon breakfast (the *thea*-ter!) we figured out some other way to get those sentences sounding right onstage and still in grammatical English. Like all real professionals, Harvey was interested in his work being the best it could possibly be, and he was grateful, and never obdurate, with anyone who could and who wanted to help.

Once Patrick Merla had typeset the plays in wonderfully readable, yet individualistic type and layouts, as was usual with Patrick's sharp-eyed work, he'd naturally found some other, somewhat less egregious, copy editing gaffes, and Harvey jumped to correct those, too.

The truth was, all three of us were being fairly low-key—which was our style anyway, or at least mine and Larry's—because while the plays were good, they were after all, *plays*. All three of us had separately published plays through SeaHorse, JH, and Calamus, and while they were selling okay, better, in fact, than many bookshop owners told us that they would, and better than almost any other plays they stocked except for Broadway hits—they weren't setting any kind of records. We didn't expect them to. Partly because, for many people, play scripts were merely that: secondary to the performance itself.

The best seller of all our books of plays, with four thousand copies out in two printings, was Doric Wilson's *Two Plays,* which I'd published, containing his seminal work, *Street Theater,* and his far more mature, newer play, *A Perfect Relationship.* But even these sold to a limited audience. Period. No matter how much Larry, Terry, and I were committed to an emerging LesBiGay theater—and we were, deeply so—we had to admit it simply wasn't that important in our new book business. Meaning our expectations for this trilogy were, well, not low, but we expected to maybe sell three thousand, tops four thousand copies. Which would be profitable for us thanks to our very low overhead and restrained costs of production.

Meanwhile, we were busily looking around for a second title for GPNy, one that would consolidate the gains made with *Torch Song* yet be more of a publishing coup. Instead, we found a collection of short stories by a Canadian author named Ron Harvie that was just too good to refuse. So, we signed up *The Voltaire Smile and Other Stories* and our brand new company went from one apparently noncommercial title to a second apparently noncommercial title. And what was the weirdest aspect of it all, none of us much cared, partly because we were happy with what we were publishing, and partly because we were otherwise occupied.

Everyone should have such luck.

———

Torch Song Trilogy had been running at the Actors' Playhouse in Greenwich Village for several months, gathering word-of-mouth and even increasing its attendance week by week when the book arrived. The cover looked OK, although I would never be happy with the cover art, and we began shipping copies to the various places that had ordered it: first the bookstores; then the general, small press distributors like Berkeley, California's prestigious BookPeople; and then the academic and library distributors like Baker & Taylor, with locations in New Jersey, Illinois, and Nevada. Most of the bookstores ordering directly were in Manhattan: Oscar Wilde, Three Lives, and the various other less gay-oriented shops. In midtown it was Drama Books; uptown, Shakespeare & Co. Little by little, as word spread, orders from other bookstores—including outlets of Crown and Borders—continued to trickle in. Note that there wasn't a B. Dalton or Doubleday or Scribner among those ordering. Although we sent them our flyers, they ignored us almost completely; and even once they began carrying our books, they seldom ordered directly.

Torch Song had been the raison d'etre and the first-listed book in GPNy's expensive and rather handsome first catalogue. This had gone out to the three hundred or so people, bookstores, and companies—usually ones that had previously bought something from any of the three allied presses. Because this was a very small operation, even at its greatest heights of success in the late 1980s, I was still handling more or less all the orders, and I pretty much knew, or could easily check, at which distributor, bookstore, or book club every copy of every SeaHorse Press and GPNy book was at any time. (This might be another reason why we never went under when other companies did.)

One bookstore that wasn't sure it wanted to carry Harvey's play was rather famous. When he died a few years back, several reporters phoned asking me to eulogize Craig Rodwell, the founder, owner, and operator for much of its time of New York's Oscar Wilde Memorial Bookshop, the first openly gay bookstore in the United States. They were clearly expecting me to say nothing but fabulous things. However, unlike the reporters who'd never heard of Craig until ten minutes before they'd received their assignment and phoned me, I'd actually had to work with, and worse, to "communicate" (the quotes are there for a reason) with this man for many years. While I did admit he was a pathbreaker, I had little else good to say about him. I think my kindest sentence to the press was, "He was driven by work and debt and penury so much that for many years he was pretty much out of his mind." But since the gay media is as hypocritical as the mainstream media, not one word of mine ever made it into print, as this man, like many others, was sanctified after his death so that the mythology of faultless GLBT heroes could continue unchecked.

I remember when Craig opened the first minuscule sliver of a bookshop— a really brave act that actually slowly paid off for him—in the untrendy and dirt-cheap East Village just off Cooper Square. His stock consisted of a handful of new books and several shelves of out-of-print used titles. I recall how hopeful he was when he moved it to Christopher and Gay Streets, off Sixth Avenue, in the heart of the West Village, where it continues to this day, albeit now under new ownership. Again, less than half of the few shelves were new books, and most of the stock consisted of out-of-print titles and used books, along with some gay magazines. Most of the openly gay people I knew bought their gay books there, and indeed bought anything there, to help Craig out. We felt it to be a community bookstore, small as it was. And as long as it continued small, all was well.

But came the glory days of the late 1970s when suddenly Craig was moving a hundred copies of *Ruby Fruit Jungle* a week, week after week, two hundred a week of *Dancer From the Dance* and *The Lure,* month after month, year after year, on top of other books, all naturally selling far better, too, with the increased store traffic, and suddenly things changed: Craig overdeveloped an attitude. A year earlier, when I was walking over to personally deliver a half dozen units of SeaHorse Press's first titles, he was easy enough to deal with. Three years later Craig was arguing with other bookstores all over the Village— his war of words against Three Lives & Company lasted for decades—loudly defending "his territory," and busily deciding which books he would stock and which not.

Two weeks after I'd delivered SeaHorse's 1981 hot-off-the-press new titles by Dennis Cooper and Brad Gooch, I got a call from an assistant—Craig now had an assistant—at the store, who phoned to say they had returns.

Returns? They didn't get enough copies to have returns. "What returns?" I asked.

She hemmed and hawed and then said it was Gooch's story collection, *Jailbait.*

How many copies were being returned, I asked. All of them: they'd never been put up for sale.

"Why not," I asked.

The answer? "Craig has decided the book isn't gay enough."

Her actual words. Craig, who by now, thanks to gay best-selling authors could hire an assistant and not be in the shop all day, had declared that he, and he alone, would decide which titles were sufficiently gay to be sold in the store.

Later on, and through some other people who knew Craig, I discovered that he seldom, if ever, actually read the books on his shelves, and undoubtedly hadn't read Gooch's. But he'd been fighting a (losing) war with the "dark forces" of Gay Leatherdom and S/M, typified for him by the work of Robert Mapplethorpe. Now the sweet and innocent (and fully clothed) youth on the cover of Gooch's first book had been shot by Robert, and in fact, was Raymond Mapplethorpe—his younger brother—who was indeed still jailbait at the time.

Knowing how Mapplethorpe's work as an entire ouevre disaffected some people, I decided not to make a federal case out of Rodwell's stupid decision and I quietly withdrew the book from Oscar Wilde Memorial. It was selling quickly enough anyway out of many other outlets, especially those on the East Side and in California, and it soon went into a second printing, so the loss was entirely Craig's. But I don't think I ever bothered the author by telling him of this disturbing, and let's face it, totally a priori, censorship.

Even so, Craig's new attitude, with its ongoing pronouncements on what was good and bad for gay life, continued unabated, at least for me, until the day we stopped selling him books. This came about in the spring of 1985 and evolved as follows.

Clever Terry Helbing, the banker's son, had shown Larry and me how to do double-entry bookkeeping for our presses, with a few extra flourishes. As a result, I could see at a glance whenever accounts were unpaid, and also for how long they were unpaid. Oscar Wilde Memorial's sales lines in both GPNy's and SeaHorse Press's account books suddenly went unpaid from thirty days to sixty. I sent out reminder notices. No check came in. Sixty days unpaid turned to ninety. I made phone calls. Craig was somehow never in. I had no trouble telling the assistant what the problem was. The bills, steadily mounting, remained unpaid.

One morning I went to the shop as it opened and brought copies of the bills for all four GPNy presses, which by now totaled over $750.00, a substantial amount for small presses. I was prepared for Rodwell to complain of poor sales, and to work out a modest, biweekly payment schedule. I had one already with me.

Instead, Craig faced me down in front of his assistant and a customer and told me he was well aware of the bill, but that as he was—and I'll never forget these exact words—"running a community service for the dissemination of gay literature," and that my partners, our authors, and I, should be "thankful for his services and not also require being paid." Following that astonishing statement, he left the shop.

So did I. An hour later I arrived back at the bookstore carrying three folded cardboard boxes that I taped back together on the shop's wooden floor. Craig still hadn't returned, which was best, but had he been there I would have done it anyway, I was so enraged. I filled those boxes with every GPNy, Sea-Horse, Calamus, and JH Press title I could find on the shelves and in its tiny inventory section. I marked them off and showed each one to the assistant ticked off in the appropriate box of our catalogue, and left it for Craig, writing

94

beneath it—"copies returned to publisher." I then dragged the boxes down the stairs to the street, hailed a cab, and took them home. Once home, I called my partners and told them what I'd done.

Reminding them even with the returns, he still owed us over $500, all of which I intended to get, even if it meant suing Craig in small claims court. Terry was irate and thankful. Larry was more sanguine, but suggested we'd never see a dollar owed to us. At our next meeting, I was referred to as the Bold Rescuer, and we joked about the matter for years afterward.

We never did sue, having far more serious (in fact, life-and-death) matters to deal with at the time than unpaid bills, and payment trickled in over the next few years, without any rhyme or reason, I think mostly whenever Craig's assistant—a nice woman who'd appeared totally appalled that fateful morning—had her hands on the checkbook and Craig wasn't around to stop her. We never were fully paid and it was only a long time after the shop had passed into other hands that I would ever step into it again.

Since Craig sold Oscar Wilde, it has changed completely. I've never done business with Kim Brinster, its new manager and guiding spirit, but from all that I've seen and heard, Kim shows oodles of GLBT community spirit and good business sense that Craig could have used.

———

Harvey's show was being prepped to go off-Broadway after being work-shopped at Harrah's, a loftlike space used mostly as a disco near Lincoln Center. Harvey told me that the show was being recast around him in the role of Arnold Beckoff. Diane Tarleton, the woman who'd played Laurel, Arnold's lover's girlfriend, would also likely remain in the cast. Harvey was concerned about finding actors for the crucial roles of his mother and the young boyfriend, but he was even more concerned about finding someone to pay the part of his bisexual lover.

Another reason he was calling was that John Glines and his lover Larry, the producers, and director Peter Pope, had decided that the play needed to be cut, to streamline it for off-Broadway. It would need several minutes cut out of each play. Harvey was panicked. The three of them had suggested cuts, each of which had cut into the author "like a knife," and while Harvey realized he was being an unreasonable playwright, he couldn't stand to see any of the lines go. What should he do?

I told him I could probably be more objective than he and yet loyal to the work, which with I was by now quite familiar, having read it a dozen times, and asked him to send me the script marked with the suggested deletions and I'd take a look? I got it in the mail a few days later and checked it over. Knowing what canny theater people the director and producers were, I wasn't surprised to see that most of the cuts made perfect sense. Several eliminating repeated information, although one or two cuts needed exposition, too, as Harvey had contended. He and I had an hour-long phone call going over the stage cuts, and meanwhile, I'd found a few other places that could use a snip and so had Harvey. Together we cobbled out the required minutes and Harvey was, if not happy, then at least not heartbroken.

As the auditions began I also began to get updates from Harvey and others connected with the production. A teenage actor, Matthew Broderick, short, cute, smart, and funny, had been brought in for the role of the boyfriend and had read so well and worked so well with Harvey that the producers and director wanted him. In his gravelly voice on the phone, Harvey expostulated, "He looked so young—what, thirteen, maybe?—that I had to ask him if he knew that the play was about homosexuality. Did a boy that young even know about homosexuality?" Harvey asked—completely rhetorically, it turned out. "Do you know what he told me?" Harvey asked. "First, he was seventeen years old. Second, he'd grown up in the West Village, gone to school there, knew everything there was to know about homosexuals. Third, both of his parents were in theater and they had tons of gay friends." Harvey sighed with relief, then added in his lowest tone of voice. "We still told him he would need his parents signature if he wanted to be in the play." Broderick got their signature, he was hired, and thus began another important American theater and film career.

Another unexpected find was actress Estelle Getty, the diminutive forty-five-year-old, who auditioned to play Harvey's mother. According to friends who were present, Estelle came onstage wearing a little Jackie O suit complete with hat and gloves, and she was absolutely WASPy, ladylike, prim, and proper. Until, that is, she read her part—at which point she became a fury, a harridan, a Jewish mother from hell.

"Absolutely, one hundred and eighty degrees wrong for the part." Harvey assured me, adding, "So, naturally, we hired her." And even though she took the play to Broadway, Harvey would feel more comfortable with Ann Bancroft, who looked and sounded just right, and who played Arnold's mother in the film version of *Torch Song*. Estelle Getty, too, would go on from the play to have a distinguished career, playing another older woman—one three decades older than she actually was (late seventies? early eighties?)—Sophia, in the television series *Golden Girls*.

But despite these great additions to the cast, and Paul Joynt being added in as Arnold's lover Alan, the group still hadn't found an Ed, Arnold's boyfriend, with whom Harvey had any chemistry, and Harvey moaned and *geschrei*ed, "I just know we'll never find the right actor for that role."

That same evening I was meeting for dinner a not very close acquaintance of many years, an actor I'd first met when I was running around Manhattan with an old friend, Broadway and off-Broadway actor George Sampson. At that time, circa 1967, one evening George and I had gone uptown to the apartment of two actors he knew from various auditions. Both were tall, WASPy, and handsome. One had just finished a four-year run starring in a major Broadway hit play, *Barefoot in the Park*. We four had a drink and a chat, and I'd then toddled off to dinner nearby with others while George had remained and a bit later on, he informed me, had a three-way with the two actors.

The lovely pair broke up maybe four years later, when one went out to

L.A. to try his hand at film while the other—Joel Crothers—remained in New York and slid into daytime television. He'd begun moving from walk-on roles as the young gardener or handyman in *One Lake George* to bigger parts as a fiancé or boyfriend on *The Secret Storm,* and in 1975 he'd become a daily recurring, and increasingly starring, role as Dr. Miles Cavanaugh in *The Edge of Night,* one of the top soaps of its day.

I'd begun bumping into Joel again on Fire Island the previous summer, 1981, more than a decade after we'd first met, but only just as we were ending that summer and closing up house. He had taken a rental not far from mine, and as we were both weekday residents—a tiny proportion of the Pines' population—we'd begun to talk whenever we'd run across each other. I'd of course remembered him and had brought up our single piece of social glue: George Sampson. By 1982, George was back in New York City, living on far East Fourteenth Street, undergoing physical therapy for his bad knee, looking bearded, shaggy, overweight, and not very smartly dressed: in other words totally different from how he used to look. No longer the faun-like beauty that Franco Zeffirelli had adored to the point of producing and directing a whole film—*Romeo and Juliet.* George now seemed far less driven and no longer obsessed with the ambition to succeed in theater—and also happier than I'd ever known him. He was only acting occasionally, and then only in tiny, non-Equity productions way off-off-Broadway, but he was a far better actor than when he'd been the focus of all eyes in a Broadway hit years before. Like his friend and my onetime roommate, Bobby Brown, George had gotten work to make ends meet in some kind of T-shirt and poster reproduction factory on the Lower East Side.

In the years between our meetings, Joel Crothers had made a name for himself in another daytime television series called *Dark Shadows,* which had become a favorite during the 1960s and was enjoying reruns in the early 1980s, bringing in syndication fees and devotedly watched by its many fans.

Joel Crothers was six foot three. At forty-one years old he was gorgeously if slenderly built, with a craggily handsome face. He had a smooth, baritone voice, and he was a talented, absolutely convincing actor. He came from a family of impossibly high intelligence and achievement—brain surgeons? astrophysicists? Some sort of geniuses. Joel himself possessed a "genius" IQ of 155, graduated college Phi Beta Kappa, and was a crossword puzzle maven, adept at chess, a brilliant tennis player, read indefatigably, followed sports closely, and who—when I reencountered him—was bored.

I was to meet Joel after work, around 6 PM, outside the ABC television studios on West Sixty-seventh Street where his soap was shooting. I was there on time, reading a *New York Times,* along with some fifty other people, most of them women. They turned out to be fans of the show and when Joel emerged along with other cast members, the actors, and especially Joel, were besieged by autograph seekers.

"Tell me exactly how you staged that to show me how important you've become?" I teased Joel fifteen minutes later, when he finally managed to escape his fans.

"It happens every day," Joel said, and for the first and last time while I knew him, he blushed.

It was during dinner that I suddenly had my inspiration. Joel had a name and reputation. Harvey needed a name and reputation to help boost his little trilogy. Why not throw them together? I asked him about the last time he'd done an important live play.

Several meals and phone calls were needed before I could convince Joel to even go to an audition. As Joel made clear, he didn't need a live play added to his life or to his resume. I countered with the usual bullshit one tells actors when one wants them in a part: he was growing dull and lazy doing television, doing the same character; he needed to branch out; he needed to challenge himself; he needed to do something different in his life.

To please me, Joel allowed himself to be persuaded to go to a *Torch Song* audition one evening, which I then instantly fled, pleading some excuse. The next day, Harvey phoned and said, "Where did you ever find this creature? He's gorgeous! He's Olympian! He's Apollo! He acts with the same casualness that normal people breathe! We did fifteen minutes of parts. *Fifteen minutes!* He *is* my character Ed, living and breathing." Furthermore in just those fifteen minutes, Joel and Harvey had argued—made up, and argued again. Clearly, they possessed, both on and offstage, that much-required stage attribute: chemistry.

Evidently, John Glines and director Peter Pope agreed. There was a problem however: Joel was overpaid and lazy and he didn't want to work hard—certainly not as hard as doing six nightly performances a week in a play, especially as he was working daytimes, too. Joel confided in me that he liked the play, he liked the cast, he would even accept the relatively low Actors' Equity off-Broadway play salary—none of that was a problem, he admitted. What the problem actually was, he wouldn't say. It wasn't that Joel thought the play would otherwise affect his career and reputation. By that point, he didn't care what anyone thought. By talking to him further, I figured out that Joel felt that he was slumming: doing everyone a really big favor.

But then, that was Joel in a nutshell. He'd already made it big. And he was right: he *was* slumming. At last, however, he and the Glines worked out a deal. Joel would perform for the initial four-and-a-half-month run at the Actors' Playhouse. And nothing more. No matter what happened.

I caught a preview a few days before the newly shortened and recast play opened in the West Village, and the show was terrific. Estelle and Matthew were strong enough to balance, if not erase, Harvey onstage—no mean feat. And Joel was perfect. His size, his looks, his voice, his professionalism, and his natural panache made Harvey look if not diminutive, at least cut down some-what in size, which the play had needed.

I missed the premiere as I was off somewhere, and it wasn't for a few weeks after I'd returned and settled back into my duplex that I heard from my partners that *Torch Song* had opened to terrific reviews and great ticket sales. Business was picking up more for the show every day, based mostly on word-of-mouth.

When *Torch Song* moved to the Little Theatre on Broadway in mid-June

1982, Court Miller replaced Joel as Ed, and Fisher Stevens replaced Matthew Broderick, who had gotten a starring role in what would become a cult-classic film, *Ferris Bueller's Day Off*. That summer, as the play soared, I kept waiting for Joel to say something, to question his decision not to be in the Broadway version a tiny bit. He never once did; his biggest enthusiasm was saved for the tennis championships. He'd bought a battery-operated portable TV that he took to the beach, where he watched every moment of the Opens. The play ran for three and a half years and, of course, also became a film, but by that opening, alas, Joel was only a memory—part of the play's earlier production.

———

A hit Broadway show however meant to us at GPNy that books had to be delivered to the theater, since had Terry negotiated through John Glines that the Little Theater would sell our book of the play.

It also meant that the book had begun to sell again all over the New York metropolitan area—not merely in Manhattan, but in Newark, Trenton, and Fairfield County, Connecticut. We were now selling first two, then three, then four times as many copies per week as we'd ever sold. We would soon need more local delivery, both to the theater and to the bookstores. The Little Theatre was moving about one hundred copies a week—and would do those kind of sales throughout the run of the play. The bookstores were each selling forty to fifty copies each per week, and they too needed on-the-spot delivery. Taking cabs with a carton on the other seat when I was headed uptown for dinner or a show, as I'd sometimes done before, was no longer an real option.

Larry came up with a solution: Tony Fish.

I don't think I ever knew Tony's real last name. It was Italian, I remember that, but different than the name printed in sea blue on matte silver on the side of the truck he arrived with at our warehouse space one afternoon to pick up a stack of cases of *Torch Song* and cart it around town with me. I'm not sure if the owner of the truck, a bakery, was Tony's uncle or cousin or some other relation. What I do know is that it was definitely a fish truck, definitely used daily to haul marine life to and from the Fulton Fish Market, recently reensconced in a fancy new market downtown as part of the ongoing development for the historic theme park to be called the South Street Seaport. Hosed out every day after work, the truck still smelled like fish, and after an hour and a half inside it making deliveries, Tony and I smelled like fish, too.

Larry never quite made clear how he knew Tony. At the time, Tony was living with a woman, although he flirted with me and almost every other halfway decent-looking guy he encountered. Larry said in later years that they'd had an affair before Larry had met Richard and settled down. Or had Tony and Larry's friend "Ruby" had the affair? I could never get Larry Mitchell's past and present lover situation untangled. Larry was born under the sign of Cancer, the sign that holds on for dear life, and Larry tended to keep his ex-boyfriends, tricks, lovers, perhaps even his past enemies, close to him in his daily life, in a sort of generalized hippie love scene.

Tony was just under medium height, with a cute, if not really worked-out body. He had a great Italian face, with big brown eyes and curly, partly prematurely graying hair. An actor—had he been in one of Larry's early plays?—he took odd jobs to make money, and this one day per week was just one of them. Tony was high-spirited, fun loving, optimistic, and great to be around. That first afternoon together in the truck set the tone for the following year or more that we used Tony Fish and his borrowed truck. After a few times, however, he went out without me. Why not? He was completely competent. But I do remember that he would seldom park directly in front of the theater, or bookstores, to unload, and thus I doubt that anyone knew they were getting books where only a few hours before swordfish and dace had lain in ice.

———

Torch Song Trilogy opened on Broadway and by the fall of 1982 had been nominated for a slew of Tony Awards. The following March, the Tonys aired on television, and we were all treated to the surprise and delight of Harvey winning a Tony for best play of the year. Before this, and for the first time since it had opened, business at the Little Theatre had slowly begun to slump. The award should ensure another year's run for the play. Publicly, Harvey thanked the producers of the play, and his publishers, Larry, Terry, and Felice, by name, adding that all of us had believed in his play before it was completed, polished, staged, and even before he believed in it. It was a lovely tribute and we were touched.

When ten minutes later, a stunned and thrilled John Glines got up to collect his producer's award—he thanked "my lover, Larry, who God knows has put up with a lot from me because of the theater." It was the first acknowledgment on television, in from of millions of viewers, from one gay man to his partner. It turned out to be a great, and very gay, evening in the theater. All of us couldn't have been more pleased: foresight, intuition, along with loads of talent, work, and professionalism, had turned three small plays by an unknown drag queen into the theatrical event of the year. Harvey Fierstein's grace and candor helped make him a star and also spokesman for gay rights that night, a double role that he has held and utilized with poise and fervor ever since.

What none of us at GPNy were prepared for was the orders that avalanched into our office as a result of the award. I'd suspected the Little Theater and the Manhattan bookstores would need more copies and had already prepared invoices for them. Early Monday morning after the Sunday night award ceremony I had called Larry to get Tony Fish and the truck ready for an earlier-than-usual-in-the-week delivery. The theater and the bookstores ended up tripling their orders. And phone orders by the score began coming in. Every small- or medium-size distributor phoned, needing a new shipment of the play. We'd just begun doing business with Bookazine, New York City's biggest daily book distributor, with a giant warehouse in the Bronx, and it ordered a large quantity of books. BookPeople in Berkeley, Baker & Taylor, and the Distributors in West Haven, Connecticut, three regional offices, also quickly phoned in substantial reorders. At the end of that Monday, I looked at our orders, checked our warehouse stock, and panicked. I phoned our printer's rep, Alvin Greenberg.

Alvin congratulated us and reminded me that we'd been smart enough to have already ordered another printing, by now already printed, bound, and ready to be shipped the following week. Big sigh of relief on my part.

Tony Fish came early, on Tuesday instead of Thursday, and we stacked most of the books we had into the truck. The bulk of those would go to Bookazine, the stores, and the theater. I'd decided to send only a few boxes to the two small-press distributors. The printer could ship the bulk of their orders directly to them in a week's time.

For the next two months, anytime Terry Helbing or I stepped out the door to go anywhere, we were carrying handfuls of smaller boxes, packets, and jiffy envelopes full of *Torch Song* orders to be mailed out at a nearby post office. And whenever anyone I knew came in and then stepped out the door from my apartment, they were given a handful of single-order, padded Jiffy packs to drop in the closest corner mailbox. The second printing sold out in three months, and a third, of five thousand copies, was printed. That too was sold before the year was over, and a fourth printing of another five thousand was set to go.

So it was that Gay Presses of New York was launched, its first title a critical and commercial success. *Torch Song Trilogy*'s fast and high sales volume would allow GPNy to publish other new titles more rapidly and better than we would have been able to do previously. It would pay for three new books instead of one in the coming year. It would open all kinds of doors for us—and for future small gay presses too, Bookazine Distributors being just one of them. Barnes & Noble and Borders, two chain store conglomerates making headway across the U.S., suddenly had to have an account with us, and we began flooding them with our catalogs.

And we were able to take a little bit of revenge, too.

Many bookstores and chains in the South kept urging us get our books to Ingram, a mainstream distributor in Tennessee that serviced them daily, as Bookazine did for those in the Tri-State Area. I myself had phoned there several times, spoken to the buyer for small press books, and had been unceremoniously shunted aside. I'd even been told, "We're Christians. We sell Bibles here. We can't have homosexual books around for just anyone wandering by to see stacked on our warehouse floor."

A week after *Torch Song* won the Tony Award, I got phone calls from Ingram. I waited until several had piled up, then I phoned back, all cream-and-molasses sweet. "Why ever would a big company like you, and a Christian one at that, be calling little old, Godless, sodomitical, big-city us?" I wondered.

Embarrassed, the buyer said he had had many bookstore calls for Harvey's plays and wanted to order them. I reminded the buyer that Ingram did *not* have an account with us. Would they like to open a account now? He said that yes, they would. I told him all about our discounts for various size orders, our shipping fees, and our sales and return policies, adding, "And if your check our catalog you will see that our policy with all new accounts is to ship a mixed order of no less than five titles from our catalog of twenty-five so the company can see what sells best."

I sweetened the pill, saying that I would aid him in selecting exactly which of GPNy's popular titles were most ordered already within his usual distribution area based on previous direct sales to bookstores in New Orleans; Memphis; Shreveport, Louisiana; Vicksburg, Mississippi; and Frankfort, Kentucky. This also alerted him to the fact that if Ingram did get behind GPNy titles, they might produce many more sales, of other titles, than he'd at first anticipated.

It worked. Ingram sold and reordered *Torch Song* as well as three SeaHorse titles—my poetry book, Dennis Cooper's poems, and Doric Wilson's plays—and one JH press title: Jane Chamber's *Last Summer at Bluefish Cove.* Within a year, Ingram was carrying most of our line. As new titles came in I would ship the no-longer-quite-so-hesitant buyer a copy. Once he saw that we were mostly selling literature, Ingram began ordering a variety of titles from our list. Soon we were even included in its annual small press catalogue. I never pushed our more outré titles on them; they always paid their bills on time and ordered carefully and intelligently. Soon they were getting new titles directly from our printer based on catalog orders or phone orders they'd made to me.

Being distributed by Ingram meant that GPNy had broken through the South's unspoken commercial-book sexual-preference barrier. We were possibly the first small gay press to do so, and we opened the way for the GLBT presses that followed.

5

GPNy: Acessing the Gay Past
and Some Possible Futures

The success of GPNy's first book meant other people would know who we were. When applying to the first New York Small Press Book Festival at the 7th Armory later that year, all we had to say was, "We published *Torch Song Trilogy*" and we got in.

We took a small table at the show and had a gigantic poster made up of our logo. Larry Mitchell and artist Joseph Modica were responsible for getting that ready, Terry for doing all the arrangements and payments. And I was assigned to make another poster, one that held art work, or possibly just the covers of some, if not all, of our books.

Because by then, the four presses actually did have close to twenty titles and it was more a matter of finding which ones fit and looked good together—along with photos of some of our authors—than anything else. I'd already been doing all of SeaHorse's and my own share of GPNy's page and book cover layouts so I took on the extra work. And I was quite happy with the result—it's now part of the exhibit that travels around the country. So, with the ten-foot-tall logo and the smaller poster in back of us, we sat, the ever-changing landscape of our books themselves stacked in front of us.

We sold only a few copies, but we handed out dozens of our catalogs—the very first one we'd put together, since we would only update them every year and a half or so. And we had to admit, and people around us at the Small Press Book Festival had to agree, it was all very stylish, very professional, and we looked . . . well, we looked as though we'd arrived.

By 1983, SeaHorse definitely *had* arrived. With five books in print, Sea-Horse was the forefront of gay publishing—an admittedly small field that included my partners' own companies, Alyson Press, Gay Sunshine Press, Gay Men's Press in England, and a half dozen not openly gay yet gay-friendly smaller presses like Grey Wolf. With its five titles, Calamus had its own distinct profile. And in the few years since its formation, JH Press had four books out. Our combined imprint had *Torch Song* and Harvie's *The Voltaire Smile and Other Stories*, with more on the way.

Explaining how the four presses worked to interested parties first at the Armory, and thereafter everywhere else, I—somewhat irreverently—explicated it thus. "We're like the Holy Trinity in Christianity: The Father, The Son, and the Holy Ghost, all of them separate yet united as—God. For us, it's SeaHorse, Calamus, and JH Presses. All separate, yet, immanently we're all united as—GPNy." Some people, having little clue what the Holy Trinity was, shook their heads, and moved on.

It was my ever-social ex-Violet Quillian Chris Cox who'd brought both Dennis Cooper and Brad Gooch to my attention. Cooper's poetry book, *Idols*, had gotten good reviews and was selling in a second printing, and we were happy with each other. During the summer of 1981, he visited me at my Bay-side summer rental in Fire Island Pines on Midway Walk with a boyfriend or trick—I was never sure which—and they stayed overnight in the second bed-room, unused midweek by my housemate, photographer Larry Lapidus. As Dennis was a serious vegetarian, I cooked a specialty dish consisting of whole wheat noodles, chick peas, and walnuts, served with salad, wine, and dessert. The wine got to the ocean-exhausted boyfriend who fell asleep. Dennis and I then talked.

He told me he'd begun writing prose seriously, and that he thought it was as good as his poetry. Some of his prose had recently been published in an underground chapbook, titled *My Mark,* and either Chris Cox or Tim Dlugos had given it to me. But, Dennis said, some of his strongest supporters within the hip poetry scene of the day had told him not to do prose, to stick to poetry. But Dennis felt he should write more prose, which would allow him to explore in more depth the themes, tropes, and characters he'd addressed with verse. He described a few of the stories he was writing and I said straight out that if they were as good as his poetry, I didn't see why he—and SeaHorse— shouldn't publish them. Dennis thanked me, but he remained extremely nervous about his decision to move on to prose. So over the next year or so until the publication of the book that he would title *Safe,* I found myself constantly shoring up his decision and reencouraging him.

Even so, his anxiety about this new direction—remember, this was an age of fine poetry—was only somewhat calmed when I agreed to publish Brad Gooch's short stories at the same time. Brad had been a young male model of note around Manhattan when I met him through Dennis. Brad was lovers with up-and-coming filmmaker Howard Brookner, and several of his short stories had come out in relatively obscure journals.

It must have been one of my very rare generally contented moments. I laid out the money and more important all the effort needed to launch two SeaHorse press books at the same time. I even agreed to throw a book party— a first for the press. Dennis and Brad worked hard, forged connections, and did what they could to make the book launch itself—and their books—successful. They provided terrific cover photos by Jack Shear and Robert Mapplethorpe, and they put together a wonderful party guest list: young, hip, cute, and clever.

Finding the venue for the party, however, was up to me, and for this I used what Dr. Tom Reynolds now insists on calling my "A-List Pines-Flamingo-Studio" connections. Chip Glass was a few years younger than me and my pals, slender, glib to the point of slippery, and (my pals all assured me) quite experienced as a party giver. He was vaguely connected with a half dozen of the most recent club openings—Bonds, for example, in the former men's clothing store on Times Square, a great space that should have lasted longer.

Chip knew who I was, and when I approached him with the project he took me on a tour of several Chelsea spaces.

"Chelsea is happening, the Village is dead," he declared without the possibility of argument. During the course of several afternoons, he propositioned me repeatedly, and changed costs so quickly I had to write them down on a pad, but he did come up with a great space: a long-closed Episcopal church on Sixth Avenue and Twentieth Street he and his pals were soon to launch as a discotheque and that needed publicity. It wasn't quite finished. I didn't need all of it anyway, so I would get a big discount, if, of course, I let him blow me, too.

Like the young everywhere, he was utterly heedless of history. "This is a first. A disco in a church!" Not so: in the late sixties, there had been, rather infamously, Sanctuary, in a desanctified Roman Catholic church in Manhattan's West Forties, where transgenders writhed near naked amid gigantic candles on what had recently been an altar while people dropped acid and danced. But I needed a fabulous space for a cocktail party, and Chip's place, with its exposed-brick, two-story connecting chancery, fit the bill exactly. The bar would open for one hour—when the owners would be paying, then close. I'd pay the rest of the party.

I sent out invitations featuring both book covers to everyone in publishing. Bennett Cerf of Random House. Bob Silverstein of Knopf, Dick Snyder of Simon & Schuster, Juri Juravich of Harcourt Brace Jovanovich. Robert Giroux of Farrar, Straus and Giroux. And of course, also to my own friends and coevals in the industry. My intent was to announce to everyone who counted that there were new players on the publishing scene and that a new generation of gay writers—following the Violet Quill and its contemporaries—had arrived. I invited individual reviewers and the media in general. Dennis, Brad, and Chris Cox sent out their own invites. But one never knows who'll attend a party until they actually show up.

Somehow the stars were aligned right and people showed up. A lot of people. The right people. I don't know whether it was curiosity, free drinks, or whether they wanted to meet Dennis and Brad or look at the new club space, but they came. While the highest echelon of New York publishing demurred, many others did show, and that was all I really wanted. On top of that, every lesbian and gay writer I'd ever heard of was there.

Chip and his partners were so pleased—"Is that Fran Lebowitz? I *love* her!"—that they left the bar open for *three* hours, not just one, and they also opened the allegedly unfinished dance floor in the nave and half of the upstairs balcony. That *was* Fran Lebowitz, yes, telling me how much she'd loved my novel, *Cold Hands* (actually it had been written by Joe Pintauro and I had nothing to do with it). I thanked her.

I turned to meet the publisher of Viking, and several editors—gay, straight, and whatever; they all seemed to know one another from Avon and Putnam and Grove Press. I put review copies directly into the hands of important newspaper and magazine book editors. Dennis and Brad were surrounded by their coteries and looked like they were loving it.

When Bob Lowe arrived, I pointed Brad Gooch out to him, revealing his huge crush on Bob. "Yeah, yeah, he's cute," Bob said. "Let's go eat. Just you and me," he warned. "No gang!"

———

Working as an editor or publisher with other authors could be a pleasurable experience or, if they possessed one or two strong character traits, it could end up being by turns interesting, intriguing, or even very weird. Several authors out of those I published over the years stand out for how utterly individual they were to me during the book process: Clark Henley, author of *The Butch Manual,* a 1982 SeaHorse Press title, and one of its best sellers; Robert Scott, author of GPNy's novel *The Finding of David* (1984), a manuscript that arrived unsolicited in the mail; Robert Glück, whose third book, *Jack the Modernist* (1985) came via recommendation from several other SeaHorse Press authors, especially Dennis Cooper; and cartoonist Howard Cruse, whose series, *Wendel,* had been running in the *Advocate* for several years before Larry Mitchell and I contacted him and asked to publish it as a book. And of course, there were also the poets.

I'd had to publicize SeaHorse Press to get customers, bookstores, and distributors, in short to sell books, and Larry, Terry, and I went out of our ways also to publicize Gay Presses of New York for the same reasons. With the expected result: we were soon receiving author inquiries, telephone calls, and letters from agents. To all, we would explain that we were a small press putting out only one or two books per year. No matter. The inquiries, phone calls, and manuscripts continued to arrive in far greater numbers than we could ever deal with.

I looked over everything that came in and tried to read fifty pages of it. If it was from someone I knew or had heard of, from a friend, colleague, or student of someone I knew, or from an agent, I often read the whole thing. This often meant spending several hours per day reading new stuff. A lot of these "books" were sometimes really just thoughts jotted on paper. The agented manuscripts were better but tended toward coming-out stories, which we thought had already been done to death. We were looking for books and authors we weren't familiar with.

That's how GPNy's second author, Ron Harvie, had come our way—although he'd had a story in *Christopher Street,* none of us were aware of that until we signed him up. That was also how Robert Scott came our way. His manuscript arrived in the mail at GPNy's post office box with a cover letter and return postage, like dozens of others. The subject matter was intriguing enough: *The Finding of David,* he wrote, was a novel of love and politics in America. David is arrested for "solicitation" in a gay movie theater and cannot face the certain destruction his misfortune will bring to the political career of his closeted bisexual lover. The novel was set in Chicago and its environs.

In early 1983, when we received the letter and book, this was a theme no one else would touch. It sounded like something we'd be interested in.

I read *David* and it was good without having especially new or exciting writing. It needed line editing and maybe a little bit of cutting, but it read very professionally, moved with good pacing, had nice plot twists, strong characters, and it was set in the Midwest, another strength, since we were trying to reach out to that little-noted area in the gay lit of the time. I gave the book to Terry, who liked it, too. We talked to Larry about it, and decided the book would make a statement about our press not being New York–centric (despite its name), and that we definitely weren't afraid of explicit sex. This was particularly important, as *David* would be the first novel GPNy published. I wrote to the author in southwestern Kentucky, accepting the book and laying out our terms.

A correspondence, then a phone relationship developed between me and Robert Scott. It turned out that *The Finding of David* wasn't his first book, but his third or fourth effort. He was worried about certain aspects of it. And he was concerned about the book coming out under his real name. We told him that we were, after all, an *openly* gay press, as evidenced by our name, but if he felt that he needed to use a pseudonym that was—while not great—possible.

I'd thought he might need a pseudonym because Scott seemed to live in a smallish town in the South—not in ultraconservative Mississippi, but not in Chicago or New York, and the subject was, after all, homosexual. But as our conversations went on, I changed my mind about that and began to wonder if it wasn't because Scott was married to a woman with whom he had a family, although he said that he was gay. Over the nine months or so between the time that GPNy accepted the book and sent out a contract and the time I began to prepare the manuscript for publication, Scott became comfortable enough with me to one day reveal that while yes, he was living in the South, and yes, he was married with children, the main problem was entirely different: he was working a day job—and had been for a decade—at a local state prison where he was a guard. And if that wasn't complicated enough, he'd also been involved in a gay relationship with a convict in that prison for two years— someone originally in his cell block, in fact. He was now in the cell block of a close friend, also a prison guard, who not only knew about the affair, but who himself (while also being a married father) had had several affairs with inmates.

"Yowsza! Yowsza!" I remarked to Larry Mitchell, explaining Scott's situation.

"Those Southern boys sure do get around," Larry commented.

Somehow or other, clever Robert Scott managed to get the people around him so excited about the fact that he was publishing a novel with a New York publisher that no one seemed to care what its subject matter was, or that the publisher was GPNy. I did, however, do him the favor of making *The Finding of David* a "SeaHorse Book," and leaving Gay Presses of New York on the book as a logo. After that, any book I brought into GPNy also became a SeaHorse Book, especially as I slowed down my own press's rate of publications after 1985. But if you look at the copyright page of *The Finding Of David,* it clearly reads as having been published by the Gay Presses of New York. I guess that didn't faze anyone around Robert. Daddy, hubby, and prison guard was happily published.

He obviously wouldn't be doing any personal appearances around the book, so it was on its own. But then he mailed me an article from a northern Alabama newspaper, showing that he had indeed done a reading in a medium-size town's bookstore there, where it turned out he had personal connections. So he even managed to get publicity out of it.

The Finding of David had GPNy's first all-color—and thus more expensive— cover, with a beautiful and graphically brilliant painting by Ron Fowler. It was widely reviewed—in the *Advocate, New York Native, Bay Windows, Washington Blade,* and *San Francisco Sentinel*—and sold nicely. Even so, and for no particular reason I could ever figure out, it didn't really catch on. It ended up selling its first printing of about three thousand copies, but went no further. Later on, we figured out the reason: while it was well written, nothing about it was in the least bit literarily special or unique: it could have been (it probably *should* have been) published by Dell, or Signet, or Avon paperbacks and been on airport racks across the country.

That was a bit of a lesson for all three of us. Despite believing and hoping that we were publishing accessible books for all readers, what we were really publishing well was literary material aimed at small, specific, or odd readerships. Separately or together, we would never put out anything as close to mainstream as this novel again.

Robert, meanwhile, seemed happy with his book and not displeased with his royalty statements and the small yearly checks. He was writing another novel about his prison affair that I asked to read and that he promised to send. Months and then years went by and I never received anything. I did get occasional phone calls, though fewer. He always claimed he was busy with his growing children. He told me he'd ended the affair with the convict. Then there were family health problems. I may have phoned him once before we closed down GPNy; I definitely wrote to him, reverting the book's rights, but I never heard back. I also never heard that he sent his new book out to anyone else, and he never tried to locate me thereafter (people write to me all the time via my publishers.) I only hope that he is well and flourishing.

Perhaps the oddest thing about my entire publishing experience with *The Finding of David* came about when I began to carefully go through the book line by line, paragraph by paragraph, page by page, as editors must. At first, I wondered if it was just something I was being extrasensitive about. So I gave the manuscript to Larry.

"You're absolutely right," he said. "It's subtle, but inescapably there."

I worried all week, then made one of the two most difficult phone calls I'd ever made as a publisher to an author. I got Robert Scott on the line and told him that I'd been going through the manuscript and that I knew he hadn't done it intentionally at all, because by then I knew he was a good guy, but there was no doubt about it: the book was racist. We couldn't possibly publish a racist book.

Scott was stunned. I'd carefully reread and underlined wherever I thought the problem occurred, and I began reading him those passages out of context, and then in context.

He was, naturally enough, aghast. "Can it be fixed?"

I thought it could. I told him I'd send him two chapters I'd redlined. In some cases it was so subtle, so pervasive, that it was only as a pattern that the racism was in any way evident. Most of the fixes were simple, i.e., unfailingly negative words, phrases, and thoughts whenever African Americans were mentioned or present, but never positive ones. I thought it probably wasn't even conscious on his part. I wasn't sure how old he was. I'd assumed he was in his midforties, which meant that he'd grown up in the South during the forties and fifties. He might have just absorbed all those negative attitudes with his daily life. Of course, that didn't make it any better—or at all acceptable. But there it was.

My main fear, of course, would be that Scott would get those chapters and not see what I was getting at, which would have jeopardized the entire project. But I was relieved when he phoned a few days later and said, "Jesus, Felice! Thanks. This is why prejudice is so insidious. You can't even see it most of the time in yourself, in your words, or in your attitudes. Help fix the book. And I'll work on fixing myself."

———

Poetry remained important to me and to SeaHorse Press, and after Cooper's *Idols,* I ended up publishing four more poets through the press, each of them unlike the others. For three of those poets, SeaHorse published their first official "real" book, and each one of them went on to have a career, some of which are ongoing today.

Mark Ameen was a young man from Boston, of Lebanese-Italian extraction, and you can guess how physically beautiful that meant he was. He was also sweet. He was a good writer, too, a poet, and later the author of poetry-theater-performance pieces in the East Village scene in the mid-1980s and 1990s. Despite that venue, Mark was serious about his work, and ambitious too. SeaHorse published his first poetry book, *A Circle of Sirens,* in 1985. Parts of that were later taken up by Gay Men's Press of London's book *Three New York Poets* (1987), and selections also appeared with many new poems in Ameen's compendium, *The Buried Body: A Trilogy,* put out by Stan Leventhal's Amethyst Press in 1990. Reviewing Ameen's one-man show, *The Seven Pillars of Wicca-Dick: A Triumph,* in the November 27, 1991, *New York Times,* Stephen Holden called it a "twisting, effusive, broadside," and concluded that in the end it was more a revelation of "Ameen's dense poetry than a true theatrical representation." Not at all a bad thing, in my opinion.

Another poet, Rudy Kikel, had moved from Manhattan to Boston, where he became for many years the arts and lifestyles editor of *Bay Windows,* that area's gay paper. I'd loved his poetry, which I had read alongside my own in various magazines and quarterlies of the day, from the smaller gay quarterlies to tonier ones like *Ploughshares.* Rudy had already put together a chapbook of work in 1980 called *Shaping Possibilities,* verse in the sophisticated, questioning, allusively stylish vein of James Merrill and Richard Howard. SeaHorse ended up including those in his first collection, *Lasting Relationships* (1984). That was enough to launch him. Through other publishers Kikel put out a second collection, almost a sequel, titled, *Long Division* (1992), and in 1997, a third, differently themed volume, *Period Pieces.* Completely different from those, and more about his family's original European background, was Kikel's next book, *Gottscheers,* in 1998. In 1994 Rudy also edited one of the better collections of gay male poetry, *Gents, Bad Boys, and Barbarians;* in 2002, a second volume came out under the title *This New Breed.* Both Mark's and Rudy's collections from SeaHorse sold out their printings and received excellent reviews.

Although we'd seen each other around New York gay literary circles for a decade, it was only after he'd moved to New England and we working together on the poetry book that I realized that I recognized Kikel from before: since childhood. I asked Rudy and he agreed that he felt the same about me. We played what I call "Jewish Genelaogy," or "Did you go to so-and-so school?" for months on end, going all the way back to kindergarten and covering everything including doctors and dentists in whose office waiting rooms we might have seen each other. In each and every case, we were two or three neighborhoods apart, sharing absolutely nothing in common except the borough of Queens. I still felt I knew him from early youth and I would periodically rack my brains for the connection.

I'd bought a Stickley-style distressed-oak bookcase from the 1920s for my study that I decided to keep near the apartment's upper floor door, and someone gave me an apt and handsome ceramic bowl I used to keep change, keys, eyeglasses, etc., immediately at hand when needed. One after-noon while grabbing change from it while going out the door, I was stopped in my tracks by a completely Proustian moment: I was back on Long Island, aged ten or eleven, and I was about to leave the house I'd grown up in, and I began to rummage in the (much shallower) bowl my mother used to keep on a low table near our front door to get change. My mother was sitting, reading a magazine nearby. As I reached for the change, she said—and years later I heard her quite clearly—"Leave a dollar for Rudy, the paper boy."

Later that day I phoned Kikel and asked if he'd ever had a paper route in Queens. He had, for the *Long Island Daily Press*. We received that afternoon paper for years, and it devolved that Rudy's paper route did indeed include my family's old address. Mystery solved.

———

Three other SeaHorse poets stood out for different reasons. The first I met while in Los Angeles at a book party for *An Asian Minor* at Unicorn Books in West Hollywood, at that time a legitimate, nonpornographic bookstore. I was talking to someone when the cutest guy in the place tapped me on the shoulder. I'd of course noticed him when he'd come in, as he was classically handsome, slender, dark haired, with pale eyes, a great face, and an amazing abdomen, clearly visible since he wore a Hawaiian shirt completely unbuttoned to show off his pecs and chiseled, washboard tummy. He also looked vaguely familiar.

"I'll be with you in a second," I said to the handsome young man, "but whatever you do, *do not* button that shirt for at least the next five years."

That statement did it, he later told me. With those words, I'd revealed myself not as the hoity-toity New York writer or stuck-up Manhattan small press publisher I might have been, but instead as someone who enjoyed the better things in life. In this case the better things in life meant poet and some-time porn star Gavin Dillard. So even before we really began talking, Gavin knew he wanted me to publish his first book.

What that consisted of, according to Gav, was a series of short love poems about a relationship he was in the middle of. Similar to, but not quite haiku, he said, they reminded him of Emily Dickinson, of Sappho. Fine, I told him, send them to me.

He did a few weeks later and I read them. Then we spoke on the phone. "This may sound weird," I told Gavin, "But this book isn't quite finished. It's possibly only two-thirds done. Before you speak, let me just say I love what you've written. Unfortunately, from what you've written, I also think I'd like to see the poems you write in the next few months before I consider this for publication."

What I didn't say—it would have been too cruel even for me to utter— was that I thought that the relationship he was writing about was too hot not to cool down. I expected it to begin to go to hell quickly. The poems he then wrote would conclude the book's downward narrative arc. Gavin insisted he was done with the book. I told him I'd get back to him once SeaHorse had space on its publishing schedule.

Several months later, a new, longer, manuscript arrived on my desk. Gavin accompanied it with a short note that read more or less, "Well, you were right. The affair is over. But at least I got a book out of it."

He'd retained the original title, *Notes from a Marriage: Love Poems.* And that's how SeaHorse Press published it in the spring of 1983. It was fresh, it was young, it was a lovely book. Not earthshaking, not about to put anyone on the literary map. Even so . . . I art directed it carefully, again using Patrick Merla's exquisite—and this book's interior really was exquisite—typesetting. I selected a pastel green and white cover, with an unexpectedly soft and sexy cover photograph of two men with their arms around each other taken by John Preston, former *Advocate* editor and author of the S/M classics *I Once Had a Master* and *Mr. Benson*.

I was leaving an early copy of Dillard's book at the offices of *Christopher Street* and the *New York Native*, hopefully for someone there to review, when publisher Charles Ortleb stepped out of his office, took a look at the slender little volume, and read a few pages. From the expression on his face, he clearly considered it to be the merest of gay piffle.

"What you should do," Ortleb suggested, "is publish porno. It's the only way you'll make money." With a reaction like that, I spent the rest of the day wondering why I even bothered to be a gay publisher. SeaHorse Press had not been started to make money. I tried to point out to Ortleb that it was more interesting and exciting to publish something that wasn't porno, something literary even, and then to break even financially. But he wasn't interested in hearing that.

At first, fate seemed to support Ortleb's point of view: sales of *Notes from a Marriage* were slow, if steady. All the more of a surprise when pre-Christmas bookstore orders for the book turned out to be high, and then in January, orders rose even higher. The book went into a second printing a year later, and continued to sell steadily and well, especially around Christmas and Valentine's Day—as a gift book—year after year.

Gavin had begun doing more public readings on the West Coast, from the book and from his other poetry, and he soon sent me a second collection, *Waiting for the Virgin*. He supplied a sexy near-nude full-color author photo for the front cover, and that book came out in 1985. Once again it sold nicely, although it never reached the figures of *Notes*, which had taken on a life of its own.

I soon began hearing from others that Dillard had a new persona: the Naked Poet. Utilizing his good looks, he was doing readings in the nude. If he did any on the East Coast, I must have been out of town, alas. He also took over his own publishing. His company, Bhakti Books, put out his third volume, *Pagan Love Poems,* in 1988, and in 1989, *The Naked Poet: Poems 1970–1985* included some from the SeaHorse Press volumes.

Shortly thereafter, Gavin published *In the Flesh: Undressing for Success,* a memoir of 1970s and 1980s Hollywood (1989), in which he named names and revealed who was gay. A few years later, he and I had traded places: he was now the editor requesting poems from me for two quite good anthologies: *Between The Cracks: A Daedalus Anthology of Kinky Verse* in 1996, in which I had three poems, and in 1999, *A Day For a Lay: A Century of Gay Poetry,* in which I had two more.

By that time, I'd come to realize where I'd seen Gavin before I'd met him. A copy of the porn film *Stryker Force* starring that nineties porn icon Jeff Stryker came my way, and as I played it, I realized I'd seen it years before in some backroom venue or other, and there was Gavin, oddly enough, up a tree, masturbating.

He'd settled down with a partner, first in Bolinas, California, the Marin hippie town that time forgot, and later on in Maui. At the time I'm writing this, Gavin Dillard's play, *Bark,* has been running a year in a theater in West Hollywood.

———

I think I can safely write that Robert Peters is one of the most prolific, versatile, potent, and—despite having dozens of books published—also one of the most unjustifiably neglected of American writers of the twentieth century.

Peters grew up in the 1930s in a poor rural family in northern Wisconsin, became a soldier in World War II, and received a Veterans Administration–financed education leading to a doctorate in literature. His first published book, *The Crowns of Apollo: Swinburne's Principles of Literature and Art, a Study in Victorian Criticism,* put out by Wayne State University Press in 1965, seemed to promise a typically prosaic academic career like those littering scores of American colleges.

Then Peters's youngest child died. And, as he tells it in his memoir, *Feather: A Child's Death and Life,* he became utterly conscious for the first time: Peters became an aware person and a poet simultaneously. He soon divorced his wife, moved to California, and at Disneyland of all places, he met a much younger man, poet Paul Trachtenberg, who became his life companion.

When I first began reading Peters in various gay poetry magazines, he'd already put out several unusual books of poetry, including *The Sows Head and Other Poems* (1968), *Hawker, Hawthorne,* and *Shaker Light: Mother Ann Lee in America.* In all but the first book, the poet concentrated on a single unusual person who was eccentrically religious or spiritual. As a professor of English and writing at the University of California at Irvine, Peters had also written two volumes of criticism of the U.S. poetry scene, *The Great American Poetry Bake-Off: Series I* and *II,* probing and searing looks at what was being published and what was being hailed as good. The volumes told the truth: no wonder the books ended up being controversial.

In 1982, Peters was in the midst of one of his most fertile creative periods, writing fiction, poetry, and drama, sometimes even mixing them together. I'm not exactly sure how it was that his next manuscript got to me. Possibly there was a query letter. I do recall getting the sheaf of poems, sitting down to read one or two while I waited for Bob Lowe to arrive for dinner, finding it very difficult to pull myself away from them to go out with Bob, and after dinner, feeling compelled to return and read the entire book.

If literature is supposed to bring you to new places and inside different minds, *What Dillinger Meant to Me* certainly succeeded. The setting was hardscrabble farming land in Wisconsin in the 1930s, the story about growing up in an overlarge family with barely enough to eat. The milieu was rendered with photographic precision, seamlessly, without pity or sentiment, using rural English, with perfect rhythm and diction. It was like reading some pre-Homeric Greek odist: that ancient and deep! The glamorous overlay to this less-than-basic lifestyle, of course, was the existence of John Dillinger, the star gangster of the 1930s: *the* gangster as far as the media of the time were concerned.

Entire newspaper and radio newscast fortunes were made following and reporting on Dillinger's bank robberies, his shootouts, his hard-bitten, bleached-blonde molls; the pranks and close escapes of the tall, slender man whom women hankered after, poverty-stricken men admired, and FBI head J. Edgar Hoover demanded must be caught. The spring Dillinger moved to rural Wisconsin, he became an instant avatar and erotic fantasy figure in the young farmboy/poet-to-be's life. By the time Dillinger was ambushed outside a double feature movie theater some months later, he had become Depression America's legend. And as Peters showed in the poems, he'd made his mark: Peters was now destined to lust after tough guys.

What Dillinger Meant to Me is classic Americana. It included some poems from an earlier version of *The Sow's Head,* but was really unlike any of the other literate, ironic, infra dig poems Peters usually wrote. Worlds away from his previous volume, *Picnic in the Snow,* poems in the voice of Ludwig, the (allegedly gay) mad king of nineteenth-century Bavaria. *Dillinger* would give birth later on to Robert Peter's equally wonderful memoir with similar material, *Crunching Gravel* (1991) but, in fact, it stands alone. It's only in the last few years, now that Peter's said that he is retiring as a poet and has put out a final batch of poems, (along with his partner, Paul Trachtenberg, and neighbor poet Barbara Hauk) in *Makar's Dozen* (2006) that he's once again remembering and bringing back to life those early days of his life in marvelously incisive work: over half of the new poems in that collection form an homage to a kind of life that once dominated, and that has now all but vanished, from the United States.

I did what I could to make Peter's collection as unique looking as it was poetically unusual. Michael Grumley had recently begun to draw using a new style of thin, light lines, and he told me he'd always wanted to do a portrait of Dillinger. His version, a sepia pencil profile placed cameo-like within the setting of a Roosevelt era ten-cent piece (as in the commonplace Depression-era lament, "Buddy, can you spare a dime?") was remarkable, singular, and positioned the book to get it at least bookshelf attention. But despite all that, and even with the few gay poems inside, *Dillinger* was never recognized as the terrific book it was. Reviews were few. Sales were half those of less talented writers.

Unstoppable, Peters followed up *Dillinger* with the life story of another, far more malevolent being: *The Blood Countess: Erzebet Bathory of Hungary (1560–1614): A GothicHorrorPoem of Violence & Rage,* and a few years later, with *Báthory: A Play for One Performer* (published in one volume in 1987). But while Dillinger was a figure of Peter's past, somehow or other the Blood Countess became the poet's present. During the 1990s, the tall, heavyset, ultra-masculine Robert Peters *became* Báthory, the "Hungarian Vampiress," onstage. The play premiered in poet Paul Evangelisti's backyard, but then went on to more legitimate stages at the Fullerton Art Museum and Venice's Beyond Baroque in California, the Loeb Center at New York University, and the Don-nell Library in New York City. It was even filmed for television in Australia. Actor Anthony Roman also presented *Báthory* at Long Beach, California's Beneath the Bridge Theater. But it was Robert in full makeup and costume as the fascinatingly bizarre woman that was the real discovery.

It was then that I first met Peters, years after I'd published him. And I have to say, watching that witty, wise, and gentle man become that gothic harridan onstage was an excellent lesson in recognizing and giving free rein to the dark side of literature. Luckily, I was able to put all that aside, and we became friends and have remained so to this day.

Once again, Peters was ahead of his time. *Báthory* was not a hit. The book of poems was more of a curiosity, and he returned to what had worked in the past. In 1989, he put out another book of commentary, *Hunting the Snark: A*

Compendium of New Poetic Terminology, a book still used in graduate classes today and deemed by some to be indispensable. He followed that in 1994 with *Where the Bee Sucks: Workers, Drones, and Queens of Contemporary American Poetry,* another slap at the crassness of what was by then becoming a much debased literary form. He was writing more prose too: *For You, Lili Marlene: A Memoir of World War II,* and *Snapshots for a Serial Killer: A Fiction and a Play,* about Randy Kraft, a typically Southern California version of the psychotic breed that seemed everywhere in late-twentieth-century media, responsible for killing dozens of teenage boys.

Now that he's done writing, Robert Peter's oeuvre looms large. Although it's still unclear who the major American poets of the second part of the twentieth century will end up being—Merrill? Bishop? who else?—Robert's work belongs up there. And to any graduate student looking to make a splash: you couldn't do better than to plan your doctorate around his memoirs, poetry, and plays.

———

Around the same time as I was beginning to publish Robert, I met a neighbor of mine in our local West Village post office, poet Edward Field. He came over and introduced himself and commented upon what good posture I had. Perhaps, I replied, it was because I had been doing hatha yoga since 1968. It turned out that Field also did yoga daily. He was a quite handsome man twenty years my senior, and I had definitely noticed him around the neighborhood for some time, walking closely next to another, slighter fellow. I'd guessed they were partners and they were. But that wasn't why Neil always remained so close. He had lost most of his sight by then, and their way of walking about together was designed to not draw attention to that fact— which worked surprisingly well; I'd certainly not guessed.

I had read several of Field's books of poetry since the 1960s. My favorites—now classics—were *Variety Photoplays* and *Stand Up, Friend, With*

Me. In a lecture (then a printed essay) titled "Whitman's Sons and Dickinson's Daughters" about lesbian and gay poetry that I'd given several times to various organizations, I used to quote in full and discuss Field's delightful poem "Pacific Octopus Lover." And it turned out that while quite peripatetic—they lived half the year somewhere other than Manhattan, as I did, but usually in more exotic places, like North Africa or Paris—when in New York Edward usually stayed right around the corner from me in that giant building on Manhattan's West Side Highway that filled a complete block, complete with an art gallery and a gay synagogue—Beth Simchat Torah—where I'd read and where I also usually voted.

Before becoming artists' housing, Westbeth had been the RCA Radio Laboratories. There, during the late forties and early fifties, British scientific genius Alan Turing devised and then perfected the diode tube that led to the personal computer that has revolutionized all our lives—that is when Turing wasn't soliciting and boinking merchant sailors from ships docked directly across the street, which he reportedly did at a furious pace in the late 1940s. Among people I knew living in Westbeth were poet John Ashbery, artist David Alexander (Richard Howard's partner), poet and academic Joe Cady, and anthropologist and writer Tobias Schneebaum. My own attempts to get into the building had failed. At first I was too unknown to have the publication requirements and to have connections to the right people to recommend me. Then, when I did have the requirements and knew the people, I found out I was earning too much to fit Westbeth's strict financial requirements. But I was glad to know Edward and Neil, and we soon became friends.

We began talking about SeaHorse Press putting out a collection of Field's poetry. The one he had in mind was to be titled *Frieze for a Temple of Love,* a truly erotic collection of poetry, although more polymorphous perverse than simply gay. By the time I read the manuscript it was about 1986, and SeaHorse—and GPNy, too—was prescheduled for at least two years ahead with new titles, besides needing to put out third, fourth, and further reprints of *Torch Song* and my own *Ambidextrous*. It really was a case of too much success, and thus too much work, for the three of us to handle.

Even so, I soft-scheduled *Frieze* and hoped it would happen. I even approved potential cover art, drawings a friend had made of the photos from the erotic friezes of the cave-temple of Ajanta in India that Field liked. I got his manuscript copyedited and ready to be typeset. But we never signed a contract, and that was unfortunate. Had he or I pushed for one, the book might have actually gotten done, if only because it would have *had* to be done.

The problem was that from 1988 on, GPNy was thriving and backed up with new projects and reprintings. I'd also gotten back into writing my own books, needing more income to support my lifestyle, which cut into the time and money I could give to the presses. Then Terry Helbing had an accident that put him totally out of commission and dropped his work, including all of JH Press, on my shoulders. In addition, these were the years in which people around me who'd been healthy began seroconverting, and people who had already been ill several years with HIV/AIDS began dying. The latter group included my younger brother Jerry, several very close friends, many acquaintances, four members of the Violet Quill Club, Bob Lowe, and George Stambolian, editor of the *Men On Men* series.

By the time I had managed to dig myself out of all the funerals, the memorial services, the grief, the blue funks, and all the extra work handed to me, Larry Mitchell had begun to lose his eyesight due to macular degeneration. Soon I was operating all of GPNy by myself. I was also trying to research and write *Like People in History, Dryland's End,* and *The New Joy of Gay Sex,* three enormous books, all of which I felt I needed to complete before I, too, seroconverted, got ill, and died.

Something had to give, and it ended up being the presses. I contacted Edward and told him that because of illness and death, we would no longer be publishing his book, and he was free to take it elsewhere.

In the meantime, Edward hadn't stood still. He arranged with the venerable Sheep Meadow Press to publish a much more important book than ours would have been. *Selected Poems: From the Book of My Life* came out in 1987. An even bigger and more prominent collection, *Counting Myself Lucky,* came out of Godine Press in 1992. Then in 1998, a decade after I was supposed to have done it, Black Sparrow Press put out a collection titled *A Frieze for a Temple of Love* with, oddly enough, all the poems from what was to have been our collection *except* the long title poem. Unlike me, Edward is an easy-going person with what I consider a somewhat saintly temperament, and so despite my failure to come through, we have continued to remain friends over the years.

————

Robert Peters and Edward Field may have been established writers. The next author I became associated with was a legendary one, and our connection would take modern gay publishing back to the earliest decades of the Twentieth Century. I'm talking about GPNy's re-publication of Charles Henri Ford and Parker Tyler's 1933 book, *The Young and Evil,* thought by many to be the first true homosexual novel, and probably the first "coming-out" book. Gore Vidal had told me it had been out of print for a long time and was in need of reissue. The truth was a bit different: the book had never been officially published in the U.S., but had in Paris, by Maurice Girodias's infamous Olympia Press, and had been reprinted by Olympia again in 1960, at which time it slowly entered the U.S. via various sub rosa distributors. The authors in the 1930s were two cheeky young men, one of whom would go on to become a noted American film critic during a time when that was a great novelty. And in fact, Parker Tyler's books, *Sex in Films, A Pictorial History of Sex in Films,* and especially *Screening the Sexes: Homosexuality in the Movies,* were pioneering volumes, lodestones for all that was sexually ambiguous or erotically quirky in Hollywood.

Tyler's coauthor was an even greater figure in the international art world. Charles Henri Ford was only fourteen and his sister Ruth Ford sixteen when they wrote to Gertrude Stein and asked for some of her poems for their just-begun literary quarterly *Blue*. These two young Southerners of great precocity and beauty felt their talents were hidden under various bushels in the Mississippi of the 1920s and no sooner had Harriet Monroe, who published *Poetry* magazine in Paris, written to compliment them on their magazine's first issue and invited them to look her up next time they were on the *rive gauche* then they had entrained to New York. They were soon crossing the Atlantic on their way to France.

Once arrived, the young Fords' beauty and brilliance, along with their verve and intelligence, did the rest. They were invited everywhere by the Parisian intellectual set, photographed often, brought out to recite their own (more often Charles's) poetry, and they became fixtures at the Stein-Toklas residence on the rue de Fleurus, at Harriet Monroe's salon, and in various other ateliers of *la vie de bohème*. Ruth soon returned to New York, where her acting talent landed her Broadway roles, leading eventually to starring parts, including premiering plays by Tennessee Williams. Her career only settled down a bit once she met and married the dashingly handsome film actor Zachary Scott in the 1950s and moved to Hollywood, where she rested on her laurels while her husband made terrible, extremely profitable cowboy and pirate movies.

Her younger brother Charles, however, remained in Paris, where he soon attracted the attention of the surrealist painters and photographers then ruling the Parisian art world. Eugène Atget photographed the licentious youth exiting a famous Montmartre *pissoir*. In the photo, an advertisement picturing a devil's long, lascivious tongue extends across the foreground and appears about to enter young Charles's fly, which he's hurriedly buttoning. Being very handsome and blond and pale blue-eyed, Charles soon conquered men and women alike—even the "Amazon" author, Djuna Barnes, who'd just become famous for writing a much-hyped novel titled *Nightwood*. According to Ford, he moved in and began a sexual affair with Barnes around the same time that he was sleeping with most of the gay or bisexual male artists of Montparnasse. While Barnes certainly helped him as a writer, both aesthetically and by getting his work known, according to Charles, she was definitely the lover and he very often the busily fleeing beloved.

He threw Barnes over completely when he met a magnetic and muscular Polish-born painter then enjoying great popularity. I knew of Pavel Tchelitchew much later for his remarkable Museum of Modern Art painting *Hide and Seek.* But earlier he was considered one of the top Paris Surrealists of the 1930s along with Salvador Dalí. And according to Charles, the "absolutely impossible person that turned out to be Pavlik" ended up being the only person Ford admitted to having been in love with, and was the major emotional affair of his life.

I discovered this information from Ford himself when I contacted him in the mid-eighties. I'd mentioned his name and the novel once again to Larry Mitchell at dinner, and with typical modesty, Larry replied, "I think I know someone who might know how to contact Ford." Indeed he did know someone: Steven Watson was a scholar of the Americans in Paris period, and had written about it at some length in *Prepare for Saints: Gertrude Stein, Virgil Thomson, and the Mainstreaming of American Modernism.* I knew Watson better, however, as the author of the definitive study to date of the Harlem Renaissance. We met, we spoke, and it was Watson who told me the next time Charles happened to be in the U.S., and Watson who gave me Ford's phone number at the Dakota Apartments in Manhattan.

There, on a cold spring morning, I walked past the spot where John Lennon had been gunned down, got through the formidably uniformed concierge/doorman inside his black wrought iron "cage," and went to visit for the first time the legendary Charles Henri Ford and his partner, a somewhat younger man named Indra Tamang. The apartment was located under the eaves of the famous nineteenth-century Central Park West building, reachable only by a second elevator, obtainable on the next-to-top floor, next to those used for the rest of the apartments.

His flat proved to be two artists' ateliers combined: two pre–World War II artist studios with various bright windows and dormers, a small galley kitchen plunked within, an added-on bathroom, and many different storage spaces hidden under what was never clearly either empty or enclosed spaces. Light and cheerful, the studios consisted of a sitting-cooking-dining area and a separate double sleeping area with central open space for artwork. Several of the dormered nook areas were big enough to also hold work tables or desks. It was all done in rather dark wood and somberly painted walls, littered with prints, paintings, and wall hangings, many of them Nepalese, Indian, or Tibetan. All the daybeds and chairs had heavy filigreed or Asian-patterned materials thrown over them. The lamps and other fixtures were faded brass and very old bronze. It seemed very much a pre-modern artist's studio not unlike those in black-and-white photos I'd seen of Whistler's atelier or Matisse's studio.

When I first met them, Charles and Indra had just arrived from their home in Khania on the Greek island of Crete, had stopped off briefly in Paris, and told me they were only staying in the States a few weeks. I showed Charles several GPNy books, left him our catalogs and our reviews, and told him Vidal had recommended his 1933 novel for reprint. I needed to know first: exactly how the rights situation of the book stood, and second if he were willing to let us reprint the book.

From what I'd been led to understand, Ford had been ill, or was perhaps still ill. At eighty years old, he looked both very distinguished, clearly still handsome, yet quite frail. Naturally, I was worried and I hoped to get at the least an understanding on paper between us.

Ford said he was interested in a reprint, and he declared that with Parker Tyler long dead without living heirs, that he, Charles, possessed full authority for handling all business regarding *The Young and Evil*. With that settled, I was assured that I wouldn't run into any rights problems.

But if I'd hoped to settle matters quickly, I was to be disappointed. Charles asked me to send him contracts at the Dakota and told me he would look at them. Meanwhile, I told him how much I could offer as an advance, at the same times apologizing that it was so little.

"Not really a problem," he assured me. "One reason I'm here in the States is to arrange the sale of my papers to the University of Kansas's library." He expected that to net him a great deal more than what I could offer. Even so, another $3,000 wouldn't hurt his pockets, either. So I was optimistic.

Due to GPNy's scheduling, the actual publication wouldn't happen for several more years, and since neither Charles nor I were in a hurry, I soon got to know him and Indra better, which led not only to using Tchelitchew's art, but also to an unexpected friendship between me and Charles and, to a lesser extent, of course, Indra.

Indra was a native of Nepal, and on their second return to Manhattan they let me know that he and Charles had apparently made their most permanent home in Katmandu for many years, with biannual forays to Paris and Khania. We knew several people in common. The West Coast poet James Broughton had spoken well of me—which rather surprised me to hear, as we'd met so briefly. Even more unexpectedly, the artist Paul Cadmus, whom I'd only met once (and flirted with) also had good things to say about me. It was clear from Charles's conversation that he still frequented artistic circles wherever he went, although most of them were populated by visual artists, and so beyond my usual range.

How Charles actually lived remained forever the purest speculation to me. With all those homes around the world, I naturally assumed he was quite well off. But a year after our first encounter, following what the newspapers said of East Asian political turmoil, Ford and Indra once again appeared in Manhattan, this time for a much longer period of time, with Ford reporting that they now considered themselves political exiles and definite personae non gratae because of something he wouldn't discuss, evidently having to do with either the Nepalese royal family or with the pair's harboring independence-seeking political revolutionaries in the capital.

Shortly after that, I heard from someone else that their Paris flat was for sale. And a few months later, someone else mentioned that the house in Khania had been sold. What had been the source of Charles's income anyway?

Steven Watson and I surmised it had been Tchelitchew's artwork, and that it had all been sold or by the 1990s the market for it had pretty much dried up. Once he was settled in New York, Ford did arrange a tasteful show in a chic European owned art gallery on Madison Avenue, a small Tchelitchew retrospective with only two demi-masterworks—at which copies of the reprint of *The Young and Evil* were also on sale.

But what soon became clear was that Charles Henri Ford was back in the U.S. pretty much for good, and that following two rather difficult years, including one of surgeries about which he would not speak, that Charles was at work again, at poetry, at his varied collages, and also on a volume of memoirs, to be titled *Water From a Bucket* (a title never quite explained), which he quickly assured me was already promised to a university press, lest I get my hopes up.

I'm guessing that Charles, who was about as canny an operator in the art and literary worlds as anyone I've ever met, and more effetely ruthless by far than any mere Hollywood starlet or Broadway producer, was establishing a niche for himself back in New York.

Work on our book went fairly easily—we were photographing and reprinting the Girodias edition page for page. And we were adding Steven Watson's introduction, a good piece of writing that would put the novel into full historical and aesthetic context. Charles would vet that essay in advance, naturally, and he would carefully look over the typeset pages of the finished book, before it went off to be printed and bound.

The only question we faced was how to present the novel visually. I'd shown Charles enough cover art of the books SeaHorse and GPNy had done to demonstrate the fact that cover art for me it was really crucial to a book's success.

We were sitting in his Dakota flat one day when the question came up once again, and Ford suddenly had a flash of insight—or of remembrance.

"You know, Fell-eese, when the book was first done, Pavlik painted a series of watercolors for it," Charles said.

I hadn't known this and I doubted that anyone but Charles did, now that Tchelitchew was dead.

"Pavlik tore apart a copy of Maurice's edition and sewed it back together, with these new pages added in, on which he painted the watercolors," Charles recalled.

My heart skipped a beat. Was there any chance that he actually had that copy handy?

In fact, he had. It was in a steamer trunk that had just, at last, come over from France, filled with things from the sold Paris flat. The three of us got up, went to the trunk, and opened it, Indra and I holding it open as aged Charles rummaged around and at long last emerged with the book. We sat back down to tea as Ford leafed through it, then handed it to me to look through.

"No one's ever seen it but Pavlik and me," he said. "He was so enamored of me at the time," he added. "He begged me not to show it to anyone else."

The drawings and watercolors were not only wonderful, they were totally period—the classical Picasso, Cocteau, Calder period of the thirties—and they were also sexy and hot, including one rather impressionistically soft-hued aquarelle of two men sixty-nining.

The book was in amazingly good condition considering how old it was, but then it was a handmade book, the pages taken from the original, and all of it, including the artwork pages, stitched together within a handcrafted leather jacket.

"Will any of them do as a cover?" he asked.

I thought the one with the sailor boy and Abraham Lincoln figure would do nicely. It was saucy, period, and easy to reproduce. I said so, and he looked at it again and agreed it would be fun.

Then I asked if he thought we might use all the watercolors for the reprint inside the book, not spaced out amid the text as Tchelitchew had originally done—that would be too difficult for the bindery, and too expensive to do—but bound together, as a portfolio.

To my amazement, Charles agreed, adding "but of course, I can't let the book out of here, it being such a memento."

Since Charles was a professional photographer himself, I would send a professional photographer and together they would shoot the artwork and we would work off the negatives.

When I discussed this with Alvin Greenberg, our printer's rep, he became excited. Even more so after I showed him the negative: this was real twentieth-century art by a famous painter. Of course, they were wonderful drawings and watercolors, and they were beautiful, and even the one of the guys sixty-nining were in Alvin's conservative, fairly straight-laced opinion, "high art." He made it easy for us to present them as an open-out portfolio bound in at the end of the novel.

The publication of *The Young and Evil,* a "SeaHorse Book" from GPNy, ended up being one of the highlights of my publishing career, one of which I'm quite proud. I wish it had been more widely reviewed at the time. It sold only its first printing and thus just managed to break even financially. But Gay Men's Press in the UK bought the British rights and also put it out. So it was unquestionably worth the expense and effort.

Partly because of how easily and well we worked together, Charles and I remained close until I moved out of New York in 1995. When I interviewed him for *Chiron,* a literary quarterly in tabloid form, I discovered that he'd been born a few weeks before my mother. In certain ways, Charles felt I was very much like the son he'd never had, having his easy-going ambition, practicality, and general optimism about life.

He would phone me up with questions about people, institutions, or foundations, and he always knew I would tell him the unvarnished truth. Once he'd moved back to America for good, he realized that New York City was fairly unlivable during the summer. He'd heard me speak of Cape Cod, where my partner and I spent a second summer in September and October each year, and so one March day, Charles organized an outing for Indra, him, and me. I rented a car and drove us up to the Cape, where he had a half dozen potential summer houses to look at. He paid for the car, gas, and even got us a free dinner and overnight stay at a friend's house near Falmouth. But although he liked the Cape, he wasn't crazy about Provincetown, and none of the houses we looked at would do for Charles's very specific, albeit unspoken, requirements.

Two months later, he phoned to tell me he had found a summer house out in Montauk, not far from those of Edward Albee and Peter Beard, whom he knew and liked and felt to be central to some sort of simpatico artistic-social set. But, he added, this had its own problem attached to it. The only real way to come and go between Manhattan the far tip of Long Island would be to drive. He no longer drove, and Indra didn't know how. He asked me to teach him. I demurred, recommending a driving school—to no avail. Charles insisted, then made me promise to teach Indra as well, and he rented us another car and said we would all drive out to the end of Long Island to do it there.

The next phone call I received before we were to go was a secret one, from Indra, in another room while Charles napped, who told me that he knew how to drive already, that he'd obtained a learner's permit, taken courses, and passed them, but that Charles insisted that he learn "American rules" and simply would not hear of him driving around without my specific tutoring and aid. This calmed me somewhat about the upcoming trip.

So the three of us embarked upon another long, overnight car trip, dropping off Charles at Peter's while I found an empty road and put Indra through his paces. He was a little rusty, even with an automatic, but he picked it up quickly, and I soon had him driving through East Hampton and along the flowery, estate-dotted lanes of Amagansett until he began to feel comfortable. I even had him drive the four of us to dinner and back that night, with me in the front seat at Charles's insistence (of course), loudly reexplaining things Indra already knew very well.

While interviewing Ford, I realized that he'd already been interviewed and quoted so often over the years that it would be impossible for either of us to come up with anything spontaneous and fresh. Charles had so much made himself a work of art that it would be boorish of me to attempt to pick at that wonderfully polished-to-a-gleam-over-many-decades surface of his. And while I knew from others that at times Charles could be mean, arrogant, and, above all, demanding, he'd never once been anything but kind to me. Some of the real luck I've had in life is how very kind some really impossible personalities have proven to be around me—perhaps because they didn't feel in any way threatened by me or by my rather aloof self-confidence. So the interview turned out to be both a collaborative effort (i.e., my questions intrigued him) and a success: he came off as uniquely Charles Henri Ford.

Although Charles and I spoke on the phone several times after I moved to L.A.—once about the subsidiary sale of the book to Gay Men's Press in England, which took many years to pay the advance and never paid royalties—the last time I actually saw Charles was for a photo shoot he was doing in which I became a subject. He and Indra had rented a tiny midtown photo studio and he told me he was in the process of putting together a book of a new kind of portrait collage. Although he explained these to me, the only one I really came to understand was the one he did of me. He'd blown up to life-size a photo of a Roman or Greek statue's upper torso. He then placed this photo over my own torso, taping it around my bare back and lower torso. He then dressed my lower body in classical drapery, seated me in front of a scrim of a classical background, placed a laurel wreath on my brow and photographed me. I remember thinking as we did it that it couldn't possibly come out any good. But Charles seemed pleased at the time and I never asked about it afterward.

He probably would have said it was "an experiment that didn't quite work, like so many others." As an Aquarian, he was airily aesthetic-scientific that way. And that was one of his sayings. But the saying I remember most and which most summed up Ford for me, and that I try to use as my own, is what Charles said when I asked at the end of that magazine interview, "In such a long, active life, filled with so many people, do you ever regret anything?"

"Regret," Charles came back to me grandly, "is *not* my milieu!"

6

Gay Presses, High and Low

I'm not sure how I first heard about the two anthologies and their strange history.

The first time may have been at a poetry reading I attended, when I spoke with Joan Larkin, a poet I'd read alongside in the past and whom I'd published in *A True Likeness*. She mentioned that she and another woman were doing a massive anthology of lesbian poetry. For the next few years, I'd would hear about it from various women writers I knew. It sounded like it was going to be comprehensive and, typical of Larkin's taste, good. I also heard from another lesbian writer somewhat later, (Bertha Harris, I believe), that Joan and her anthology partner had also decided to put together a book of lesbian fiction.

Both volumes were needed. Whereas gay male fiction in the early eighties already had a clear—if fairly recent—history and a strong, ongoing profile, lesbian books by the 1970s were best known as pulps—paperback novels, especially the work of Ann Bannon, among others.

Partly this was because many lesbian novels were reviewed as women's literature, not separated out as gay, as for example books by Andrew Holleran or Armistead Maupin were. John Rechy, Edmund White, and I were unquestionably gay male writers, and could not easily be subsumed under the rubric of male writing. But Kate Millet's *Sita* and Bertha Harris's *Confessions of Cheru-bino* didn't shout out "gay" the way that Rita Mae Brown's *Rubyfruit Jungle* or Judy Grahn's *Edward the Dyke* had done a few years earlier; and since then even Brown and Grahn had refocused their energies, writing more generally feminist books like *Six of One* and *Another Mother Tongue.*

This state of affairs had come about because by then many lesbians, espe-cially the more intellectual and creative ones, had joined the feminist move-ment and the National Organization for Women (NOW), and they were turning their energies to women's issues and away from exclusively gay topics.

The 1978 New York gay pride parade had been one of the most trans-parent indications of how far lesbians had moved away from the close working relationship women had had with gay men during the Stonewall Riots and early gay liberation era. One of the figures from that original Stonewall Inn insurrection, Sylvia Rivera, a transsexual who admittedly dressed like a female hooker, went onstage at the parade's end along with the half dozen other gay and lesbian leaders. One of the lesbians immediately stood up and declared that Sylvia was a travesty of women, an insult to women, and refused to remain onstage if Sylvia was there too. Vito Russo, who was at the microphone, was amazed that this founder of gay lib was being insulted. Arguments ensued, got louder and more raucous, and other women stormed the stage. Sylvia and Vito—neither of whom I'd ever known to back down from a fight—naturally enough defended themselves.

All this was happening at the same time that thousands of marchers, many of whom had struggled those last few miles up Fifth Avenue and into Central Park, were looking for nothing more than a place to rest and some-thing to eat and drink. The situation had reached its most chaotic point when Bette Midler, who had been invited to entertain the crowd, grabbed the mike and began singing a cappella, drowning out the noise behind her from the onstage combatants.

People in the crowd sang along with her, then Bette's prerecorded

Felice Picano at the time of publication of *The Lure,* 1979.

Dino Di Giorlando,
first SeaHorse art director

Artist Ron Fowler, 1990

Andrew Holleran, Robert Ferro,
Felice Picano at Gaywick

Author Robert Peters

Jane Delynn, Felice Picano, Dan Diamond, Michael Grumley,
and Chuck Ortlieb at Three Lives Bookstore reading, 1981

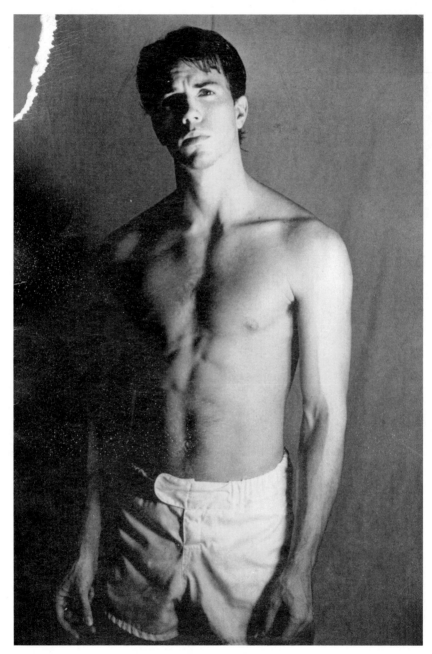

Gavin Dillard, "the Naked Poet"

LARRY MITCHELL

IN HEAT
A ROMANCE

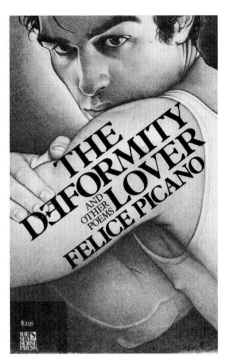

THE DEIFORMITY
AND OTHER POEMS
LOVER
FELICE PICANO

$295

THE SEA HORSE PRESS

The
BUTCH
MANUAL

CLARK HENLEY

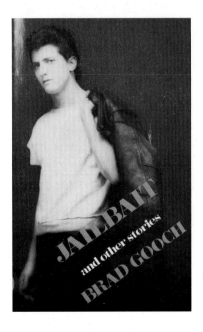

JAILBAIT
and other stories
BRAD GOOCH

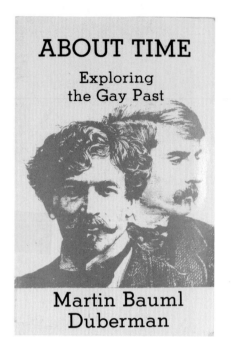

ABOUT TIME

Exploring
the Gay Past

Martin Bauml
Duberman

Jane Chambers'

Last
Summer At
Bluefish
Cove

THE JH PRESS
GAY PLAY SCRIPT SERIES

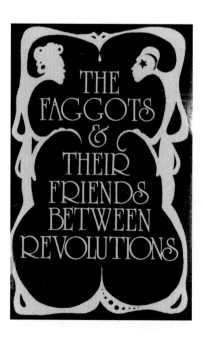

THE
FAGGOTS
&
THEIR
FRIENDS
BETWEEN
REVOLUTIONS

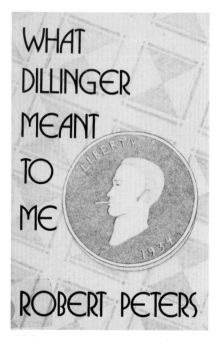

WHAT
DILLINGER
MEANT
TO
ME

ROBERT PETERS

Ambidextrous

The Secret Lives of Children

FELICE PICANO

── NOTES ──
from a marriage

love poems
── by ──
GAVIN DILLARD

MEN WORKING

stories by
RON HARVIE

JACK THE MODERNIST
ROBERT GLÜCK

Early Gay Presses of New York exhibition at the Governor Anderson
Library at the University of Minnesota at Minneapolis, 2001

background music was located and turned up loud, and she began a short concert while the stage was cleared of people, who nevertheless continued to argue.

Within weeks of the event, lesbians began abandoning the gay movement both privately and publicly. Some spokeswomen like Adrienne Rich said it was about time, that it had had to happen. Lesbians had little in common with gay men anyway she argued, since gay men were totally subverted by the male capitalist culture, had no interest in women's rights, or in fact in anything other than having as much sex with each other as possible. Some feminists adopted and eagerly shared elaborate fantasies of a secret gay male society being designed and built sub rosa, in which queer guys had sworn to eliminate all women, except perhaps some they planned to enslave as baby-making machines to produce future sexual partners. It became pretty far-fetched and might be said to have reached a bizarre climax a year or so later with NOW's ill-conceived, disastrously executed antipornography campaign.

In that grotesque project, women from NOW took the most ghastly, antifemale images of bondage and humiliation they could locate, mostly from privately sold, plastic-wrapped magazines available only in adult bookstores, and transferred them onto life-size posters. Photos of bound women, gagged with rubber balls in their mouths, blindfolded or hooded, were paraded through Manhattan's busiest streets during rush hour by feminists who all the while decried the images as pornographic and anti-woman.

A lot of people were appalled by the images. But many men and women complained that NOW itself was actually exposing them to these pornographic images for the first time in their lives, and so NOW itself had become a pornographer—a contention difficult to argue with. In the midst of this atmosphere of escalating gender war, one lesbian declared on a public stage at a writer's conference I attended that all women were victimized "any time any male on the planet" had an orgasm. Wherever Adrienne Rich, Andrea Dworkin, and a handful of other prominent lesbians appeared in public, they enjoined their sisters to flee from the "danger of gay male culture" as fast and as completely as possible, contending that gay men were more dangerous to women than even abusive husbands. Some fled their gay male friends in droves. Other women would have nothing to do with gay men for decades afterward.

Many of those same women then helplessly floundered when NOW's leaders suddenly abandoned them, publicly calling them—in Betty Friedan's words—a "lavender menace." They became even more confounded when NOW's entire lesbian wing was denounced, and when it was disbanded—an open sacrifice, the organization assured the women, that would "ensure" passage of the Equal Rights Amendment. Needless to add, that day never arrived.

Naturally, from the onset, some women would have nothing to do with this curious rift, but their numbers were few and those that I knew told me they were constantly pressured by their peers. Luckily, among that number were the owners of Three Lives & Company, who were more interested in good writing than in gender politics. Nevertheless, for the next five years at the very least, increasing, unceasing gender division dominated American urban gay life. It became more and more difficult to gather a mixed gender group for any GLBT cultural event. This invariably led to those few women who did attend the events standing up at some point to state that they felt unrepresented or underrepresented.

I'd personally become so annoyed with this particular ploy that at one such reading, when, as its organizer, I was subjected to this knee-jerk complaint, I was already prepared: I read out a list of women whom I had personally invited to the event, reading what each one had replied to me: usually a personal excuse, but in some cases simply an insult and a rejection on the grounds that the invitation had come from a man. In the midst of this recitation, the complaining lesbian and her partner stood up and left the event, followed of course by cat calls. Their leaving signified to the rest of us that they didn't want to hear anything reasonable or to help repair the problem.

The remaining men at that reading made it clear they all felt that lesbians would not be satisfied no matter what happened, and that they ought to be barred from future events a priori. Several of us, however, held feminist beliefs ourselves and thought a different tactic was needed. We openly supported NOW and the Equal Rights Amendment, which the organization was trying to pass, believing it really was needed, and that its passage could bring lesbians back into our lives and back into the gay movement. We marched and picketed with women whenever possible, and gave money to their cause.

Meanwhile many personal and professional relationships between gay men and lesbians—where they existed at all—continued to be very strained. One place where this was less true, however, was the theater, and this was typified by Terry Helbing and his personal and professional connection with innovative playwright Jane Chambers, as well as with her partner Beth Allen, and with the various women involved in turning Jane's play *Last Summer at Bluefish Cove* into a hit.

I also remained friends with a handful of lesbian writers and scholars, and I'd already signed one up for a SeaHorse Press book. Karla Jay had been part of gay politics from Stonewall and the early days of the Gay Liberation Front. She had worked with Allen Young, creating three path-breaking gay anthologies put out by a mainstream paperback house in the early and mid-1970s. In fact, while all this feminism was being taken to extremes, I was busily art directing and laying out the beautiful little book of Renée Vivien's wonderfully strange collection of stories, *The Woman of the Wolf,* unavailable to English-language readers before Karla Jay translated them from French.

By the mid-1980s, a strong reaction against the lesbian separatist movement emerged from a new generation of women who wanted nothing to do with it—especially in New York's East Village, where activists like Jennifer Levin, Ann Northrop, and Sarah Schulman were already closely associated with gay men. Later on some of these women would be instrumental in what would end up being a fight for lives, through the organization ACT UP. But that was still brewing very much below the surface of public gay life, and it would be years before it became a noted, international movement.

One day I received a phone call from Joan Larkin. She was clearly upset, although not at me or at GPNy.

Joan and Elly Bulkin, another lesbian poet, had worked for years—in Joan's case, close to a decade—on two monumental lesbian literature anthologies, undergoing the countless hassles, humiliations, and near-disasters involved in being the editor of a compendium of such scope. I well knew what this entailed, since several years earlier, I'd put together the collection *A True Likeness.*

Joan and Elly had had even more to deal with than I had: first, they had to navigate the volatile political waters of feminism at the time. Second, they had to cope with women changing their minds, not merely about a line or sentence or poem, but about whether they ought to be included in the books at all—there were cases in which contributors couldn't decide if they were lesbian, bisexual, or straight, and therefore whether they belonged in the books.

(In later years, after GPNy had taken on the publication of these books, we would receive letters from women who had appeared in the two volumes informing us that they had since married men and begun raising nuclear families, and wanted their names erased from the cover and their writings taken out of the anthologies. We replied by mailing them copies of their signed releases agreeing to publish their work and represent their names, which managed to quash all further correspondence. But after all, those books hadn't started off as GPNy titles. They'd been commissioned by Daughters Inc., a fairly new but successful women's publishing house with strong feminist connections and allegedly impeccable feminist politics.)

Over the following year, Joan and Elly saw the anthologies through copyediting, typesetting, proofreading, and jacket design. Stressed but satisfied their books were finally on press they had then waited for the books to be printed and bound, which they had been, by a company in Springfield, Massachusetts. All they had to do was wait for the books to arrive.

They waited, and waited—but the books never came. Soon, even the phone calls Joan and Elly made to Daughters Inc.'s Back Bay, Boston, townhouse office were no longer being returned. One day they discovered that the publisher's phone had been disconnected. They contacted other women they knew in Boston and in the Northampton area, and the truth emerged: Daughters, Inc. had gone bankrupt, shut its doors, and the officers had split for parts unknown.

And the two anthologies? According to Elly Bulkin, they were printed, bound, boxed, and ready to be shipped. They were also sitting at a printer's warehouse in mid-Massachusetts, and had been for several months.

What Elly and then Joan spelled out for me was an author's, editor's, and anthologist's worst nightmare. Joan almost wept as she read me the table of the contents of the two volumes over the phone. Not only were all the important lesbian authors there, so were up-and-coming ones I knew and liked—Dorothy Allison and Jewelle Gomez among them. I told Elly and Joan that I would discuss the situation with my partners and see if there weren't something to be done.

I called a rare GPNy dinner meeting and we three got together in an Indian restaurant near Cooper Union. There I presented Elly and Joan's situation to my GPNy partners, whose jaws dropped, just as mine had. But what could we do? At this point, Elly and Joan's names and reputations, as well as years of work, were on the line. They didn't expect to see any more money, although it would be nice if they did. What they really wanted was to get the books out of that printer's warehouse and onto bookstore shelves. They wanted us to rescue the books from the printer.

We agreed that I would call to find out how large the ransom would be and whether we could possibly raise the amount.

The printer was surprised to hear from me, and kept asking "How well do you know these ladies?"

Not well, I admitted. I asked what was he planning to do with the books. "Nuthin'. You want 'em? All ya gotta do is pay the printing bill."

The printing bill wasn't cheap. No wonder Daughters Inc. had gone under—I'd never have used that printer. But the cover price of the two fat books wasn't cheap, either—$10.95 and $11.95, at a time when most trade paperback novels were going for $6.95 and $7.95. I did some math and figured that if we paid him the printing costs, we'd be selling the books with about half our usual profit.

Terry and Larry agreed it was worth doing. Not only did we believe in the intrinsic value of this historic project, but it could bring GPNy street credibility among women readers, and just as importantly bring us good karma. Should the books go into a second printing, we'd manage a better price from the printer, maybe make a profit, and then be able to pay the two editors' royalties.

What made it an easily done deal was the timing: we were about to send our new catalog to our own printer. We'd been working on it for months; all we'd need to do was add another page to advertise the lesbian anthologies. I had a copy of the book in hand by then, and as much information I needed. In a day the new page would be laid out and ready to go.

Phone calls were made to Elly and Joan telling them our proposed line of action. I contacted the printer and told him we would pay for the fiction anthology immediately, and, we hoped, the poetry anthology shortly thereafter. To recoup at least some money on what he'd probably feared was a total loss, he agreed to the deal. He even had a delivery truck bring the books down to us in New York during its next run at no extra cost. Elly and Joan were relieved that it had worked out.

But how could we get GPNy's logo on the book? Could we affix decals to the spine? Or cheaper yet, inside, on the title page?—if only to blot out the name of the original publisher. Terry looked into the cost of the decals and discovered they would be inexpensive. But putting decals on all 2,500 books for both titles would be far too much trouble. So the books were distributed by GPNy with Daughters Inc.'s name on them, just as printed. Only the distributors and the booksellers knew the truth—and the reviewers, since the review copies went out with GPNy's logo on its publicity packet and stationery. Word of the rescue soon got around the GLBT community anyway.

The fiction anthology sold well, and we eventually went back to press for a second printing. The poetry anthology followed within ten months. The books were well reviewed in the gay media, but if there were reviews in feminist or lesbian journals and newspapers, they weren't in any of the ones Terry, Larry, and I, or our woman friends, scanned for years afterward. I've no idea what anyone among the feminist separatists thought of what we at GPNy had done in making the books available.

Nor did we enjoy an ongoing relationship with Elly or Joan. We would inform them by letter of whatever new was happening regarding their books, and while the poetry collection sold much more slowly, both anthologies were down to a handful of copies by the time we closed GPNy's doors in the mid-1990s. We'd didn't hear back from them, even when we sent out a letter reverting all rights back to them. They were probably happy the books were out and wanted to forget the whole experience.

For GPNy, it turned out to be an all-around good deal. We had, in effect, inherited two big collections for which others had already done all the work, and excellent work too—a rarity in publishing. Still, I never discovered whether they came to us only after having been turned down by one or more of the other women's presses that were around at the time—Firebrand, Persephone, Beacon, and Naiad come to mind, most of which probably couldn't have afforded such a rescue or published more popular, genre works—or if Elly and Joan were fed up with the feminist press they'd originally signed up with and had come directly to GPNy, figuring that although we were men, we were said to be smart and have money, and seemed to know how to publish and sell good books.

———

If that encounter with women's books might be seen as a particularly lofty moment in of GPNy history, this next relationship, hard on its heels, lies a lot closer to the gutter. However, it also fulfilled one of my unspoken dreams since junior high: to become, in the most literal sense of the word, a smut peddler. All thanks to the Reverend Boyd McDonald.

I first noticed his name several years before, when in the late seventies someone handed me a remarkably unremarkable-looking sixteen-page pamphlet, its type and black-and-white photos printed poorly on mediocre paper folded in half and barely held together by staples. Titled *STH* or *Straight to Hell,* its subtitle tickled me exorbitantly: *The Manhattan Review of Unnatural Acts.*

The anecdotes presented therein were about as louche an assortment of sex stories I'd ever encountered, with titles like "Marine Takes It Up the Ass— And Likes It!," "Fey Farm Boy Forced to Suck Six, Including Family Horse!," and "Prep School Boy Sniffs His 'Nauseating' Underpants." But also featured were articles on art, culture, the media, and even politics. Occasional smaller stories would tackle current affairs, with titles like "DaVinci Beats Vatican Anti-Sex Rap," "The Heartbreak of Indigestion: Senator is Helped off Congress Floor," and one of my own personal favorites, along with a photo of then–First Lady Nancy Reagan deplaning somewhere with the now-classic caption, "Do Her Hemorrhoids Rule the Oval Office?"

The articles, some in the form of news items, others in the form of first- or third-hand reports, were salacious, juicy, for the most part working-class tales of innocent lads lured, tricked, coerced, or paid to perform homosexual acts with others. They usually went rapidly from initial surprise and disgust to habitual and obsessive fornication, including orgies. No part of the anatomy or function of the body escaped the editor's purview: the more perverted and gag-worthy the better. Some of the entries were letters—perhaps real ones after the first few issues, although all had undoubtedly undergone transformation via McDonald's not very subtle editorial hand, and all were probably kicked up a notch or two, although he always swore to anyone who asked that they were real. The result was sexy, smart, funny, and provocative.

As a sideline, *STH* also fulfilled a rather gaping void in gay lit. Most of the writing available, even twelve or thirteen years after Stonewall, was written by middle- and upper-middle-class guys. I can think of half a handful that wasn't—John Fox's *Boys on the Rock,* comes to mind—and we at the four Gay Presses would make a special point of publishing several more working-class books, including SeaHorse Press's man-boy love novel, *Street Boy Dreams* by Kevin Esser, and Calamus Press's story collection, Ray Dobbin's *Don the Burp.*

By the early eighties, even before AIDS had much of an impact on our psyches, the question of gay male sexuality had become a major issue in gay politics and in gay life, and the centrality of sex to our lives continued to cause manifold problems to the movement and be a dilemma defying any easy solution. The Stonewall movement, after all, had begun as a sexual liberation movement. Years after the formation of the Gay Activists Alliance and the Gay Liberation Front in 1969, I would bump into founding members like Marty Robinson and Jim Owles around Manhattan, and in catching up with them, it was their sexual escapades, their recent sex experiences, and who they thought was hot sexually that formed half of our conversation. And they were by no means the only ones. Sex was simply very important, and thus very commonplace, among my generation.

"Gay liberation" had, for many gay men, meant the unrestrained legal freedom to have as much queer sex as possible. In contrast, for many lesbians of the sixties and seventies, sex seemed to be one of many issues after job equality, career opportunities, health care, and child care. Whether this was actually true or not—the lesbians I knew were as horny as I was—it was still the public face of lesbianism and one reason why gay men and lesbians were so often at loggerheads whenever they were expected to pull together around issues supposedly important to both.

Lesbian and gay magazines and newspapers were naturally enough chief among the fundamental and persistent sites where the issue of gay sex was fought out between the genders, and at few papers more so than at the high-profile *Advocate*. For years, the national biweekly had been printing personals columns in the back. These had exploded in size, complexity, and daring as more and more gay men came out of the closet. For every female personal ad there were twenty, then fifty, then a hundred male ones. Those ads also became more explicit in tone and language. S/M, bondage, and humiliation scenarios, water sports, fist fucking—you name it, men did it and sought others who did through ads. Women complained. If the *Advocate* was supposed to be a political paper for all gays and lesbians, why did women have to be subjected to these awful, disgusting ads?

The reason, of course, was that the ads had begun to pay off in a big way. As the 1970s progressed, the income from the *Advocate*'s personals advertising began to approach the income of its newsstand sales, then of its subscription sales, then grew to equal the two combined. The result was higher pay for writers, the hiring of full-time reporters in Washington, D.C., and part-time international reporters, new respected columnists, and big-name authors—like yours truly—doing more features. It also paid for a noticeable physical transformation. The *Advocate* changed format, switched to better paper stock, and got slick, full-color covers. As a result, its publisher could approach more mainstream advertisers, bringing in even more income through new openly gay advertising agencies.

The two sides of the conflict seemed to slide further and further apart. And every local gay paper that had sex ads had to deal with the issue. Sales of the *Advocate* to women's bookstores and female subscribers dropped alarmingly. For a brief period, publisher David Goodstein decided on a compromise: he would move the personals ads to a separate section, an inset printed on yellow paper, that would be available on newsstands and in subscriptions—but only if you specifically ordered it.

That inset itself began to grow. But for many male readers, some of the beautiful and sexy men that had been regularly pictured in ads for movies, porn stores, books, and various sex toys in those ads, had now vanished from the regular pages of the magazine, which for many now looked sanitized—and kind of boring. Now gay men began withdrawing from the biweekly, canceling subscriptions and no longer buying it. This was a far bigger problem than women leaving, since male readers outnumbered female readers so greatly to begin with. What to do?

A brilliant solution was found: *Men,* a whole new Liberation Publications Inc. (LPI) magazine clearly intended for a single-gender audience, filled with articles, fiction, true stories, and sexy, nude photos, all in full color on high-gloss paper, and with pages of porno ads and sheaves of personals. Women need not read, or even admit, its existence.

Men came out in 1985 and from the onset it was a huge success. Within a decade, LPI had introduced another magazine, *Freshmen,* concentrating on younger men, and a few years after the even racier *Unzipped,* with its emphasis on the stars of the gay male porn industry who by 1990 had become icons of gay male culture—Al Parker, Ryan Idol, Jeff Stryker, and Joey Stefano, among many others. These magazines were equally successful: one early editor in chief of the three "body mags" once confided that he personally delivered checks for over $60,000 to the main *Advocate* office every week. Clearly sex sold. For many, it sold better than news, reviews, features, or even those minor television celebrities pictured on the cover of the *Advocate.*

Around the same time that *Men* was launched, the venerable *New Yorker* magazine published its first story with gay content—young David Leavitt's "Family Dancing," the first story he ever published. Except, of course there was nothing at all gay about anything in the story, except that the author told us that the narrator was gay. But he wasn't in a gay relationship. No relationship or sexual incident he'd experienced are referred to or noted in the tale. The story is about his mother dying.

But it soon led to a raft of writers who'd been sitting on the fence suddenly coming out with their gay-but-not-really-gay collections of stories and novels. Most interesting of them all remained Leavitt himself, partly because he was a better writer than most. His novel, *The Lost Language of Cranes,* in contrast to his early story collections, was a gay novel with gay content, and with sexual content to boot. No matter. *New York Times* fiction reviewer Michiko Kakutani liked the stories but not the novel. Over the years (and with the exception of his fine bildungsroman *Martin Baumann*) booksellers have told me that it is Leavitt's most out-there sexual stories—*Arkansas: Three Novellas,* for example—that gay men have loved and that I believe will eventually stand as his literary legacy, rather than the more mainstream books that appealed to straight reviewers like Kakutani.

At the other end of the spectrum, otherwise sane writers of the underground who once were literary outlaws then declared themselves to no longer be "gay" writers. While one can only admire any artist who wants to stretch, aspire, and write for everyone, it can rebound harmfully, as many of them have found out. I don't notice many of these so-called literary outlaws reaching bigger audiences or writing significantly better books now that they are no longer "gay" writers.

All this to preface that Gay Presses of New York's founders were at the time extremely aware of the question of how much sex to publish, and let's face it, of fulfilling our own desires as gay male readers to read more and better gay sex in books and plays. And thus, our very specific determination in the mid-1980s to counteract this ongoing antisex and publish more sexually explicit material. Larry Mitchell's novel *In Heat* (GPNy) and Bob Herron's very funny and sexy comic novel *Moritz* (Calamus) was the result. Terry Helbing signed on New York playwright Robert Chesley, who had moved to San Francisco and there instantly expanded his sexual material and sexual topics in his new plays *Stray Dog Story* and *Jerker,* both of which Meridian Gay Theater produced and JH Press published. SeaHorse had Dennis Cooper's sexually transgressive *Safe* and *Closer* as well as Gavin Dillard's works.

Even so, there was room to push the sexual envelope even further, and *Straight To Hell* seemed to promise exactly what we were missing.

When I asked around trying to find out who its author-editor, Boyd McDonald, was, oddly similar reports came back. He lived in a single room occupancy on Riverside Drive and One Hundred Thirteenth or Fourteenth Street. He was a man in his fifties. He'd graduated Harvard Summa Cum Laude, and gone to work as a copywriter for a prestigious advertising agency, where he'd risen to vice president in a few years and had become an alcoholic. After a decade or so, he'd left the ad agency and ended up homeless on the Bowery. He'd since kicked booze and was now living on welfare and "editing" this deliciously outrageous magazine, using the alleged "technical" aid of a few friends. The title of Reverend was from a mail-order ministry somewhere in South Carolina, either an affectation, or more likely—given how atheistic he would prove to be in his writing—a slap in the face toward all organized religion, which McDonald openly disdained.

Boyd garnered so much underground cachet with *STH* that pathbreaking publisher Winston Leyland at Gay Sunshine Press in San Francisco decided to turn the magazines into books. He'd put out the first one, *Meat,* in 1978, and it had been so successful he'd followed it with three more volumes: *Flesh, Sex,* and *Cum.* It was one of those improbable success stories—I'd even bought one of the books and read it cover to cover.

I'd then promptly forgotten about them until one afternoon when Larry Mitchell phoned and asked, in the most hesitant and tentative of voices, what I thought of Boyd McDonald and his books. I told him I loved them. Did I know, Larry asked, that the first one had sold eighteen thousand copies and the second one was already at fifteen thousand? I didn't. These were big numbers for a small press. At SeaHorse, only *The Butch Manual* had come close, at 12,500 copies, and although *Torch Song* would eventually sell over forty thousand copies through GPNy's edition (and many more through book clubs and mass-market paperbacks), it was a special case. What would I think, Larry drew out his question a very long time, of GPNy becoming Mac-Donald's publisher?

I'm not certain which of Larry's friends eventually introduced him to Boyd McDonald. John Reed, the cute punk typesetter he used a lot for Calamus Press, may have been the connection. Or it may have been East

Village art director Joseph Modica, who'd designed the GPNy logo, and who Larry also used a lot. What I had to know was whether Boyd had any more material. "Hadn't those four books he did with Winston Leyland used up all the published issues of *Straight To Hell?*" I asked.

Larry's response was that Boyd had *boxes* of more stories, reports, and anecdotes; he'd been collecting them for years. My next question was obvious. Why was Boyd changing publishers now, after four titles?

As far as Larry knew, the answer was that Boyd also wanted to put out a collection of humorous, sexy essays and anecdotes about movie, TV, and rock music stars whose lives and careers he'd been following, in some cases literally since they were boys. These heartthrobs included TV stars Ricky and David Nelson, and filmdom's Victor Mature, Robert Mitchum, and Richard Widmark. That book, already finished, was to be titled *Cruising the Movies*, and would also be filled with photos and movie and television stills of the hunks. Someone—Joseph Modica, John Reed, or maybe "Ruby," another of Larry's pals—had read the manuscript and thought it was priceless: pure Boyd McDonald. But according to Larry, Winston Leyland had absolutely refused to publish it, demanding instead from Boyd more of the best-selling semiporn.

I read the manuscript of *Cruising the Movies* and loved it. It was the kind of affectionate satire that would fit GPNy perfectly, one we could all be proud of. I gave it to Terry, whose only comment was, "I've had a crush on Ricky Nelson since I was three." He also liked it, finding some parts of it a bit more raw than either Larry or I did.

Larry had also sweetened the pot further by telling us that Modica would art direct and even lay out each McDonald book, for his usual fee to Larry. Meaning that I wouldn't have to lay it out. And since many photos were being used, it would be a big, complicated make-up job.

Finally Larry had even already discussed a first printing of five thousand with Alvin Greenberg, the printer's representative for Terry's press and for *Torch Song.* Larry surmised that we would eventually sell ten to twelve thousand more. At a cover price of $11.95, that would be profitable indeed.

I agreed to the deal, and we decided that we would send out our first-ever multibook contract, for two of MacDonald's usual compendiums and *Cruising the Movies,* all to be published over a period of two years.

None of us had actually seen the Reverend McDonald yet (Larry had talked to him on the phone). But within a few days of our decision Larry met with him, and a few weeks later, once I'd sent out a contract, Boyd said he wanted to get together with me to go over some aspects of the agreement. I was hardly prepared for the experience. I'm not sure what I was expecting when Boyd rang my bell one lovely spring morning. What I saw when I answered the door was a man in his midfifties who looked like a grown-up version of Alfalfa from *Our Gang* comedies, complete with plastered-down hair, dressed much as I'd seen William Burroughs dressed in photos, although both a lot nerdier and also more dissolutely. Boyd was slightly taller than average, thin, and wore dark and rather featureless clothing which was nevertheless semiformal: a dark gray, almost black sports jacket, nonmatching dark gray or black slacks, and a shirt of the same ilk. He also wore a hat, which was clearly out of date in the mideighties, even in Manhattan.

We sat down in the living room and drank fresh coffee I'd just brewed in my Chemex. He smoked an extravagant amount of cigarettes and went over the contract section by section with me, trying to make sure that he understood everything.

What had made SeaHorse Press and then GPNy so desirable as publishers was that we were all authors and wrote up author-friendly contracts and sent out author-friendly royalty statements. I'd discovered that SeaHorse was offering first-book contracts with the same cash advance for most first and second book authors as literary heavyweights like Knopf, Houghton Mifflin, and Farrar, Straus and Giroux, and with better royalty breakdowns. We had other author-friendly paragraphs in the agreements as well. In most cases we held on to author's rights to film, foreign rights, and theatrical productions with a fifty-fifty split, with the understanding that should any *real* theater or film project ever come through, we would reassign the rights back to the author for the grand sum of one dollar. Meanwhile, our authors were protected from unscrupulous producers, who would in the meantime have to go through us. (By this time, I had read and even overwritten more than a few theater and film contracts for my own books.)

The contract discussion with Boyd lasted about an hour, and couldn't have been more pleasant. Virtually every point I brought up to explain, Boyd accepted without much comment. I wondered for weeks after why he'd come by at all.

Immediately upon Boyd leaving my apartment, and although I had awakened, had coffee, and showered that very morning, only an hour or two before our meeting, as soon as he'd gone, I felt that I had to go downstairs and take another shower.

Explaining how well the meeting had gone to Larry later on, and how baffled I'd been by its necessity, I also mentioned that second shower. Larry laughed and then reminded me, "Well, after all, he *is* New York's dirtiest old man." At which point I realized that yes, even though we were sitting some ten feet apart and were fully clothed, discussing a contract's minutiae, I'd felt all the while as though Boyd's tongue had come out and licked me from head to toe. Talk about personal affect!

Two months later I received a phone call from the Reverend Boyd McDonald. Earlier that week, I'd sent him an advance check for the first of the two compendium books that we were to publish, to be called *Filth!* The check was, as we'd stipulated in the contract, for $1,500, with a second advance payment of the same amount due to Boyd when the book was printed and distributed for sale. As I made small talk I kept wondering if I'd screwed up in some way. Terry had given me the check, and I'd sent it out with a cover letter explaining it was the first part of the advance payment, and inviting him to call with any questions. Now he was calling. But why?

So finally I asked, "Did you get the check I sent?"

He had, Boyd said. That's why he was calling.

Did he understand that he'd get the second part when the books were ready to be sold? I asked.

Well, that was just it, he said. Now, what was this check for?

I only half panicked. I explained that according to his contract, he was receiving an advance of $3,000 total against royalties for the sale of *Filth,* and that we would provide a full royalty statement around January of the year following the publication of the book, and every January thereafter. Those would show the total sales for the previous year and whether the royalties exceeded the $3,000, which they probably would. Then he'd get a check for the balance. Meanwhile he was getting half of the $3,000 now and half upon publication, which we thought would be in August.

There was a very long silence on the other end of the phone. Then Boyd said the oddest thing I ever heard during all my years of publishing. "You mean I *get paid* for doing this?"

"Sure," I responded, not fully understanding his question. "You get ten percent of the cover price of each sold book, unless it is sold abroad or at a much lower discount. But in general, yes, you get about a dollar twenty a copy."

"And this check is . . . ?" he tried.

"That check is payment in advance for the first approximately one thousand five hundred copies sold. A second check will come to you in August. Then in January more money will come to you if the books have sold over three thousand copies, and so on, each year after that."

"Oh," he simply said, so absolutely tonelessly that I wondered what in the world had happened. "So I can cash this check now?"

"Yes." And thinking of how many bottles of Irish whiskey it might buy, should he fall off the wagon, I added, "Better yet, put it in a bank account. Say a savings account. And earn a little interest on it."

He told me he didn't have a bank account, so I said I'd tell him how to open one. "Or better yet, one of your friends could help you?" I suggested, as he seemed fairly out of it.

He provided me with a new bio note and said he would also send a new photo taken of him sitting on his stripped-down bed in his stripped-down room in his single room occupancy.

The new bio read, "Boyd McDonald was born in South Dakota in 1925. 'I was a pioneer high school dropout, leaving school to play badly in a traveling dance band. I was drafted into the army, graduated from Harvard, and came to New York, where my principal activity was taking advantage of the city's public sexual recreation facilities. As a sideline I worked as a hack writer at *Time, Forbes,* IBM, and even more sordid companies. . . . I recently beat my own meat almost constantly for five days and was in ecstasy. I mention this to show the kind of sustained, conscientious dedication that goes into *STH,* and the anthologies.'"

Later that day I phoned Larry and told him of the phone conversation we'd had, suggesting that whoever had been Larry's link to Boyd should be contacted fast and should be persuaded go with Boyd to open a bank account.

Larry agreed and said he'd do that, but he was unusually thoughtful as I repeated that morning call's very peculiar particulars. He asked me to repeat what Boyd had said, and when I did, I heard a distinct intake of breath on the other end of the line. "Well, you understand the implications of that first state-ment," Larry asked "When Boyd asked, 'You mean I *get paid* for this?'"

I was almost too horrified to answer. "You mean he never received an advance for any of the four books he did for Gay Sunshine Press?" It didn't surprise me too much. I'd heard that Winston Leyland kept his cash rather close to his vest, especially once the company and magazine had become his sole means of support.

"Well, that much we now know for certain. It's the *other* implication."

And now I saw what Larry was implying. "You mean that Gay Sunshine sold over fifty thousand copies of his books and Boyd apparently never saw any *royalties?* No! That's impossible. It cannot be."

"Darling! *Nothing's* impossible," Larry said, in that dark baritone of his.

Sure enough, when the first copies of the book arrived and shipped to our warehouse, I mailed out two copies to Boyd with a check for the balance of the advance, and got yet another puzzled phone call from him and had to reexplain what advances against royalties were.

The book arrived toward the end of September, and was distributed for the next four months. It sold well. But as GPNy paid royalties only on paid sales, and Boyd's sales were just shy of fulfilling his advance, he didn't get another check until February of the following year when *Cruising the Movies* went to press. Again I was forced to explain to Boyd what an advance was, and as this was lower—for $2,000—*why* it was lower. I don't believe he phoned when the second advance went out a few months later, but he certainly phoned me in late January of the following year when he got a check for over five grand in royalties for *Filth!*

This time I couldn't help but ask, "Boyd, didn't your previous publisher send you checks like this? You know, on a regular, annual basis?"

As usual with Boyd, I couldn't get anything like a straight answer. And I didn't press him. *Filth!* was in its second printing by then, with ten thousand copies in print, selling so steadily we'd probably go back to press for another four thousand copies soon. I was flabbergasted. I phoned Larry and repeated the conversation I'd just had.

By then Larry had heard through the friend who'd introduced them that whenever Boyd needed money he would pester Winston. Then he would get a few hundred dollars at a time. But he couldn't pester him but a few times a year. I never discovered whether this was true or not.

In five years, GPNy would print a total of five of Boyd's titles with total sales of over thirty-nine thousand units (*Cruising the Movies* being the relative deadwood at a respectable 3,200 copies). Boyd earned over sixty grand from us and we were happy to pay him. I'd like to think that his old age—he died of emphysema not long after the last title was published—was made easier because of his relationship with GPNy. I heard he went out more and was seen at clubs and other places. He even came to a famously ill-starred dinner at my place once along with his solar opposite, Quentin Crisp. But that's for another book.

Volume two of the GPNy line of Reverend McDonald's compendium was indeed titled *Smut,* and so I could with full justification finally refer to myself in the media as an author, activist—and smut peddler.

7

SeaHorse and GPNy Create and Discover the New Gay Nonfiction

I'd met Clark Henley briefly on that same book tour to L.A. for *The Lure* when I first encountered Dennis Cooper. Clark was my age, tall, gawky, and in no way hip. Years later I would find out he came from a Nob Hill *Social Register* background, his sister in the same San Francisco debutante class as the controversial heiress Patricia Hearst. Clark, however, looked anything but, with his oversized glasses; puffy, frilly, long-sleeve shirt; and Travolta-esque bell-bottom pants with cartoon-big yellow shoes. But he was bright-eyed and well spoken, and got my attention when he asked if I'd have any interest in publishing a book of photos, lists, and comments he was putting together about how to be butch.

When I turned and silently looked him up and down, he quickly added, "Not that *I* claim to be butch, naturally. . . . It's satire. *Social* satire!" He added more details, none of which I could picture. But I handed him my card and said sure, send it to me.

A month or two later, I got a phone call from poet and writer Michael Lassell, whom I knew through Bob Lowe. (I first met Lassell either at some New York party or at a Unicorn Bookstore event.) Michael very formally informed me that Clark Henley was a very close friend, a great wit, and a total darling, and that he had written a brilliant satire on "the new gay drag—and how to do it" and wanted to send it to SeaHorse Press. I told Michael that I recalled meeting Henley and told him once again to send it.

A few more months passed. When the manuscript finally arrived, it had lots of little envelopes filled with numbered and lettered black-and-white snapshots that fit into corresponding boxes on somewhat amateurishly laid out pages. It took me an entire afternoon to put the whole presentation together. I didn't read it till the next day, but I was already intrigued—and laughing. Partly because about three-quarters of the photos—"butch" in leather with whips and chains, and "nelly" in hairnets, heels, and flowered aprons—had one model: recognizably Clark himself. (The others—usually of cute, hunky, and yes, butch guys in underwear, bathing suits, and shorts—were, I guessed, Clark's friends or tricks.) And partly because that morning I'd awakened in the flat of a fuck buddy, looked in his refrigerator for something to drink, and encountered the following and nothing else: one box of amyl nitrate poppers; one jar one-quarter filled with mayonnaise. No milk. Not even a Coke.

One of the photo pages in Henley's book, which I'd seen only the day before, had been captioned, "The Butch Refrigerator," and cautioned: "Remember, less is more." It pictured a box of poppers and what looked very much like a quarter-filled jar of mayo.

This guy was onto something.

I sat down with the laid-out photo pages on my downstairs butcher-block table, and I read the text. This how it began:

No one was born Butch. People were born babies and promptly burst into tears, which was most un-Butch. Yet when some people grew up they became inescapably Butch, while others are still sitting on the sidelines waiting for a miracle. Here it is, *The Butch Manual!*

It was funny. It was witty. It simultaneously adored and denigrated the entire gay male clone extreme. For example, according to Clark, when invited to a party, a nonbutch gay man might say the following, "Thanks dear, but I wouldn't be caught dead with a polecat wearing a tutu in that neighborhood, never mind enter that ghastly building in that horrible shade of yellow, or that apartment, which I'm certain is designed to death in reused Mylar and old Angelo Donghia castoffs."

By contrast, Henley assured us, Butch invited to a party would respond "OK," and then lose or forget the invitation.

An explanation may be needed for why, in the 1970s, gay men suddenly became "butch." Why they sported large amounts of body and face hair, dressed badly in torn jeans, clunky, uncomfortable engineer boots and Air Force or motorcycle gang jackets and why it was that they walked around like they had kielbasa-size dicks and grapefruit-size testicles. The answer is that the pose, the attitude, and especially the outfit got—and facilitated—sexual action, anywhere and anytime. It also had political implications. After the Stonewall Riots, many gays intended on being treated as regular guys. Thus the emphasis on macho clothing, attitudes, and facial hair—beards and mustaches dominated the next gay decade. Thus the dropping of all potentially feminine characteristics. Thus, eventually, the loss of the entire wonderful world of camp.

Clark contended that we'd gone too far in this direction.

Once his book was accepted, Clark went into a fresh panic, and dithered for weeks over my few and simple editorial suggestions. At last, I yelled at him, he handed them in, and I sent it out for printing. The blueprint pages arrived and Clark tinkered and dithered with those, too. I yelled again. The book was at last printed, delivered, and sent out.

Before this, I'd been placing ads in the few existing gay magazines and newspapers that reviewed books. Generally I paid for these with cash or, if I knew the editors, with trade—freelance writing in exchange for the cost of the ad. The Butch Manual was the first book I published that required no such trade: being so visual and so funny, it would be featured on its own. After a little bit of arm twisting, the *Advocate,* the *New York Native,* the *Washington*

Blade and, surprisingly, *Playguy* (which featured some of the very butches Clark was mocking), excerpted the book or featured it in a column.

Keep in mind that *Torch Song Trilogy* had been published for a year or so already and while doing well—over four thousand copies—it wouldn't really pop as a bestseller until after it won the Tony Award a year later. Henley's book became one immediately. A first printing of five thousand sold out in its first six months; a second of five thousand more went in the next six months— records for my tiny company. I did a third run of three thousand copies, and eventually the SeaHorse Press sell-through was over twelve thousand, excellent for a small press.

A little more than a year after publication, I received a phone call from the sub rights editor at New American Library (NAL) expressing interest in reprinting the book. She sounded and acted as though she were doing me the biggest favor, so I told her I wasn't interested. A week or so later I received a letter from an editor at NAL/Dutton Books. Dutton had recently been absorbed into the NAL empire. Politely, the editor explained that his boss, Arnold Dolin, was putting together a line of gay trade paperbacks to be called Plume. He loved Henley's book and wanted it for the line. I phoned the editor and he was even more polite and enthusiastic than before. I called Clark, read him the letter, and laid out what I thought were the advantages and disadvantages of this republication, both for SeaHorse and for him.

First, I admitted that our sales had begun to slump. NAL ought to reach a far deeper market than SeaHorse could because its distribution was so extensive, so it should sell many more books. We'd both make money—splitting the profits fifty-fifty—by essentially doing nothing. I would keep my edition in print as long as feasible, but I expected NAL's to blow the SeaHorse edition out of the water. (It didn't.) The editor had said, then confirmed in writing, that they'd do virtually nothing to change the way the book's interior looked. They would probably alter the cover slightly, although he definitely wanted to retain the photos of Clark as Mr. Butch on the front cover, with Clark in stiletto heels, rhinestone glasses, and a babushka, trying to lift a weight, on the back.

After much soul searching and, I'm guessing, discussions with Lassell and other pals, Henley OK'd the deal.

Three months later, I had still received no contract from NAL. Six months later, someone read to me from *Publisher's Weekly* a blurb about how the book was to come out the following month. Incensed at this further ignoring of us, I called the editor at NAL and instructed him that he was about to publish a book without a contract: an illegality. He was aghast. Two days later the contract arrived on my desk.

When I called that same sub rights person who'd originally phoned me, she was once more snotty and rude. A minute later she was astounded to hear me say, "I've received the contract and I've looked it over. I'm assuming the book is at the printer as we speak. I've got eighty-four points I would like to discuss with you on this contract:" What I meant was that I had eighty-four problems in a seven-page agreement.

We spent hours hammering out something vaguely acceptable, until a realistic agreement was achieved. The upshot was a book less handsome, though a bit more commercial looking, than SeaHorse Press's version. They totally screwed up the joke on the two covers, however, using only one photo of Clark in semidrag on the front. While the editor loved the book, the sales people didn't—or at least they didn't seem to know how to market it. Although it came out less than two years after the original, and while it was still hot in the SeaHorse edition, it only sold another twelve thousand copies via NAL, about a third of what I had expected. Clark, however, was thrilled: he was in bookstores across the world.

He'd already begun working on his follow-up book, temporarily titled *When Queens Collide,* the flipside of butch—femmeness or sissyness. He worked on it for the rest of his unfortunately short life, never quite getting the tone right, never quite achieving that fine balance between humor and vindictiveness he'd earlier achieved. But then, unlike me, Clark also worried about offending people.

The messages about his health from L.A. worsened during the mid-eighties, just when I was feeling the worst effects of AIDS among my own set. Clark Henley died in 1985. Aside from our publication, he had earlier done the black-and-white illustrations for a new version of Clement Moore's classic poem, *The Night Before Christmas*. Talented artist that he was, it's *The Butch Manual* that remains Henley's testimonial. It's one of the few perfect and true artifacts of its gay era, and I'm proud to be associated with it.

———

"Don't even think of writing autobiographical until you are forty years old!"

That's what I commanded my adult class of budding authors at the Writer's Voice Workshop at Manhattan's West Side YMCA. It was February 1984, and in my defense it was the second fiction writing course I'd taught that year and thus the second time in a year that I'd found myself up to my eyes in mostly bad autobiographical fiction that I was then forced to read. One woman in the class smiled. She was in her late fifties and worked as a CPA and of all of them, she alone was writing what I considered an interesting account of her youth—in the 1940s, as a Greek resistance fighter against the Nazis on a small Aegean island.

I knew that I was wildly overstating my case. Thomas Wolfe, F. Scott Fitzgerald, J. D. Salinger, John Knowles, and many other writers I admired had written exquisite fiction about their early lives while they were still young. But I hadn't. Neither had most of my friends who were, by 1984, published authors, even though it was supposed to be the traditional way to make a name for oneself.

On the other hand, just the summer before, at the age of thirty-nine, I'd begun writing what would end up being the first part of my first memoir and I was intensely aware that I believed I'd accomplished a kind of breakthrough in the form and simultaneously how grateful I was that I'd waited so long to write it. I'd written my first, still unpublished, novel in 1971, and published my second one in 1975. In the decade since I'd put out six novels, a book of short stories, a book of poetry, a novella, and edited an anthology. I felt that this was the minimum experience needed to write autobiographically. I was grateful because through those previous ten books and ten years, I'd done a great deal of writing, thinking about writing, talking about writing—including with the members of the Violet Quill Club—and pondering about writing. What I'd only been partly aware of was that after ten years and ten books I was ready for a major change in *how* I wrote.

By 1983, I had published in a variety of genres, but not autobiography. How is it I came to write *Ambidextrous?* Because whenever I told Bob Lowe about my life between ages eleven and thirteen, he assured me that my experiences were unique—more like those of a man in his twenties than a child of eleven; he would ask me to tell him the story again, in more detail. And because the memory of one particular year and one particular relationship with a teacher remained stuck inside me. It was a problem that needed to be solved.

What I related in *Ambidextrous* ended up far less genial than the anecdotes I'd told Bob. The first part of the book was about how, by being different, I'd nearly ruined my life at the age of eleven, and how that had determined my life thereafter by showing me that even as a little boy I could have cruel, implacable, irrational enemies; that not only could I not depend on anyone else to defend me against my enemies but more crucially, that if forced to, as I had been, I could defend myself—and in so doing become as ruthless and relentless as any tyrannical adult.

I began writing *Ambidextrous* without seeing any of this. Those revelations arrived as both a shock and as eureka moments. What I did know was that the story of Mr. Hargrave, my fourth grade teacher, trying to change an essential quality in myself—my fundamental ambidexterity—into conformist, right-handed writing, was as galling to me three decades later as when it had first occurred—and as symbolically fraught. I didn't understand why or what it meant. But one afternoon I forced myself to relive the experience and was amazed by how strongly I still felt the old resentment. I decided I must write what I recalled.

For the first time ever as a writer, I turned myself into an experiment, complete with a theorem: If X is so, then Y ought to be . . . what? I had no clue, but I gave myself a month and twenty thousands words to work it out.

"Basement Games," as I named that first section, took thirty-five days to write and came out at 22,000 words, and I found that in order to explain to Bob (my only reader of this text, remember) why and how what happened between Hargrave and me was so important, I had to drag in the three Flaherty girls down the street, other kids in my class, books I was reading at the time, my dentist, and all kinds of other people and incidents.

Even before I was done, I knew two things. By focusing so tightly on a few incidents and on the guerrilla war between Hargrave and myself, I'd somehow created a larger atmosphere—an ambiance. By telling this simple story, I'd evoked an entire world and time to which I'd not given much thought in the intervening years. Unlike Proust dipping his madeleine into a tisane and inadvertently recalling decades, my portal into the past was a deliberate delving into a long-closed mine, and I was shoveling out all the debris, and at the same time noting all the slag until something valuable announced itself—an excavation.

Actually, I made three discoveries, the third being that by writing "Basement Games" I'd only touched on the entire story. Because after writing about one memory, it became clear that my transformation from a conformist kid from Long Island into the war protesting integrationist/student radical/gay liberationist that I became in the 1960s was merely kick-started by that incident. If I was to at last address the issue I would also have to write about the two crucial years that followed and a dozen other people, especially the boy, then the girl, who became my first lovers—and so parts two and three of the memoir.

"Man is the only animal that blushes," Mark Twain wrote. "Or needs to." I discovered the truth of that as I wrote about my twelfth and thirteenth years. I'd forgotten my glue-sniffing sex sessions over pictorial gay porno with the boy I called Ricky Hersch, or the orgiastic sex with the class ice princess and how I discovered that her father, wounded in World War II, was watching us from another room via a series of optical effects. I'd forgotten how a short story I'd written about the latter situation had caused a scandal when I'd entered it in a citywide school writing contest and how that, too, had affected me. Indeed, I—and those around me—had plenty to blush about.

Meanwhile, like most lazy writers, I decided that I'd done enough. I gave Bob and my agent "Basement Games" to read. They liked it well enough but felt it was unfinished, that more was needed.

"More?" I asked, knowing full well there was plenty more. Even so, I dithered for months. Then I went back and reread what I'd written. I found that what was in "Basement Games" was not only absolute honesty in writing, but the other characters were far more interesting than the portrait I was able to draw of myself as an eleven-year-old. I was barely a person, whereas they, from the monstrous Hargrave to the sirenlike neighbor Flaherty girls, were all distinctive. I also discovered while writing the memoir that although he was the first evil genius in my life, Hargrave had also done me a big favor: he had forced me to act as an individual for the first time in my life; he had set me on the road to being the man I eventually became.

"Basement Games" was loosely chronological, riddled with chatty, explanatory digressions that moved forward, back, and all around in terms of time, place, and subject. Up until then, I'd only written tightly plotted, tightly structured novels. In comparison, this memoir was a mess. And yet it had a certain texture, based not on plot, but on the voice I had discovered to tell the story. I found I really liked this new texture and so I decided to see how flexible and useful the new voice could be.

"A Valentine" was a second novella-length memoir about the very next step in my sexual, social, and intellectual development: entering junior high. It detailed my first group of friends, my first homosexual experience, and my first drug experience—airplane glue. It was as digressive, as unplotted, as textured, and as full of characters as the first part. And as I wrote I allowed myself to remember, to dig more deeply, to expose whatever I happened upon, including a few humiliations which, like any real historian, I then faithfully recorded.

From there it was a cinch to find the next developmental step—the ninth grade and my first real emotional relationship. While writing part three, titled "The Effect of Mirrors," I also rediscovered how I'd first become a writer. And why I'd almost immediately ceased being a writer. All of which I'd forgotten. Self-recognition came about through experimentation—it was how I realized how I'd gone from being a nonreading, nonwriting child to being an avid reader and fairly good writer, and how I went from being a naive virgin to a practiced fornicator and petty pornographer, from a nobody to an individual. In short, I figured out how this particular character, Felice Picano, had come into being, different from yet more or less recognizable as the one today.

Once the three pieces were put together, to my further surprise, they cohered. They not only related to each other, but they built upon each other. I titled the result *Ambidextrous,* which in its original hardcover edition was subtitled *The Secret Lives of Children.* I only discovered the structure I used as I wrote the book: it wasn't based on form, on genre, or point of view, but instead on me discovering the voice of the child I had been, interspersed with my adult voice, with both of them needed to tell that child's story. *Ambidextrous* is one of my strongest books partly because it used this newly discovered-in-process structure: I've since decided I have to discover the structure as I go along whenever writing a new book.

But how did this book end up with GPNy, when I was an author at Delacorte/Dell?

I'd gotten wind that my editor and strongest supporter there, Linda Grey, was about to move to another house, which was no surprise, given how badly treated she was by the men senior to her. This was especially horrendous given how hard she worked and how much money she made for the company. So I was casting around for another publisher. When I'd settled at Delacorte three books previously, I'd had interest from a half dozen editors, three of whom were quite serious.

My first two readers for the memoir—Bob Lowe and Jane Rotrosen, my agent at the time—gave no indication that this book's reception would be anything unusual. For that I had to wait for the first editors who read it. The manuscript went to four mainstream fiction editors who had read my previous novels, and according to Jane were fans of my work. Not one of them wanted *Ambidextrous*.

They told Jane I'd written about ordinary, literate, middle-class, preteen suburban children as sex-starved, drug-abusing pornographers capable of almost any crime. This, according to them, was heresy.

I'd prettified nothing. I'd written of beautiful Lynn, who spurned the adoring, froglike Myron, and whose love life thereafter seemed cursed. Ricky Hersch, my book's male Lolita, became a highly decorated Vietnam War hero before being killed in action. The four editors thought my portraits harsh and cynical; the one of Ricky was even called unpatriotic.

Today, the criticism my book received then seems silly when it isn't hypocritical. Now if you're *not* a bulimic, drug-addicted, serial murderer—or her victim—don't waste your time on a memoir: no publisher will want it.

Even so, with several mass-market paperbacks and a new, more literary novel (*Late in the Season*) just out in paper, the handwriting on the wall was clear: my agent told me to put *Ambidextrous* away and go to work on a new commercial novel. I told her I'd work on the novel, but I knew the memoir was good and I wanted her to sell it—I didn't care to whom.

It took me some years to piece together what happened next, but somehow or other someone in her office had seen a GPNy title and suggested that Jane send my book to them. Larry Mitchell and Terry conferred and made a small offer for hardcover rights. And when they'd all made the deal, Jane told me about it.

It made sense for GPNy: *Deformity Lover* had sold well and brought income into SeaHorse Press; four years later my novella, *An Asian Minor,* written half as a favor to artist David Martin, also sold well. My GPNy partners knew of my small press sales figures when they had signed up my short story collection, *Slashed to Ribbons in Defense of Love* in 1983. My first collection of short fiction, the volume consisted of eleven short stories, all but one of which had been published before in magazines as diverse as *Blueboy, Drummer, Christopher Street,* the *Philadelphia Gay News, Gaysweek Arts & Letters,* and *Cat's Eye,* a literary quarterly. The unpublished tale was "Baby Makes Three," meant originally to be in a volume along with *An Asian Minor* and *Looking Glass Lives.* When I first considered putting the volume together I was calling it *Gay Tragic Romances,* envisioning the title in a bubble above the face of a tearful, cartoon-pretty guy—like a Roy Lichtenstein painting. I think I changed the title because the new one sounded better.

Slashed to Ribbons debuted during a particularly fortuitous year, one of those sudden efflorescences of the short story that occurs every few decades. In this case, it was fueled by the necessarily short-lived literary minimalist movement that brought Raymond Carver and Donald Barthelme to prominence. Their work, and that of Anne Beattie, another short story expert, and to my amazement, my own most recent book, were featured on the cover of *Writer's Magazine* that spring under the headline "Short Story Renaissance," with flattering minireviews of our books within. No wonder mine went into a second printing in a year, and into a third two years later.

It also set me up as more than a poet or novelist for years to come, giving me my first taste of purely literary—rather than commercial—cachet. The first title of mine that editor Scott Brassart reprinted at Alyson Press in 2000 was that very collection of stories (with *An Asian Minor* added). Since their 1983 book publication, some of the stories have been anthologized again and again; and several have been turned into theater pieces. "Hunter," however, is the real winner, with seven appearances in other anthologies so far.

My partners at GPNy figured that as my memoir was even better than those previous three books, it would do even better. The decision to publish it in hardcover was a dual one. It would definitely help our profit margin. I don't know how much it's changed since, but in the 1980s the cost of a hardcover added maybe another 50 percent onto the costs of a bound trade paperback—something like another $1.25 per book. Meanwhile, instead of selling it for $7.95, you could ask almost double the amount—in those days, $14.95. A nice profit, indeed.

That I was a hardcover author was clear. SeaHorse had done a hundred *Asian Minors* in hardcover and they'd sold quickly. GPNy published three hundred hardcovers (along with three thousand trade paperbacks) of *Slashed to Ribbons in Defense of Love* in 1983 and those sold out, too. And in those times, there was allegedly a difference between having your books come out "between boards" or being—as the Beatles song put it—a "paperback writer"—the latter was far more working class and common. You didn't have to be a genius to figure out the next step. GPNy used another of my books that was not a mainstream best seller to make money—*Late in the Season,* in its handsome trade paperback.

Ambidextrous however would require GPNy's first paper wrap cover—for a few hundred hardcovers—and for that I went to the man who'd become our artist-in-residence, Ron Fowler.

Gay Presses of New York published *Ambidextrous* in November 1985, in an edition of six thousand hardcovers. The book was eventually widely reviewed in the gay and lesbian press—and was virtually ignored by the mainstream press.

When I urged the book industry's bible, *Publishers Weekly,* to review my memoir, sending them several galleys and reminders—after all we had the Tony Award–winning play on Broadway on our list!—the paragraph it finally printed showed that the reviewer had read maybe the first six pages of the book. He hadn't a glimmer of the rest of the content, never mind the subversive material therein. Or maybe he had read it, and for some reason chose to gloss it over in the review.

The reviewer for the *Manchester Guardian* in England, however, had read all of *Ambidextrous,* and he'd definitely gotten its radical point—and been infuriated by it. "Mr. Picano," he publicly instructed me via the pages of the paper, "well brought up eleven-year-old children do not have sex. They do not use drugs. They do not purvey pornography."

I wrote back and suggested the reviewer look up the word "memoir" in his dictionary, defined in my own copy as "a report or record based on a writer's memory of events that occurred during his life." I had had sex, used drugs, and been a pornographer as a kid: ergo kids that age had sex.

But even the allegedly hip American gay press wasn't sure what to do with the book. I suppose it's a sign of exactly how radical *Ambidextrous* was, as, twenty years ahead of its time the book was neither gay nor straight. Instead it was as accurate as I could recall it, a memoir of three years of my life and of the people around me. The first sexual liaisons I'd had had been with little girls and had been their doing entirely, as I'd been blissfully ignorant of sex before then. The second series of experiences had been with a boy my age, also more knowledgeable, and had involved our using drugs in the form of airplane glue—another strike against me. The third relationship with a girl classmate had been with the "ice princess" in a class of intellectually gifted children. Looking back on it now, it must have seemed to some as though I'd put together a list of the sacred cows of adolescence a page long, and then gone out of my way to demolish them one by one within the confines of one little memoir. Even worse, I'd done so with complete and utter ruthlessness—parading as naiveté.

To say that I was deeply disappointed in the general lack of mainstream critical reaction to the book and the misunderstanding with which it met would be playing it down. I was devastated. I thought the book would move me onto another literary plateau. But how could it, when no one would even publish it . . . review it . . . read it? True, the book was translated into German, under the wonderful title *Doppelbegabueng*. I even gave way after three years and allowed Plume to republish *Ambidextrous* in trade paperback in the United States. England's Gay Men's Press put out its edition in 1989. It was published again in the U.S. by Richard Kasak Press in 1995, in a mass-market edition, and then Hayworth Press reprinted it in 2002 as part of my memoir trilogy. Yet to this day I've not gotten past my bitterness over the book's debut.

In the two decades since it was first published, my childhood memoir supposedly became one of the books that a few generations of lesbian and gay youth read during their coming-out process. The fact that *Ambidextrous* has never been out of print for thirty-one years is some very small gratification.

———

During this time, I'd become acquainted with that consummately sophisticated critic of French literature, George Stambolian. I knew that he was a professor of French and interdisciplinary studies at Wellesley College. I would learn that he'd attended Dartmouth College and received his PhD from the University of Wisconsin. I'd perused his study, *Marcel Proust and the Creative Encounter* (1972), and the volume he coedited with Elaine Marks, *Homosexualities and French Literature* (1979).

But rather than the unquestionable intellectual those texts represented, it was the sensual side of Stambolian that I ended up connecting with. He had noticed me, he told me sometime later on in our friendship, in the spring of 1978, while he'd been out walking his dog, Bodo, quite early one Sunday morning: I'd been coming home from a night out dancing and drugging. As I unknowingly passed him, I had my arms around two other men, dressed like me, out all night like me, George said. Clearly, we'd looked to George like we were on our way to one of our homes for a ménage à trois to screw away the rest of the weekend. This moment had intrigued George and he would refer to it—and to glimpses of me together with the young artist Scott Façon he had at the Pines—as being critical to our connection and to our friendship, even though we never had sex, seldom spoke of it, and never did more than exchange friendly kisses when greeting.

This was the era of semiotics, of Roland Barthes, Michel Foucault, and Jacques Derrida, the philosophical era of things not being "in and of themselves" as Kant had thought a century earlier, but instead of things being signifiers for many other things that were unsayable or indescribable or otherwise unapproachable. I took it all with a grain *de sel.* No matter how much Jacques Derrida explained how books wrote themselves utilizing me and the culture at large as mere tools, I knew how much labor I really had put into each story, poem, novel, and play, and I refused to cede an iota of credit to any such nebulous notion as an "age."

Nevertheless, I did find the semiotic chic lit thought of the 1980s to be amusing in a corrupt, *fin de siècle* kind of way, and I found George as one of its more finely tuned representatives: charming, brilliant, knowledgeable, and sensitive—although at times he became mired in that mentality academics often harbor. During a driving trip to his summer place in East Hampton, he waxed rhapsodic about Joseph Conrad's novella *The Heart of Darkness,* calling it "the greatest short story in the English language." I'd just reread it, along with several other Conrad novellas, and had found it murky and overwritten, especially in comparison to his *Typhoon* and *The Nigger of the "Narcissus,"* to my mind far better stories. It turned out George hadn't even read those works. Yet he had no trouble making his blanket pronouncement. Another time, I was rereading *The Guermantes Way,* and I began talking about how I'd at first been delighted, and then disappointed, to notice Proust's "lumber"—the rather bare-bones, joist-and-beam framing devices he'd used for the hundred-page-long afternoon party in the long first chapter. George couldn't believe I would fault the French *maître* for shabby structure. He grew incensed, livid; he almost chased me home.

George had been doing in-depth anonymous interviews with gay men for *Christopher Street* magazine, one of which had even found its way into that bastion of *Nouvelle Vague,* the seminal quarterly *Semiotext(e).* He wanted to interview me, not as Felice Picano, but as a specific Stambolian type, in my case, "a self-made man." I never actually understood what this term signified, even when the interview came out and I read it. But it somehow fit with Stambolian's other in-depth interviews: "With a Handsome Man," "With a

Deformed Man," "With an Intellectual," "With an Artist," "With a Dying Man." For George, the very anonymity he provided would offer not so much cover for further excavation and discovery as a screen behind which various kinds of personae and scenarios might more easily develop and flourish.

Read as a whole, the interviews really do work; they are amazingly intimate and stimulating, in a way somewhat similar to Boyd McDonald's, Robert Peters's, and Dennis Cooper's image worship—enticing by being so bold, so bald, so totally out-there honest. It didn't take any kind of genius on my part to see the interviews all together in one volume. George needed to do one more, with a young heterosexual man of his acquaintance, to round out his series of portraits. *Male Fantasies/Gay Realities* came out in 1984 as a SeaHorse Press book, in trade paperback along with two hundred library binding copies, and sold quickly.

While well reviewed, the book was never really recognized as the incisive piece of semiotics it actually was, probably because the unvarnished homosexual content was still too inflammatory. I don't think it ever made the leap into academia he had hoped for. Stambolian brought me a photograph to be used on the cover that I liked and used. It pictures what is evidently a very sexy nude guy whose torso is totally covered with a plaster mask; I think it's a terrific visual correlative for the constant, excellent uncovering that takes place within the book.

Through my own contacts, George soon made other connections among gay lit people, which is to say, outside of academia, and there his charm, intelligence, reputation, and knowledge helped him get chosen to edit what would turn out to be the most consistently well-reviewed as well as the best-selling anthologies of gay fiction, *Men On Men*. The first *Men On Men* book came out in 1986, published by NAL/Dutton's ongoing Plume line, and featured most of the members of the Violet Quill Club, together for only the second time after my own 1981 anthology sold over twenty thousand copies and was soon followed by *Men On Men 2* (1988), *Men On Men 3* (1990), and *Men On Men 4*, which I helped George edit and, because of his ongoing illness due to HIV, for which I wrote the introduction, using several interviews with him as a basis.

It wasn't long before George was appointed a member of the Advisory Board of the Lesbian and Gay Studies Center at Yale University, and it was because of his influence, along with that of scholar John Boswell (author of the seminal *Homosexuality, Sexual Tolerance, and Christianity* (1981), that The Violet Quill Club's papers have been collected at the Beinecke Rare Book & Manuscript Library there.

Male Fantasies did more than tilt George's focus away from academia and French writing toward American writing and gay literature. It made him intrigued enough to try his hand at other kinds of writing himself. Coming into daily contact with people like me, Andrew Holleran, and Robert Ferro also helped demystify the enigmatic springs of creative writing for George. Although he never did so easily nor fluently, George began writing fiction. At times he'd shoot himself in the foot by deciding in advance in what great author's style the tale would be written. But eventually he fought through that mistraining and found his own voice. Two of Stambolian's short stories were published: the French-influenced "Encounters" in *Christopher Street,* and, in 1994, his perfect piece, "In My Father's Car," eventually published in *Lavender Mansions,* edited by Irene Zahara, several years after his death.

Even though both tales cost him much pain and effort, it's not too difficult to believe that had he lived longer, George Stambolian might have written enough stories to fill a book. I know I would read it. Reading especially that last story, I can hear George's urbane, questioning, and amused voice. But it's not much consolation for losing him.

———

Like Stambolian, Martin Duberman had been on my radar for some time. He was a great-looking guy, evidently very smart, a multitalented writer (drama, prose, history, and later, autobiography)—altogether an intellectually accomplished man. Even though we got together socially several times, the electric spark that makes connections solidify was somehow missing. However, during one of those coffee dates in Marty's sunny Chelsea flat in Manhattan, he brought up the subject of some old texts he had happened upon over the past few decades while nosing around in various collections and libraries, researching and preparing data for his published books.

By 1984 when we first met, Duberman's books formed an astonishing contribution anyone would be proud of, ranging from his integrationist texts *In White America* (1964) and *The Anti-Slavery Vanguard* (1965) to his Bancroft Award-winning biographies of Charles Francis Adams and James Russell Lowell, to his influential counterculture-era study *Black Mountain: An Experiment in Community* (1972). Several of Duberman's plays had been produced, including one about Beat writer Jack Kerouac. These had been collected in *Male Armor* (1974). At the time I met him, Marty was at work on what would turn out to be the key biography of the giant twentieth-century African American actor, singer, and activist, Paul Robeson.

Duberman was an academician, but unlike Stambolian he was definitely openly liberal, left-leaning—to some a socialist. And unlike George, Marty was already known to a larger public. Duberman's first publication of an openly gay work, through Gay Presses of New York two years later, would end up redirecting the focus of his writing and his life's work from the Left to gay rights, from the American past to the many hindrances, humiliations, lies, and indignities of the American gay past—including Duberman's own.

The lock-opening for Duberman began quite slowly, almost unnoticeably. He'd alluded to his collection of old texts several times and he'd even shown them to me in his flat, shopping bags of them tucked into a corner of two overstuffed bookshelves. In a series of phone calls, he began explaining who wrote them and what exactly they were. Fascinated, if not utterly persuaded, I agreed to look them over, toward possibly making some kind of book. Marty made it clear that between teaching and doing his Robeson research and writing, that he wouldn't have the time to organize it himself. But if I selected what I thought was the most intriguing and significant of the material and then structured a book out of it, well, we just might get something done.

One afternoon he arrived at my flat with two overflowing shopping bags he'd dragged downtown in a taxicab. Over the next few weeks, whenever I had spare time, I'd try to decipher the texts. Many of them were early Veloxes, photocopies, mimeographs, even xerographs—barely legible, badly copied—of writings that Marty had stumbled across in library historical collections. Most were handwritten—letters, memoirs, diaries, stories. It took me a few months, but at last, I had read them all and selected a dozen texts. Marty recommended one or two others. We decided to print each text as it existed, arranged chronologically, with an introduction by Marty. The first text was from eighteenth-century New Jersey, a Revolutionary War autopsy report showing some surprise that one particularly brave and effective solider fighting the redcoats was actually, when unclothed, revealed to be a woman. Marty would write about similar stories, and about cross-dressing in general, among both men and women, as reported in American periodicals of that period and earlier.

One of the best pieces was a mid-nineteenth-century correspondence between an esteemed and powerful upper court judge and a businessman he'd somehow come back into contact with after a long time. The letters reminisced jocularly about their time together as young men, sharing the same bed, and how the judge remembered being awakened by his friend's "long, fleshen pole," on many mornings. The tone of the letters was suggestive, open, sincere, and a little bit salacious. Was he trying to reawaken the other's interest again? Who knew? But as Duberman was careful to point out in his explicatory text, while many young men slept together in those days out of thrift, to conserve heat, and because of a shortage of beds, this was proof that sleeping together did actually include sex. This remains an explosive issue today, as various studies show Abraham Lincoln shared beds with other men, not only as a young man, but also in the White House.

As important as these and other eye-opening pieces were, so was a long memoir filled with homosexual incidents written at the turn of the twentieth century by a wealthy individual able to travel the world and indulge his tastes that we included. And once Marty had shown me some forty pages of the journal he'd kept in the late fifties as a college student, we also decided to include this amazing document, which detailed how the young Duberman sought psychotherapy to try to cease being a homosexual.

Although I was only a few years younger than him, for me being gay had been nothing earthshaking. When I decided I was gay in 1966, it had been just another way to rebel against my parents, their generation, the state, and "the man." For Marty, accepting his homosexuality had meant loss of place, reputation, and importance in his family, as well as probable sexual slavery to thugs and complete degradation. No wonder he longed to escape.

About Time: Exploring the Gay Past was put out by GNPy under my SeaHorse Book imprint in 1986. It was a big book in many ways. I'd worked on it from the very onset, selecting the materials, guiding Duberman not only in what he should include but in how he should write about it, reselecting and reediting along the way as the book took on a life of its own. Like all SeaHorse books, I art directed it and laid out every page. I also spent months collecting nineteenth-century images, finally selecting two idiosyncratic, very handsome daguerreotype male heads and torsos that I then reproduced in bronze ink against a pale cream-white background to resemble older periodicals. I used characteristically nineteenth-century newsprint type faces for all of the book cover's lettering and text.

Working with Martin Duberman was a great experience. Even while overworked, he met deadlines we set together. He was professional at all times and he went out of his way to contribute and to make the book a good one. In the end we were equally proud of it. And in his dedication page, Marty gave credit to me—without whom, after all, the book would not have been written.

I wish I could say the same about his literary agent. From the beginning, Frances Goldman was a problem. She never acknowledged that I was the driving force behind the book, and while I didn't require a formal acknowledgment of that fact, I did require cooperation. She evidently believed that since we were a small press and Marty a big author, that she could call the shots—which she did as frequently as possible. She held up the contract for weeks. She tried selling the book to another publisher after it had come out, which was illegal as well as unethical. She never really understood what the book was about, why Marty was doing it, or why it was being done through GPNy, rather than through Knopf—which, lets be honest, two decades ago, and possibly even today, wouldn't have touched it with a ten foot pole— "fleshen" or otherwise. I'm not sure what her relationship with Duberman was, but Goldman evidently had more influence than I'd thought. She continued to annoy me in various ways after the book came out—every week after the book's publication, in fact.

She would phone me with new criticism. "*The New York Times* hasn't reviewed the book. Send them another copy," she commanded. I doubted they would review a gay history book, but I duly sent another copy. (It still wasn't reviewed.)

"It's a bestseller. Put out another printing," she demanded the following week. Of course, I knew exactly how many copies of the book were out, where they were, how many had sold, and to whom.

"It's selling nice and steadily; however, it's not a bestseller," I noted.

The following week she was at it again. "So-and-so needs *About Time* for their book club. The head told me himself!" I'd already contacted the club and sent them a copy. No one had returned my call, which meant he was not taking the book.

This went on week after week until I stopped taking Goldman's calls. But soon her letters began, and they were even more bothersome.

Somehow she convinced Marty that the book needed to be longer. By now, his massive Paul Robeson biography had come out and had gotten its front-page reviews. GPNy had hoped to ride its success but in fact saw no impact on sales. His agent insisted that our book be reformatted. The late eighties were a particularly bad time, both for me personally—four members of the Violet Quill Club died within fourteen months of each other, after awful illnesses—and also for Larry and Terry. The last thing I needed were demands from this person. I ignored the phone calls and letters. Then she asked me to release the book's rights back to him so that a larger publisher like Knopf or Vintage could republish it in an expanded edition and get it the attention it deserved.

Finally I'd had enough. I phoned Marty and asked if he himself really wanted the rights to *About Time* back. By then our edition was almost sold out, and either we would do the new edition, or someone else would do it. He seemed unaware of the situation, and promised to phone back. He didn't. When I called him again, he said, "Maybe I'd better take the rights back."

I conferred with Larry and Terry. Larry summed it up. "We don't need the book, and you certainly don't need that agent in your life." I wrote and reverted the rights back to Duberman.

About Time was republished, not by Knopf, not even by Vintage, but by Meridian Books, like Plume, an imprint of NAL/Dutton, in 1991, my own sometime publisher. It was the same book I'd put together, minus, of course, the dedication. If the book received major reviews or scads of new sales, I never heard about them.

But *About Time* became a turning point for Marty. He stopped doing big, historical bios and has since put out five more books. *Hidden From History* (1989), a second volume of texts and commentaries, was a sequel to *About Time. Cures: A Gay Man's Odyssey* (1991), was a continuation of the journals and texts he'd put out in GPNy's book. The next three were also gay themed. *Midlife Queer: Autobiographical Essays of a Decade, 1971–1981* (1996). And most recently, Duberman published *Left Out: The Politics of Exclusion* (2001) a discussion of how homosexuality was expunged from socialism in the U.S., and, of course, *Stonewall* (2002), a history of the key political event in contemporary gay history.

And so, like George Stambolian, Martin Duberman's experience with a small gay publisher helped redirect him more deeply into himself, his past, and into new areas of gay literature. I've no idea what happened to that agent, but I later discovered that she was also behind another, earlier, GPNy mess. Sarah Schulman had brought her first novel, *After Delores,* to us to publish. We'd been looking for bright new lesbian writers to support. We liked the novel and offered Sarah a contract. The book ended up going to Beacon Press, but only after we had made an offer, sent out a contract, and were awaiting Sarah's signed agreement. Guess who her agent was?

8

The Ones That Got Away:
Cocteau, Purdy, Vidal . . .

Although the combined Gay Presses of New York were expanding and doing solid business, all was by no means perfect. What was wonderful could have been truly fabulous if several projects headed in our direction had actually worked out. Several of these undertakings concerned male authors who had already reached a pinnacle in their work and reputation; another concerned a colleague of mine from the Violet Quill. There were still other possible hit books that we were never able to put out. And then there was Harvey Fierstein's second hit on Broadway, *La Cage Aux Folles,* for which he ended up controlling absolutely zero publication rights.

Tolstoy said, "Happy families are all alike; every unhappy family is unhappy in its own way." So, too, the stories of all near-miss publications are different. The Russian's dictum suggests that these unhappy stories are more fascinating than their sunny counterparts. That may or may not hold true here. I'll let the reader be the judge.

———

I had been taken to a madly overcrowded party in someone's ultrasmall one-bedroom apartment in the former St. George Hotel in Brooklyn Heights by a bevy of my younger writers—Dennis Cooper, Brad Gooch, Tim Dlugos, and David Trinidad. I was about to turn around and leave when Christopher Cox caught me by the shirt and dragged me out to the building's corridor, refreshingly cool and blessedly nearly empty, save for two elderly gentlemen. They resembled retired library clerks, each holding tightly onto vastly oversized umbrellas, despite there being no rain cloud in sight.

Had I ever met James Purdy? Cox asked.

Indeed, I'd not met him and I shook his hand. He was of one of the two elderly men, medium height, dressed boringly in a gray windbreaker, and altogether unremarkable. His face was rather pinched and undistinguished, his hair gray and lank. His partner looked identical, except for the color of his windbreaker. With his insistence on being social, Chris said to Purdy, "Felice is a big fan and he's been itching to meet you."

Now this was not strictly true. In fact it was more like a much extended piece of typical Southern courtesy-flattery by Chris, who being from Alabama, was infrequently, at times disconcertingly, given to such outbursts of overadulation.

Chris worked within some tiny puzzle piece of the huge Random House empire, and to keep in touch over the years since he'd broken up with Edmund White and the VQ Club had disbanded, he and I usually met for lunch somewhere around his office on East Fifty-first Street. It had been at one such lunch that I'd mentioned that I'd been reading Purdy's non-gay themed novels, including *Jeremy's Version, I Am Elijah Thrush,* and *The House of the Solitary Maggot.* These books, set in the Midwest, felt very Southern. Rather than those he was better known for, they seemed to be his major works.

Like many people everyone my age, I'd come to Purdy through the books that had made Purdy's name in the forties and fifties: *Malcolm* and *Cabot Wright Begins,* which I could take or leave. In the sixties, however, I'd been knocked over by the amazing, the astonishing, *Eustache Chisolm and the Works,* a novel of S/M love and mystical sex that I thought raised Purdy into the vanguard of gay writers, although even he admitted that book was an aberration. Since then, he had written the chain of novels I've mentioned, as well as *In a Shallow Grave,* which had received respectful if generally bewildered reviews. No longer a prodigy, Purdy was considered by some to be a shooting star whose trajectory was over, and by others as a writer who'd failed to reach his potential.

My enthusiasm for *Eustache Chisolm* was enough to prompt Chris's overture, and in a few minutes, he told Purdy about SeaHorse Press. In turn I took down Purdy's phone number—he lived a few doors away from friends of mine in Brooklyn Heights, several streets from the party into which new arrivals would periodically arrive, filling the hall with noise as they crammed themselves in, like college men crowding into a telephone booth a generation earlier. During a silence, Purdy intimated that he might have something for SeaHorse Press. I said I'd phone him.

A few days later I called, and Purdy said he'd been thinking of a collection of his unpublished plays and short stories. He was not very forthcoming with details. After a few minutes of conversation I found myself enmeshed in his verbal lacework, composed of unequal parts of overcivility, irrelevant questions, and obfuscation. All attempts at clarification, I would learn, were pointless. Purdy did rack what he claimed was his admittedly poor memory for the venues where the plays had been performed. Of the short stories he said even less. He did however say he would look around and send what he had.

Even so, once I'd hung up, I figured if we received one play of the caliber of *Color of Darkness* or Albee's dramatization of Purdy's novel *Malcolm,* we were set.

He sent them, two months later, in a pale blue folder. I read them, the day after I got them, with a growing sense of excitement tinged with unease.

The three plays were short, even for one-acts, and they read like typical Purdy, with a dreamlike quality of "action" and bizarre, dreamlike characters operating within an equally dreamlike setting. According to their cover pages, all had been performed at one time or another over the past few decades around the country, and all in theaters I'd never heard of. The stories were likewise typically strange and either not quite clear or somewhat winsome. There was absolutely not one thing among them, story or play, that was particularly remarkable: nothing, certainly, equal to his best work, or even to his best-known work. Still, it was James Purdy at his most characteristic, and his readers wouldn't be startled or in any way disappointed by it.

I phoned Larry Mitchell and asked him to decide for himself. We agreed that a collection of Purdy's unpublished work, even at this rather sleepy level, would be a feather in our cap. We couldn't really count on selling a lot of copies. But would Purdy even consider an offer of $2,500 that would mean selling approximately two thousand copies? To suss out Purdy's expectations I called Chris Cox who said he understood that Purdy was short of money and would accept our offer. It still embarrassed me to make it.

Another matter, until then totally minor, became increasingly important, concerning who actually owned the publication rights of these short plays. From my own playwriting, I knew that one had to file a copyright notice with the U.S. Library of Congress for every finished play—or later, every "refinished" draft in which I'd revised more than 20 percent. And that one was thereupon, at some later date, issued a proof of copyright.

Copyrights also existed for books, of course, but books were published with that information on the back of the title page, there for anyone to see. Such was not the case with a play unless it, too, was published, which hadn't been the case with Purdy's. I was told that some theater programs had had the author's copyright printed, which would do as proof.

I phoned Purdy, told him my partners and I liked the book, and that we could publish it the following year. One request I had was that Purdy supply us with the place and year of publication for each of the published stories, and send photocopies of the copyrights for the three short plays. What I thought was a standard request was met by utter mystification. I explained patiently about the stories. After several minutes, he grasped that I needed to print previous proof of publication in the book. About the plays' copyrights, he had absolutely no idea.

I tried another tack. Did he perhaps have a drama agent who had handled the plays? Yes, and he named Helen Harvey, the very agent who'd first handled Harvey Fierstein. The mere mention of her name sent panic through my body. Our book had already been out two years in its GPNy edition when I discovered that Helen Harvey was selling the publishing rights to Random House. Rather than fly off the handle, I suggested that James look among his papers for the copyright notice *before* contacting his agent. But he promptly threw another monkey wrench into the conversation by asking me why the copyrights were needed. We were back to square one.

I calmly explained that in order to legally sign a contract with any publisher, he needed to prove he actually owned the publication rights to the plays.

Of course he owned the rights, he countered. He'd written them, hadn't he?

I told him about Harvey Fierstein, who had written the adaptation of the movie *La Cage Aux Folles* for Broadway on a commission from a producer and yet failed to receive any publication rights in his contract. I went on to explain how some theater managers, directors, producers, and impresarios purchased commissioned plays and that they, not the writers, then owned the copyrights. If GPNy were to publish Purdy's plays and he did not hold the copyrights, we could be literally sued out of existence, a risk we didn't take lightly. After a half hour making this point to Purdy, he agreed to do as I'd asked and locate the copyrights.

Four months later, I lunched with Chris Cox who asked what had happened with Purdy, and I told him of our phone conversation. "Oh, darling," Chris began, "You can't publish those plays without knowing who holds the copyright." Before we parted, I asked if Chris could gently nudge Purdy in the appropriate direction.

A few weeks later, I received photocopies of the six Purdy stories to be part of the collection, each one clearly stating where and when it had been published previously. Slow progress, yet, still, progress. I left a message on Purdy's service thanking him profusely, adding how much we were looking forward to getting the copyrights for the plays and moving ahead with the collection.

That was the very last any of us ever heard from James Purdy.

————

If trouble found me in the case of Purdy, I actually went looking for it with Gore Vidal.

One day, while I was in A Different Light Bookstore, I heard owner and manager Norman Laurila telling a customer that Vidal's novel *Myra Breckenridge* was out of print. Norman had tried to order it repeatedly, only to be told that Random House had no plans to reprint it. All three of us in the store thought this was a scandal: another sign of how mainstream publishers ignored the gay market. When I was leaving, Norman said offhandedly, "Why don't you republish it through SeaHorse?"

My immediate reaction was to scoff. Who, me? Publish Vidal? Come on.

But a week later I mentioned this to Robert Ferro, and he said his new friend Walter Clemons, a book critic for *Newsweek,* knew Vidal, perhaps had even interviewed him, and would probably know how to get in contact with the self-exiled novelist. A few weeks later I received Vidal's address in Rome, where he lived most of the year.

Gore Vidal is such a legendary figure that it's difficult to say how and why I felt I could approach him. Innocence? Stupidity? Bravado? Who knows, exactly? But I felt I could and so I did. Partly, this was over my real ire at *Myra* being unavailable. I think Vidal's essays are magnificent, but except for *Burr, Myra Breckenridge* is the only fiction he's written that I think any good. There is nothing like it in our literature. One would have to go back to Max Beerbohm or Laurence Sterne, among the British, to find its match. Certainly nothing in American lit comes close to its combination of style, wit, and satire.

In writing to Vidal I composed one of the most careful letters of my life. I addressed him as "Mr. Vidal" and "Sir" throughout. I wrote that I'd become aware that his novel was out of print and not slated for reprinting. GPNy was a small yet respected publishing house devoted to gay-themed literature, and while we couldn't pay much as an advance, we would do a professional job, keep the book in print forever, and solicit his input in every area of the process of reissue, right up to the completed product—words I knew from experience any writer would delight in reading from a prospective publisher. I also mentioned that we were speaking with James Purdy, a writer Vidal admired, about printing a collection of his work.

I didn't fully expect to hear back from Vidal and so I was slightly astonished when a letter from Rome, in its *pneumatique* blue envelope. *"Caro Felice,"* it gushed (or camped), as though we'd known each other forever. He thanked me for my interest, and then went on to lay out the problem that was keeping *Myra* out of print. It was a short novel, and he wanted it to be packaged with, and sold together in one volume with its sequel, *Myron*. Vintage Press, he said, was uninterested in doing that. He added that he'd been in Cleveland, Ohio, giving a lecture, and that he'd been struck by how "wide in the girth" American youths were, even the handsomest and those with otherwise remarkable bodies. He much preferred European youths, with their slender torsos. He went on for a very long paragraph about the hips of younger Italian men. I thought this switch of topic odd, but amusing.

I considered *Myron* a dog of a book, but I would print it if it meant getting Myra back in print. Larry and Terry agreed, and I wrote back saying it could be arranged. We knew, of course, that.

It had struck both Larry and me that we might indeed never get the book if only because, by providing him with an offer, Vidal could use that offer to go back to Random House and get from them what he wanted: the tandem volume.

And after many months of hearing nothing about the status of the project, that's what eventually did happen. Meanwhile the letters between us became monthly. In each of mine, I hewed as closely to the subject as possible. In his, however, he barely gave a sentence to our putative topic—publishing his book—instead using the body of the letter to comment at length upon more, much more than American asses: how television was ruining American minds, how much people abroad hated the U.S., how no one paid attention to books or writers anymore. It was not brilliant letter writing; it was not Vidal at its best. But it was during one of these missives that he blithely mentioned that should "our little conspiracy" not come to fruition, that I might interest myself in a 1933 novel titled *The Young and Evil* by Parker Tyler and Charles Henri Ford.

I'd not heard from Vidal for months when a phone call awakened me at 4:15 AM. It took me some time to figure out who it was and what he was telling me: the editors at Vintage had at last given in and given up: *Myra* and *Myron* would be published as he wished: in a single volume. He thanked me for having gotten them "over the edge" on the decision.

The next morning, when I looked at the cover of the paperback I'd laid on the bed table, it read—"Young and Evil—Tyler/Ford," clearly something I'd written during the night, probably as a result of something Vidal had said to me. Under it, I'd also written "send *Ambi* to Rome." This latter I understood somewhat better.

I told Larry we had lost *Myra Breckenridge* to Vintage a few days later—a disappointment if no real shock. I also told him that Vidal had agreed to look over the galleys of *Ambidextrous*. Maybe he'd give us a blurb.

The next time Vidal phoned it was to say that he'd read my memoir but that I shouldn't expect anything to come of it. He wouldn't give me a blurb—he didn't give blurbs—adding dismissively, "After all, everyone thinks their own childhood and youth is significant, when in truth they were just like everyone else's." He couldn't have been more patronizing or condescending. Vidal summed up his philosophy of the memoir: "Only someone like Svetlana

Aluyevna's childhood is of any interest to read, and really only because she was Joseph Stalin's daughter."

You may imagine my surprise therefore, a decade later, when Gore Vidal published his version of my childhood memoir, *Ambidextrous,* only his was titled *Palimpsest.*

A few days after that last phone call, I bumped into poet Edward Field on Hudson Street and mentioned Vidal's early morning phone call and letters with their wildly swerving shifts in topic and mood. The soul of tact, Field said, "Well you know, Felice, writers of my generation often indulge a bit more than they ought to."

"You mean to say," I asked, "he was sloshed?"

I shut off the ringer in my bedroom, so I don't know if Vidal ever called again.

––––––

By this time, I'd begun to think about SeaHorse Press's direction over the past seven or eight years since its founding, and the shifts in the GLBT culture that had taken place. It wasn't so much that a literary yet accessible small gay press wasn't really needed anymore, although by this time virtually every mainstream house was publishing gay and lesbian fiction. My partners at their own publishing houses, were still putting out gay plays, and only a few new gay poets were that interesting to me, and most of those—Antler, Mark Doty, and Michael Lassell—had already found other publishers. Unwilling to let the name or imprint drop, since it did have a sort of cachet, I began to expand SeaHorse Press's goals and consider a different kind of book.

It was during this period that I published *The Young and Evil,* George Stambolian's interviews, and Martin Duberman. In the meantime I looked around for other likely projects. Guy Hocquenghem had suggested Jean Cocteau's *Le Livre Blanche (The White Book),* which had been recently translated and put out by Marion Boyars Publishers Ltd. in England. I contacted

Boyars, who was willing to sublease it to SeaHorse Press for $10,000, a large but not impossible sum of money—I felt I could sell ten thousand copies of this admittedly minor work by my favorite French author.

But a problem arose regarding the artwork—Cocteau's own black-and-white drawings, which were as intrinsic as the text to the book. Cocteau was still alive when he'd given Boyars permission to use the artwork. Once the artist/author's heirs got wind that an American publisher was interested in taking on the book however, dollar signs began to dance before their eyes and they asked another $10,000 for permission to use the artwork. Both Boyars and I wrote to the estate—not Cocteau's boyfriend, Jean Marais, although I guess he was ultimately the *dernier parole* on the matter—explaining that I would have to sell a minimum of twenty thousand copies of the book to break even. Their response: I would sell over a hundred thousand copies—they were certain. I wasn't. Boyars told me he'd only sold about four thousand of his own edition throughout the entire British Commonwealth over a three-year period.

Whenever I mentioned the idea for the Cocteau book to anyone I knew connected with books—distributors, bookstores, or the media—the interest level registered close to zero. Finally I declined to send off large sums of money the press didn't have, and *The White Book* was never published in the U.S., although eventually Boyar's edition slipped into the U.S. in small amounts via various distributors.

Around this time, while going through my library, I found my copy of a book I'd read a decade before and had loved: *The Story of Harold.* I originally read—and loved—in the Avon/Bard paperback edition published by Bob Wyatt, the wunderkind editor who'd run the press for a decade. He and my friend there, Susan Moldow, had introduced sixties and seventies readers to works like Richard Farina's *Been Down So Long It Looks Like Up to Me,* Steven Millhauser's *Edwin Mullhouse,* Julio Cortázar's *Hopscotch,* and Gabriel García Márquez's *One Hundred Years of Solitude,* making instant classics out of them.

First published in hardcover in 1974 by Holt, Rinehart and Winston,

Terry Andrews's unusual and very good gay novel had come out of Avon/Bard several years later with cover and color illustrations by the inimitable *New Yorker* cartoonist and Balanchine ballet addict Edward Gorey. I'd read and loved the book then, and a decade later, reread the hardcover and thought again what a fine book it was and how it ought to be returned to print. I contacted Avon, by then, alas, bereft of Wyatt, and I was redirected to Holt, where I was told the book was out of print. While they couldn't give me the real name of the author, they'd contact him and give him my name and phone number and my message. The managing editor told me that of course Terry Andrews was a nom de plume. But why it was, and why there was such complete secrecy about the author was a mystery the managing editor refused to address.

A few weeks later someone phoned and told me that he knew me, as an author, and as a neighbor. He'd seen me at the post office on Hudson Street, pointed out by an acquaintance as—in his words—"the famous gay writer." His name was Jerry—not Terry—and definitely not Terry Andrews, he assured me, but he wouldn't offer a last name either, did I mind too much? And he'd be happy to meet with me for lunch, say at the nearby Sazerac House on Hudson Street a block from where he lived.

I agreed to meet, not knowing what to expect from such espionage-like rules of behavior over a mere reprint. A few days later I sat in the third booth from the back as instructed and a jolly, heavyset, gray-haired, casually dressed man, his bright blue eyes twinkling behind granny glasses, came in, sat down, declared himself to be Jerry, and ordered lunch.

The Sazerac House was one of the oldest continuously public houses in Manhattan's West Village. The White Horse Tavern of literary fame—poet Dylan Thomas fell dead upon its black-and-white diamond-patterned floor after a night of boozing—had also been around during the Revolutionary War (and was right around the corner from where I lived). The Sazerac's narrow, all-brick back section; tiny, low-ceilinged kitchen; and wide, shallow fireplaces confirmed that it, too, was in an eighteenth-century building, when "the Village" was actually the separate Village of Greenwich, several miles north of what was then New York City. I used to go there with friends for the Sazerac's wonderful and inexpensive bayou and creole cooking: deep fried oysters, gumbo, jambalaya, and catfish fillets with red rice and beans.

Jerry was charming and funny, and while a bit grandfatherly for a man only sixty-two years old, he was intelligent, smart, witty, and knowledgeable. He also flirted with me, a fact I used to my advantage. Little by little, and only after a great deal of circuitousness and irrelevant conversation, did I begin to comprehend what Jerry was more or less telling me, why he had written *The Story of Harold* under a pseudonym, and who he was—which explained all the mystery he cloaked himself in.

It appeared that Jerry was a successful children's book author, much like the protagonist of his novel. How successful? Well there was Dr. Seuss, there was Maurice Sendak, there was Saul Steinberg, and then there was Jerry. He never told me what name he wrote under. (Because of the connection of the names, I guessed—although with absolutely no proof—that he'd written *Harold and the Purple Crayon* and the other Harold books for young children.) But he assured me he had been a successful and beloved children's book writer and lived off the substantial earnings from his books, although he claimed to have "retired." Ergo his perceived need for there being no connection in the reading public's mind between the adored granddaddy figure and the bisexual elder into worshipping working-class cock and allowing himself to be humiliated by dominant leather babes during S/M sex scenes.

I could live with that. For the purposes of our publishing venture he would be the pseudonymous Terry Andrews. If he wanted to do readings or signings for the book, for all I cared, he could dress up in leather with a black lace bustier and a riding crop. Or never go at all. I just wanted to get the book back out there. Jerry agreed.

"Is there any way we might get the Gorey art, too?" I asked. He said he knew Gorey, and would phone and ask him. But if not, he said, there were a few more of the drawings similar to the one he himself had done for the front cover of the hardback that we might include.

"Great," I said. "Let's do it."

That was pretty much the gist of four follow-up phone calls, each spaced a month apart. Actually the fourth call was maybe a month and a half later, and Jerry apologized, saying he'd been ill a week: some kind of freak stomach thing.

I sent him the contracts, and phoned leaving a message saying that he could mail them back, or I could stop by and pick them up.

"Excellent," he replied.

No contracts were returned in the mail. Meanwhile, I budgeted the book and figured I could pay Gorey something. I asked around and through Bob Lowe's ex-lover, choreographer Rodney Griffith, then with the Pennsylvania Ballet, I finally got the artist's address, and I wrote to him—on a Gorey postcard—telling him how much I loved his work. (*The Curious Sofa, The Gilded Bat,* and *The Blue Aspic* remain among my all-time favorite books.) I asked how SeaHorse Press could use the artwork he'd done when it reprinted *The Story of Harold.*

The summer arrived and I never heard back—not from Jerry, and not from Gorey, whom I was told third-hand was summering out of town near Woodstock. When I returned in the fall from the Pines, I had a phone message from Jerry's lover, who himself would be out of town for another month. Bob Lowe and I drove up to North Truro, on the Cape, renting the house Larry Mitchell co-owned with Ron Schreiber for two weeks, as we usually did. When I returned to Manhattan I phoned Jerry's number yet again.

This time I got Jerry's lover, whose voice I recognized from previous calls. He said that Jerry had died of stomach cancer three weeks before. It had come on that spring, and had run through Jerry during the summer.

I was shocked, and I let him go with my condolences. For months after, I tried reconnecting with him—trying not to be too morbidly commercial—to ask if Jerry had signed the contracts for the reprint of *The Story of Harold,* but to no avail. By the time I actually got someone to answer the doorbell of their apartment, it was the superintendent, sweeping out the empty rooms to show to prospective tenants. Jerry's lover, now presumably the heir of to the royalties to *Harold* and umpteen other titles, had left New York and headed "somewhere south," according to the super. "I think maybe the Caribbean."

I never located him again. Gorey did write back—on the margins of the very same postcard I'd sent him—saying he would release the rights to the art for the novel back to Jerry but not directly to SeaHorse, but by then it meant nothing. Without a signed contract, I didn't dare republish the book, and to my knowledge it has remained out of print ever since.

I used the autographed Gorey postcard as a bookmark until it got lost, and once at the New York City Ballet, a few months before he died many years later, I got up the nerve to go speak to him. Gorey was drenched in lavender scent. His twenty-foot-long poison green wool scarf was wrapped and rewrapped about his reed-thin body, his fluffy, floor-length faux fur coat dragging along the parquet behind him. I wanted to thank Gorey and tell him what had happened with the book and why I'd never gotten back to him.

"It was all rawther mysterious," Gorey told me. "No one could ever get a straight answer on the precise hows and whys of poor Jerry's sudden affliction." Gorey's bushy, white eyebrows danced at the last word, divided as it was in ten syllables. "Nor his quite headlong and unprepared-for demise! One doesn't wish to appear suspicious," (come on now, one adores appearing suspicious when one is Edward Gorey), "but I'm afraid it's all rawther more sub rosa than one would expect from such an apparently unexceptional personage."

Years later I went searching for Terry Andrews in the New York Public Library's various catalogs. That was the name given as author of *The Story of Harold*—with no other name attached. Had it not been a pseudonym, after all? The only other titles I ever found by any author with the same name would have fit the putative years of authorship of the Jerry I met: *Sunset in Eternity*, a 1958 self-published novel (through Vantage Press) about the dangers of alcoholism (Jerry looked kind of like a reformed drinker, and had drunk only Diet Coke with lunch), and two other titles from the sixties in a genre I would call "gift book"—*The Spiritual Cat* and *The Spiritual Dog*. I never found a single children's book title—not even *Harold and the Falsifying Author*.

––––––––

Another SeaHorse Press title that was ready to go to print in 1984 never made it. It would take a great deal more pages than I have here to do justice to George Whitmore's personality, his life, or his career, and to our short yet tumultuous relationship—I hope some day someone does tackle the subject, because George was nothing if not fascinating, and I keep finding out and recalling intriguing things about him.

Even after the Violet Quill Club ended, George and I remained in contact, although George undoubtedly blamed me for not sticking up for him in his feud with Robert Ferro and Michael Grumley, a feud I was only vaguely aware of and, frankly, supremely indifferent to.

George had already published *The Confessions of Danny Slocum* in 1980, unquestionably the predecessor of autobiographical writers like Dave Eggers and Augustin Burrows, decades before them, and I believe better. He'd been writing poetry and plays since he was a teenager and, to my knowledge, gay short stories since the mid-1970s. He mostly read those stories to us six other Quillians at our very scattered "official" meetings, and several had provoked trouble.

One about disco queens, titled "Last Dance" had pissed off Andrew Holleran who thought it was too close in theme and structure to his own first novel, *Dancer From the Dance*. Another Whitmore tale about a trick and friend of mine, titled "The Black Widow," published in *Christopher Street*, caused great embarrassment to the enraged subject of George's story, and a hard time for me, who knew him, thereafter. A third story, "Getting

Rid of Robert," is credited by no less an authority than David Bergman, author *The Violet Hour* and *The Violet Quill* Reader, as the casus belli behind the breakup of the Violet Quill—I almost wrote *Violent* Quill— although I'm not at all sure that was the cause; I think it might have been simple ennui that ended our meetings.

Despite this, George and I spoke about publishing his stores, including the disputatious ones, under the title *The Black Widow and Other Stories*, through SeaHorse Press. George lined up a dozen of them, and we signed contracts. I then copyedited the stories (lightly, since George was so touchy), and George had gotten a clean manuscript back to me. All fast, clear, easy, and quite professional. The collection was ready to be typeset and I was talking to photographers—Arthur Tress, whose photo I'd once used, came to mind— about doing cover art for the book.

Out of the blue, George phoned and asked me *not* to publish the stories. He'd been trying to find a publisher for his second novel—I'd not even known he'd written a second book, that's how far removed we'd become—and while Michael Denneny at St. Martin's Press, who'd published *Danny Slocum,* had finally turned novel number two down, someone else we knew—I keep thinking it must have been Bill Whitehead at Dutton, although George never said who exactly—had expressed strong interest in it. Great, I said. What did that have to do with the stories? Well, George told me, he thought the novel would have a better shot at being published and of him of getting a contract for it if he offered the short story collection along with it; after all the editor would know the stories, since they'd been published in a magazine and in a well-reviewed anthology.

Obviously I was pissed off: I was being spurned for a bigger press. But since George insisted that this would be his one shot at fame and fortune, who was I to stop him? I gave in, and while voicing my disappointment, I agreed, saying I hoped it all worked out for him. I sent back the manuscript of stories to George along with all copies of the contract, with "Voided" written across the top. And that was the last I heard of it.

I gave no further thought to George's story collection, but instead moved ahead with my own writing and with other publishing projects; after all, as pop diva Mary Wells always sang, "There are plenty of fish in the sea."

Only years later did I discover that the (unnamed) editor had accepted neither George Whitmore's novel nor the short stories for publication. I have to suppose that George was too disappointed and just too embarrassed to come back to me with the stories. And to be frank, I was still annoyed at being passed over. But since he never did come back to me with them, I don't know exactly what I might have done. To this day I have no idea what that second novel was, or whether it was ever fully written out or only a proposal. When I spoke to George's friend and executor, Victor Bumbalo, about the incident, many years later, he didn't remember any of it very clearly. Victor did recall that the novel in question was not George's official second published novel, *Nebraska.* That, Victor said, had first been a play that George wrote and given to Victor to look over. Bumbalo said he thought it had not worked as a play, and he had irked George by saying it would make a good novel—sage advice. It did make a very solid novel and was published by Dutton in 1987.

George's short stories remain unpublished to this day and worse yet remain unread, in a vault devoted to the works and lives of the members of the Violet Quill in The American Groups Collection of the Beinecke Library at Yale University. They and George deserve better than that.

9

Art and the Gay Presses

From the very beginning, at least two GPNy partners, myself and Larry, were devoted to uniting some of the more intriguing currents of the visual arts swirling about us to the literature we were writing and publishing. Manhattan in the seventies and eighties, and particularly the so-called East Village, was a hotbed of new art and new design. And by the time GPNy closed its doors it had established a unique, if never standardized, look for its books that remains instantly recognizable to any of us who worked for the company. I was recently in the good-sized library of Samtökin '78, the gay and lesbian community center in Reykjavik, Iceland, and with relative ease was able to pick off the shelves, by their spines alone, seventeen titles that our four presses had put out. That's probably also a sign of our far-flung reach, and how pervasive the little companies' influence was.

This happened partly because I myself art-directed so many of the books. But even those art-directed by others have the clean, strong, masculine, often sexy, as often witty, graphics and typefaces that set Gay Presses books apart from the usual small press and mainstream books of the time. Many later gay books consciously or unconsciously copied that "look."

Where we stood out the most however was in the choice of cover artists we used, whether the art was drawing, photography, painting, collage, or some combination, each book was as much a space for a visual artist to strut his stuff as the interior was for the writer to shine. GPNy credited the artist outside on the back cover, or in the case of hardcovers, on the back cover inside flap, long before it was commonly done in the industry. We also used the identical image in advertising the book, in catalogs and on posters for bookstores and the various conventions and trade shows we attended: it was a unified visual campaign. We would send out a copy of the artwork along with a photo of the author—especially if the author was young or cute—with every review copy and with every piece of book promotion that went out. Today this is so standard a procedure that no one thinks about it.

By the time GPNy was formed in 1980, there were already several venues for the gay visual arts to be shown in Manhattan, with others popping up in San Francisco and Los Angeles. Probably the most important were New York's Robert Samuel Gallery (1974-79) and the Leslie Lohmann Gallery (established in 1975, and which still exists as the Leslie Lohmann Foundation Gallery in Manhattan), as well as Stompers, and Rob of Amsterdam, which concentrated on European gay art.

For many of us this was our first look at the homosexual and bisexual presence in the late nineteenth- to mid-twentieth century. Artists like Thomas Eakins, Henry Scott Tuke, Charles Demuth, Marsden Hartley, Paul Cadmus, and Pavel Tchelitchew were revealed to be bi or gay predecessors and brothers. Photographers like Wilhelm von Gloeden, F. Holland Day, and George Platt Lynes, with their amazing male nudes, suddenly had their work shown again in books, magazines, and galleries. No wonder whenever we thought poetry, we also thought art.

But while most of these older artists were admirable, it was the newer artists we sought to expose, the newer artists whom we felt said something about what all of us were writing and publishing.

———

It was a particularly hungover Sunday morning in the seventies. I'd gotten in from dancing at seven or eight in the morning, screwed till ten, slept till midafternoon, and was at 4 PM having wake-up coffee and perusing the Sunday *New York Times*. Three pages in my eyes were arrested by two facing full-page ads for Barneys. I'd been hearing via the gay grapevine that the decades-old clothiers where our fathers used to shop had suddenly hired younger gay men (some of whom I knew) as window designers, managers, and clothing buyers. They expected to become the men's—and women's—clothing shop of the year.

The ads weren't the usual dull photos found on other pages of the paper for other stores, but instead intensely rendered illustrations in close, exact lines with tight hatching and shading, opposed to the free-form, off-the-cuff sketches then current. This was a style of illustration that later on would be called Precisionism. The perspectives were slightly odd. There were many figures per page. The bodies and clothing looked gorgeous. The women, and especially the men illustrated were in poet Ian Young's phrase, when reviewing my first poetry book—and its cover a decade later—"polished gods."

"Did you see those ads?" every gay man seemed to ask in the next few months. Adveristing hadn't used illustration quite as striking in fifty years. This new illustrator's name suddenly became clear for the very first time in one very much lighter sketch—Stavrinos. A few months later, at Flamingo, I met George Stavrinos, with some friends.

"Felice loves your work!" my pal told the squarish, dark-haired young illustrator who was laughing and dancing. "Felice is a great novelist," he added. George flashed his happy, caramel-center brown eyes at me, and as we danced he told me to come up to his studio and look at his work when I had the time.

His studio turned out to be the large sunny living room of a good-size flat facing west ("I get up late," George explained, "morning light's wasted on me") in Manhattan's West Seventies, very much a transitional neighborhood at the time. Close up, the twenty-eight-year-old was genial if not handsome, with a slightly bad complexion but nice Hellenic features, a squarish forehead, big nose, and nice mouth. And once he was in motion, he was lovely, especially because of those amazing eyes and his high, light tenor, an undeniably masculine voice.

He'd come from the Boston area, he told me, and had eventually gone to the Rhode Island School of Design. He'd graduated in 1970, and here five years later, New York was at his feet. Well not quite, but quite soon, I predicted. In fact, George would soon be asked to join the venerable Push Pin Studio, where his work was to be found in their hardcover quarterly "magazines"— in effect art books. He would go from Barneys to Bergdorf-Goodman—where he drew high fashion, and on to book covers and book illustrations; from *Blueboy* to *Playboy;* from posters to water colors and paintings. Today his illustrations sell online for many hundreds of dollars, while galleries price the few rare acrylics, oils, and watercolors of his that infrequently come up for sale from five to ten thousand dollars.

As we drank tea and I admired his stunning portfolio, George told me that he loved beautiful men; drawing and painting them was also the best way of getting to meet, know, and sometimes blow them, he added. He illustrated with many pictures and sketches he had done, accompanied by libidinous anecdotes that sounded only a bit less so in his retelling. He then said he'd like to draw me, which he did, and which led to our own tryst.

Afterward, I talked about my poetry, which I wanted him to illustrate. He told me our mutual pal had given him some of the poems already and he'd read and liked them. I told him the book's title, *The Deformity Lover,* and said I wanted someone spectacular on the cover. I'd arrange the "deformity" of the title in my own subtle way, I assured Stavrinos. He brought out a drawing he'd begun for a commercial client, who'd changed his mind before George was half done. But the artist had fallen in love with the model and the artwork (taken off a photo in an Italian magazine, he told me) and so he'd continued to work at it even without pay. The man pictured was, in a word, scrumptious: a "polished god" of the first magnitude. We agreed on a price and I took the artwork home, promising a check, which I sent in the next day's mail.

The cover of *The Deformity Lover and Other Poems* received several Society of Illustrators awards, including one for best book cover illustration of the year. I enlarged the cover to poster size, pasted it on a board and took it to my readings. I would leave it outside an hour beforehand, and always find a crowd when I got back. The cover got the book so much attention that reviews printed it full and half-page size. My membership dance club, Flamingo, decided to do a show of George's work while I read a dozen poems from the book, standing in front of the poster, before a party began one Saturday night—the only poetry reading ever given at that discotheque.

Within six months, Stavrinos was illustrating book covers for Avon Books' Paul Monette novels, and eventually for mainstream hardcover books. Stavrinos also unwittingly led a movement in print advertising, returning it to its sources in illustration. Along the way, he casually yet utterly revolutionized the depiction of men in the media. Before, the fanciest gay illustration had been erotic—this side of (when not actual) pornography. Tom of Finland, Rex, and Blade ruled the roost. After George Stavrinos, gay art was gorgeous but it was reserved—at times, glacial—and all the more desirable for that aloofness. Within a year the work of Sadao Hasegawa, Mel Odom, David Martin, and Ron Fowler was suddenly filling gay magazines, gay book racks, gay posters, and gay greeting cards, and did so throughout the seventies and eighties. I knew many of the men used as models, and the artists did not exaggerate their great looks.

Stavrinos and I worked together again—he did the cover illustration of the reprint of my second gay novel, *Late in the Season,* which GPNy put out in 1988, following the Delacorte hardcover and Dell mass-market versions. Luckily it was an already finished piece that George wanted to see in circulation, because who could otherwise afford him by then! Not us.

———

David Martin came to my attention because of his effortless looking line drawings of men on invitations to Manhattan's private dance clubs: The Loft, Flamingo, and later on, the Saint. Soon, Martin's colored drawings were gracing magazines and gay advertising. His illustration for Lighthouse Court is still used by that bed and breakfast today in magazines and gay travel books, decades after Martin employed the art to help pay his hotel bill at the gay resort. One invitation to a party I received had a typically David Martin drawing of a handsome centaur in profile. The model turned out to be author Robert Ferro.

Like George Stavrinos, who had revived illustration art for fashion advertising, David drew and painted friends and tricks and lovers. And David admitted that he had to be half in love (or was it in lust?) with you before he would draw or paint you well. Then David drew you not only well but also somehow better than you ever looked in life. The drawing he did of me in 1982 that ended up on the cover of my collection of short stories *Slashed to Ribbons in Defense of Love* I referred to as "The Breck Shampoo Portrait" because of the gorgeous hair it depicted, even better than my own at the time. That was done with David facing me at my butcher-block dining room table downstairs in my Eleventh Street duplex while I laid out and glued down sheet after sheet of interior pages for a SeaHorse Press book that I was publishing.

David came from Montana and seldom returned there. He was as far away from the idea of a cowboy as you could get. About five foot six, he'd probably had been overweight as a teenager, since he worked out constantly to obtain a cute, if still teddy bearish, body. He had wonderful, curly chestnut hair and he went bald early and ended up being very sensitive about it. He had sparkly, light-colored eyes that I recall as green, but also as light blue and hazel, too. Since David and I never had sex, I have no idea of any of his other physical attributes, but he seemed to feel like he had to do a great deal more than others to remain a member in good standing of the Pines-Flamingo crowd that we ran in, which I never understood, since he was so attractive.

David lived in Chelsea, and he used to stop by my place in the West Village at least once a month. He'd somehow developed the chiropractic ability to "crack" necks, and since I'm a type-A person and always somewhat stressed, he would crack mine every time I saw him. He would then buzz around my place like a bee, sometimes alighting, sometimes not, and often, before I knew it, he would be gone.

Each visit however contained a purpose, no matter how tiny—a question, a suggestion, a hint, a piece of information—and one day while we were having coffee, David began talking about the illustrated books of his youth, which after all had been responsible for his drawing, painting, and becoming an artist in the first place—a way to escape his being a total misfit-oddity in cowboy-country. Since I was a publisher now, David said, why couldn't we work together and do an illustrated book?

I was a very small press publisher, I reminded David. And an illustrated book was an expensive proposition. But we could make a start at one. I found a copy of a manuscript I'd written a few years earlier, titled *An Asian Minor: The True Story of Ganymede*.

I've no memory of where this literary bagatelle had originated, except that it had somehow come out of my re-encountering that well known statement of Gertrude Stein's to take old stories and to "make them new." I'd been reading Ovid's *Metamorphoses* and had come upon the Zeus and Ganymede story, and I remember thinking, *Well this doesn't seem right.* Knowing what I knew of pretty adolescent boys—I'd been one and I'd been enraptured by an even prettier one (Ricky Hersch), I couldn't believe the rape had been as simple as Ovid made it out to be. I was sure there was a great deal of wheeling and dealing back and forth, and more than a little bit of reverse psychology and probably even some real sexual politics. After all, unlike the other hundred or so nymphs, dryads, oreads, princesses, and beautiful youths whose transformations Ovid had chronicled, Ganymede had managed to obtain something unique, something not Semele, nor Leda, nor the gorgeous Adonis, nor even—though she came close—Persephone—achieved: Ganymede got to become an immortal god himself, whisked off to

Mount Olympus to become cup bearer to the gods. To me, what led up to this most fabulous transaction in Greek mythology was the real, and so far untold, story.

Add in Ovid's statement that Ganymede had been the most beautiful of mortals, and another question arose. Zeus reportedly wandered the earth looking for love, but by no means did he travel as often nor as far as Hermes, his official messenger; nor as actively as Apollo, who in his role as the Sun, after all, rose and set daily; and probably not even as often as Ares, god of war, whom we know continues to roam about the earth stirring up international trouble daily. Each of those three Olympians must have gotten a previous look-see at Ganymede. How was it that none of these very persuasive immortals, each of whom let us recall had numberless seductions to his credit, had ended up with the cutie?

My story would in fact tell of each of their encounters with Ganymede and more, it would do it from the point of view of the teen himself. He of course would be smart, and even somewhat objective, as a result of being a very minor player in a really large (albeit royal) family of which he was a most insignificant element—in my tale, Ganymede is 110th in the line of succession to the throne of Troas, founder of the city-state of Troy.

I'd begun the story in March of 1979, and I'd intended it to be part of a trilogy of long tales or novellas, including what would become the short novel, *Looking-Glass Lives,* and the novella, *And Baby Makes Three,* all of which dealt with strange, unusual, even impossible loves.

Work went fast, as I was having lots of fun writing it. I wrote it in a little over a month and I revised it in another five weeks. So it was there to give to David Martin.

Even before I handed the story to him, as I was telling him about it, I could see his eyes light up with the possibilities. It's setting was the classical Hellenic world, and so it would have many beautiful men in it, undressed *a la Grecque,* and of course many classical settings with temples with Ionic and Doric columns, etc. He already loved the idea of the story.

He read *An Asian Minor* that week and called to say he wanted to illustrate it.

He told me some of his ideas for the drawings, which I approved. He even came by with sketches, very vague sketches. There was a problem, however, he said. While David already knew the teenage blond beauty he would use as a model for the title character, and he was also fairly sure an ex-lover would model for Hermes, there were several other characters—and remember these were Olympian gods—whom I would simply have to supply myself.

This was early 1981. I wasn't seeing my second lover, Ed Armour anymore, in fact not even talking to him, which was too bad as he would have made the perfect Apollo. But a few days after David's demand for great beauties, I ended up having a quickie uptown with a former fashion model I'd met at the Pines the previous summer, whom I'd bumped into while visiting a pal in the D&D building. He had bulked up a bit, halfway to his becoming a fullfledged muscle queen a few years later. We went home together, and afterward, as he'd lolled about nude in his unmade bedsheets, still playing with himself and talking dirty to me as I tried to get dressed and get out, I saw a Kodak Instamatic on his dresser, and quickly took a half dozen photos of him.

David couldn't believe the photos, he all but drooled over them, until I pointed out that the guy was a devout bottom. When he did the drawings of Apollo for the book, David used my muscle number's body, but with a different head. Two gods down, two to go.

Zeus, of course, had to be fatherly and fully bearded. Who better, David asked, than the hottest Puerto Rican in New York, Frank Diaz? So I phoned the "Black Widow" and asked if he would mind posing for David, certain he would laugh at my temerity. Instead Frank was pleased and I guess David got to blow him, too.

He didn't get to blow Bob Lowe—at least not that time—who turned out to be the model for Ares, lovestruck god of war in my finished book. By the way, the illustration that David Martin did of Bob—he was more than halfway in love with him—for a double page illustration of Ganymede at a blacksmith's forge, is the single best representation of what Bob Lowe really looked like, better than any fifty photos of him, and for that reason alone, now that Bob is dead, very valuable to me.

Once again, Patrick Merla helped me design the books' interior, typeface, layout, and page design, which ended up being perfect, both "classical" and gracefully contemporary. I selected a slightly heavier, finer, and shinier grade of paper for the interior, and broke down and allowed David the more expensive freedom of a full-color cover, a first for SeaHorse Press. We ended up pleased with the result. *An Asian Minor* was a hit, especially given how arcane its subject matter was: "Gany-who?" I heard people ask when they first heard the title. It went into three printings of 2500 copies each.

Years later fans still talk about the book as a favorite. It was also the first title that I published in a small number of hardcovers, without dust jacket, intended for libraries, but surprisingly also sold to individuals. As there were only a hundred of those, we put in a back page, David numbered and we both signed the books. Recently, a numbered *Asian Minor* hardcover that had listed at $14.95 sold on eBay for $150!

The novella was beloved enough that it was reprinted in 1999 (alas, without David's lovely drawings), in an Alyson Press edition titled *The New York Years,* along with my stories, and again it sold pretty well.

Right after our book came out, David's career shot into high gear. Suddenly he was doing double page spreads for gay magazines like *Blueboy* and *Advocate Men,* as well as a great deal more commercial art. Freed up a bit by the new money he was earning, David also began doing serious painting again. I was hoping to buy one of his acrylics—*The Big Wave* (I even wrote a poem about it), when word came that he'd suddenly moved to Los Angeles.

I visited David in his tiny rented wooden house, high on a hill in Silver Lake overlooking the lake itself, a year and a half later when I was in California on a book tour. Like many artists who first move out West, David was intoxicated by the brilliant light, by the enormous, conspicuous topography, by the colors of the flowers, and by the fantastic shapes of the plants and trees. He was in one of his more fey moods on that particular visit, so I got less information out of him than I'd hoped for, especially about what had motivated his move, and why it had been so sudden. What I did get however were many impressions. And one impression I instinctively picked up was that David had been unhappy in New York but now he was very happy indeed and working daily—not always the case in Chelsea.

Two years later, the next time I was out West, David had moved, some thought to San Diego, and none of the phone numbers I had or got for him worked. I returned to L.A. after readings in Portland, Seattle, and San Francisco, and walked past a gallery in West Hollywood that just happened to be showing David's latest paintings.

I'd gotten hold of a copy of *An Asian Minor* on that trip, and I brought it with me to the gallery. Showing it made it a lot easier for the gallery personnel to see that I knew him and it was okay for them to tell me that David was indeed living in San Diego. In fact I'd missed him by a few days. I wrote to him. They promised to get my letter to David. The art on display wasn't illustration but acrylic paintings, consisting entirely of brilliantly colored scarlet, carmine, blood-red, magenta, yellow-gold, and hot pink bougainvillea's trailing up, over, across, and cascading down pale tan, ecru, gray, and various off-white shades of walls. All of them said California and they were simply gorgeous.

David and I spoke by phone maybe a month after that. He'd been ill, David said, but he was recovering. By then, it was the late eighties, and being ill meant AIDS unless otherwise specified. Speaking to him, I immediately felt the polar chill that always accompanied those horrible, euphemistic words.

A week later, David sent me a photo of a strange, large acrylic painting he'd done of classic male nudes in flimsy boats on a churning sea, their bodies oddly contorted, with red writing smeared over it reading, "Crossing to Safety." Then, shortly after, another painting of a blond man, with thorn-like red lettering across him reading, "Martyr"—evidence, as if any more were needed, that David had contracted HIV, was very ill indeed, and hoping for a miracle. A few months later, I heard that David had never recovered from an opportunistic illness, and had died.

No second illustrated book by me and David ever followed *An Asian Minor.* We had spoken about him illustrating *Looking Glass Lives.* I'd told him the story of that book over the phone and David had sent me a photo in the mail of a painting he had done earlier: a nude man, faced away, his lower body and legs wrapped in dark cloth, classically draped, yet somehow Gothic too, in other words in the style of the novel, and I thought, well maybe David *could* illustrate it. That photo ended up being shown to the art department and was used as the foundation from which an artist worked up a cover illustration for *Looking-Glass Lives* when Alyson published it years later. But despite that cover art, that particular short novel would have another artist work on it and thus have another story.

———

I'd been seeing Howard Cruse's cartoons for years. First in various adult comic books that circulated the East Village in the early seventies: *Bizarre Sex, Heavy Metal,* and *Fangoria,* where Cruse's funny, counterculture strip *Barefootz* was a welcome relief from R. Crumb and some of the other, heavier-footed cartoonists.

Both Cruse and Crumb made the move to the *Village Voice,* where they reached a larger audience. Then in 1980, *Gay Comix* appeared on newsstands— a comic book co-founded by Howard and always featuring his work. One strip, *Wendel,* was about a young gay man, and the plotlines detailed his relationships with his lover Ollie, his gay-positive parents, Ollie's son and ex-wife, and various other friends and family. A funny, often moving strip, *Wendel* explored a variety of gay and lesbian issues. It moved as a strip to the popular *Advocate,* where it went on until 1989, when the editors changed formats and eliminated comic strips from the magazine.

It was a natural for GPNy to talk to Cruse about doing the strip as a book.

Wendel was published by us as a book in 1985 and sold out its first printing. A few years later, St. Martin's Press continued the series with *Wendel on the Rebound* (1989); *Wendel All Together,* a compendium of the two books, along with stray strips that had never gotten between covers, came out in 2001. Why there wasn't a second GPNy printing and why we never asked for a second volume is the real story.

During our preliminary discussions with Howard about the book, he explained in great detail that the book had to be done to a particular size and no other, in order for the right number of strips to fit each page and its facing page. He specified the paper we needed to use in order to ensure that the far heavier than usual comic book inks would take but not smudge. He needed the covers to fulfill certain other exacting standards, and of course be four color. Once we had agreed to cost-check all these and get back to him, Howard said, "It would make it all easier, if I art directed the book, and laid it all out, inside and out."

This, of course, meant that he would assume a huge amount of control over the book. So Larry, Terry, and I discussed it, and thought, well why not? It would save us the work and the effort and it would make Howard happy. We contacted our usual printer's representative, the estimable and even-tempered Alvin Greenberg, and told him what we were doing. I sent him copies of the comic strip so he'd get a good idea of what we planned. We gave him Howard's phone number. They spoke and it looked like a done deal.

Because the dimensions Howard had required required an off-size, in other words, a size not readily cut and bound at most printers/binders, it would be a more expensive project. Ditto because of the weight of the paper and of course the cover stock, which was thicker and heavier than we usually required.

Wendel was one of a dozen books we were doing in our most prolific pair of GPNy years, 1984-85, and so in a way we welcomed the two of them, Alvin and Howard, working together, with so little for us to do.

Cruse got it done and out to Alvin and the printer. Howard went through the blueprints for the final book, made whatever corrections were needed, and seemed, when we spoke on the phone, if not happy, then at least not unhappy.

The book was then printed and bound, and we received two early copies by overnight mail as usual, and I had one delivered by hand to Cruse, who again seemed if not happy then not unhappy with the result.

I don't know what plans to celebrate the book the author/illustrator had previously made. If he'd planned a public event he sure hadn't told any of us at GPNy about it, and to my knowledge there wasn't one. The book had never seemed to require a send-off. It was already a very well known and well liked quantity; it had appeared in our catalog and I'd reported to Cruse that it had gotten substantial book and distributor pre-orders. So I was a little confused when Howard phoned one day and asked where the book was.

I contacted Alvin and was told the book was being shipped in a few days. I phoned Howard and told him.

"What day?" he wanted to know.

What was the difference? It would arrive and I'd get a call from our warehouse and go down and have the copies brought up to our warehouse space. That's what I told him.

No! Howard had to know precisely what day the book was coming. Then, when I'd managed to obtain that very difficult to obtain piece of news, he wanted to know when the book was being shipped, what day, what hour, what time. Then we had that info, he needed to know where in the United States, the truck actually was.

Now I'd met control queens in my day—at times, Terry Helbing could be one—but I'd never encountered anything quite like this. Had there been a signing, a TV appearance, something timed to the book's arrival, I might understand his anxiety. His was the thirtieth or fortieth book we'd published. There was a system in place. The system worked. He'd get the book. It would arrive. Despite all this, he needed to know every single detail. Details *we* didn't know. Details we didn't *need* to know.

Howard's phone calls continued daily, even hourly the last day of the three-day shipping journey, and I was freely making up things—"It's in Paramus, New Jersey, now. The driver stopped at a diner and phoned in." I even began making up hassles—an accident in the Holland Tunnel: the book would have to be delayed—if only to amuse myself.

But I wasn't amused. Two other authors had expressed similar types of publication over-anxiety—Clark Henley for *The Butch Manual,* and later on Robert Glück, for his *Jack The Modernist.* But these were sweet, self-aware people, conscious of the fact that they were acting crazy and being terrible *nudges,* and that made it a bit easier. Not Cruse.

The books arrived. Howard actually arrived at the warehouse by taxi as they were being unloaded and got his author's copies. And that's the last time Larry, Terry, or I spoke to him.

Wendel had indeed been presold by its longtime *Advocate* appearances. How small that presale was, we soon found out. The book sold its first 2,800 copies and then stopped dead. Orders thereafter trickled in literally one by one for months. Two years later, while doing royalty statements, we faced the prospect of reprinting it. The three of us agreed that there was no way we were going to have anything further to do with Cruse, not in *this* lifetime. We reverted the rights to the author. If he perused his royalty statement he should have figured out why.

———

Ron Fowler first came to GPNy's attention early on and he ended up doing the art for more of our titles than any other single artist. For years, Larry Mitchell had been a summer resident of North Truro on Cape Cod, a tiny, mostly residential village off Route 6, just south of Provincetown. He and poet Ron Schreiber co-owned a wonderful eighteenth-century house with a variety of additions put on during the nineteenth and twentieth centuries. I've described this house in some detail in part nine of my novel, *The Book of Lies;* it is where fictional author Dominic de Petrie (whom some reviewers thought was a self-portrait) lives in the novel. In fact I myself did stay at the wonderfully funky old house a few weeks at a time, usually after Labor Day, along with Bob Lowe, from 1984 to 1990, and with other friends from 1991 to 1993. Larry Mitchell, his partner Richard, and whatever other friends, family, and crew Larry assembled around him, have spent the early part of each summer there for several decades.

It was on the Cape that Larry first encountered Ron Fowler's work. A native of North Carolina, Ron had moved to New York City during the late sixties, but by the midseventies he'd fled the gay circuit party scene there, finding it far too distracting. (He was terrifically cute, with a good body and sparkling, sea blue eyes; no wonder he'd been distracted!) In P-Town, Ron had found himself a home and studio off Mechanic Street, where he lived and worked for the next twenty years, and where I visited with the sense of wonder of a child in a toyshop.

When Ron Fowler began doing the artwork for Provincetown's biggest annual street party, Carnival, he elevated those posters from disposable announcement to the realm of instant collectible classics. Larry Mitchell, in fact, had collected a few posters himself and hung them on his walls at home. That's where I first saw them, and I thought they were great, too.

A month or so later, I was in Boston doing a reading at Waterstone's and I phoned Fowler and asked if I could come to the Cape to see what he was working on. We had a blizzard the next day and I awoke in journalist/poet Rudy Kikel's apartment, facing three feet of snow on the ground.

Despite the blizzard, there did turn out to be planes flying to Provincetown, as the Cape had only gotten a dusting of snow. So I trudged through slush out to a cab, and at the airport, found myself stepping into a single engine four-seater where I turned out to be the only passenger. The pilot gestured me up to the copilot's seat, and handed me a broom to sweep snow off the plane's wings on my side.

Given this nervous-making, inauspicious beginning, it turned out to be a gorgeous sunny New England morning, a great air flight over Boston Bay with its many islands glinting in the sun and a perfect arrival. Ron picked me up in his car, and once arrived at Ron's studio I looked through all of his art he offered—paintings, drawings, posters, pastels—and realized he was the real thing.

Before I flew home the next day, I told Ron all about SeaHorse Press and GPNy and I asked him to send us sketches in black and white to consider for our second GPNy title.

Three of Canadian Ron Harvie's stories had been published in magazines and an anthology by that time, and I mailed copies of those to Fowler. A few weeks later, he sent back a sketch of a imperfect male statue, unfinished, eyeless, still being chiseled out of its stone, but for all that, astonishingly beautiful. Larry, Terry, and I looked at this illustration and at the three other sketches Ron Fowler had sent and agreed this one would work perfectly for the chiseled prose and classical poise of Harvie's stories in his first collection, *The Voltaire Smile.*

For Ron Harvie's second book of stories two years later, Fowler did a more hard-edged, less clear-cut illustration. This other book of short stories was titled *Men Working,* and the black-and-white cover art showed two working men, both hirsute, muscled, and hot, with a brilliant orange "Men Working" sign, just like that taken off your local highway project, serving as the title background.

We loved that artwork, too. So a few years later, when GPNy ended up publishing the hardcover edition of my first memoir, *Ambidextrous,* it was only natural that we would contact Fowler again and ask him to do the cover illustration. I don't know how much of the book Ron actually read before starting work—the better part of prudence is to never, ever ask. But he came up with a brilliant way of rendering not only the content of the book, but what was involved in the act of writing the book: two sets of hands—a child's holding a crayon and an adult's with a fountain pen—both of them simultaneously putting down the title on the book, beginning with the grade-school lettering of the little boy and ending with the grown-up, penned script of the man.

The cover was nominated for an Art Directors of America award (our second, after *The Deformity Lover*) and a Society of Illustrators award (our third). Thus, you can imagine my surprise and distaste two years later when I finally allowed a mainstream publisher, Dutton/New American Library, to purchase the paperback rights to my memoir. They ended up publishing the book with a bland photo that mimicked Ron's illustration of two pairs of hands, but without any of the spark, significance, or originality of his.

Ambidextrous was Ron's first full-color cover for GPNy, but in truth it was really transitional between black and white and full color. The wraparound cover art he did for the 1985 GPNy novel, *The Finding of David,* with it's striking male portrait and its brilliant use of the colors and shape of the American flag for what was a political gay novel was, I still consider, complete and perfect. I continue to believe that book never got attention on any of the levels it should have, including its artwork.

Ron would do one more book project, not so much for SeaHorse Press or GPNy, as for me. It would be Ron's triumph as an illustrator, and one of the best illustrated books of the period.

10

GPNy and the Art of the Gay Photograph

In a volume of recently published letters of Henry James there's one that's both funny and revealing. James, by then in his mid-sixties, writes about attending the memorial service for a late-Victorian poet of little repute today at Westminster Cathedral in London. Naturally the place was filled with dignitaries, and the rows around James were filled with writers and artists. Epistolary James is less than impressed. He can only write about the younger men in the rows in front of him whom he knew and who he reported were busily passing among themselves photographic images of young, unclad Sicilian men. The aging, evidently unhappy Master writes to his interlocutress in high dudgeon, remarking that there are times and places for such sensuous frivolity. Evidently, the commemoration was not, in James's view, one of those occasions.

What strikes me most about this incident is that it's so believable, and that it could happen here and now, or tomorrow. Secondarily, and equally significant, we pretty much know what those very photos were that young men such as Hugh Walpole and Somerset Maugham were passing around and salivating over that so annoyed James: Wilhelm Von Gloeden's still remarkable shots of young boys, nude or draped with furled cloth, amid ruins and upon terraces and amid authentic landscapes all reminiscent or redolent of Greek and Roman classics.

It's thanks to private collectors (and some of von Gloeden's models themselves, including the Lebanese poet Kahlil Gibran, author of *The Prophet*) that those photos continue to exist, hidden away for decades as they were from prying eyes, from prudes, and especially from Benito Mussolini's *fascisti*. The erotic photo of so many adolescent jokes has a long, ignoble, yet quite wonderful history. Mixing it with serious nude art skews the value upward more than a little. As many liberated exhibits beginning in the late-seventies showed, males photographed as sexual objects may be thought of as beginning with Thomas Eakins, Eadweard Muybridge, Frank Sutcliffe, and von Gloeden, but they were continued by men (and women) of talent, among them Imogen Cunningham, Berenice Abbott, Georges Brassaï, F. Holland Day, George Platt Lynes, Starr Ockenga, and Jacqueline Livingstone. The gay nature artist and *Life* magazine photographer Minor White showed in his work that journalism, history, and the homoerotic can come together beautifully.

By the time that my post-Stonewall generation had come out, the erotic male photos we saw were of a different order than those altogether. Our main resources were not art, but a bastard kind of art, to be found in the same big city downtown bookstores that sold gay magazines and gay-themed pulp paperbacks. Sometimes the photos were only available via mail-order ads. The American Model Guild (AMG) was the name I recall that produced the most. The artists all had names like Bruce of Hollywood, or Jim French ("frenching" was pre-Stonewall code for fellatio, as "browning" was code for anal sex, so I always wondered if it was a made-up name). The photos were usually studio bound or taken at beaches, with young men in thongs, close-fitting bathing suits, and loincloths, holding spears and shields, hoisting athletic equipment, or playing at cowboys. They were young and cute, with perfect bodies, although the "Indians" looked to be of dark Irish-American extraction.

Those photos, however, were difficult to obtain and thus rare, and so they held an erotic charge that cannot really be understood today, or in fact any time after that morning in 1981 when Calvin Klein put a seventy-foot photo of a beautiful man, nude but for jockey shorts, on a Times Square billboard, and ushered in the age of the modern male nude.

Today we can, and we do, regularly see men in various states of undress everywhere—in print, movies, on TV—with their genitals suggested when not actually visible lumps in their underwear. In 1969, young men without shirts were told by policemen to put them on or face indecency charges—unless they were at a gym, beach, or pool. The other infrequent sites for acceptable male nudity were limited to school and club locker rooms. Clearly this was a period profoundly opposed to masculine beauty throughout America and in fact the world. It was, however, an age in which nude or seminude women were displayed a great deal, almost always as festishized objects, and in the process demeaned to the point that the existence of the feminist movement seemed a natural reaction.

This however was the society, the civilization—if one can even call it that—in which my generation, including a handful of brave and daring photographers, grew up, and they were as stymied and infuriated as the rest of us who loved male beauty and the masculine figure. In his introduction to Allen Ellenzweig's pioneering book *The Homoerotic Photograph* (1992), scholar and SeaHorse press author George Stambolian writes that by the 1970s, that changed because "gay men were actively redefining themselves and transforming their bodies" in protest against this culture of antimasculine beauty and the homogenization of the corporate man in America.

Physically, this could be done by stripping nude and by streaking, or running naked through public events, which became so popular it happened once on an Oscar telecast. Or else we could remain seminude publicly as much as possible and as often as possible in other ways. Watch the 1971 documentary movie *Woodstock* and you can't fail to notice how purposely undressed that historical concert's young male attendees were; this was clearly part of that generation's revolution.

We could also dress and act as sexy and alluring as possible. Gay men of the seventies sported T-shirts one size too small that stopped above our belts to reveal our flat tummies and navels, along with Levi's 501s with the top two buttons left undone to display our groins and even a bit of public hair. Even more provocatively, we used to wear the *bottom* two buttons of our 501s undone, signifying the ease with which we could pull out our cocks for sexual action.

It was a era when straight liberals regularly declared, "We don't mind your being gay. Just don't flaunt it." But what was the point of being young, gay, and good-looking, unless you could flaunt it—and make straight guys nervous, or even better, nervously turned on, at the same time?

The photographers among us in those years that went out of their way to flaunt what we were all trying to do, and how we were sexually acting out via our appearances. They both provoked and apollonized male beauty in pictures that are so sudden, so stunning, so potent, and so dangerous with erotic charge that thirty years later they still shock, appal, excite, and humiliate viewers.

Stambolian writes in that introduction of the very strong reactions to some of this gay male photography in 1978 by critics, art reviewers, and eventually by members of the U.S. government itself, to explain how seriously (and it seems quite successfully) gay men transformed ourselves and the male figure itself into a sex object equal to that of women. He adds:

> Not surprisingly, the same criticisms were leveled at the gay novels of the period: Andrew Holleran's *Dancer From the Dance* and Larry Kramer's *Faggots,* the objects of particularly vicious attacks, both appeared in 1978, together with Edmund White's *Nocturnes for the King of Naples,* and followed in 1979 by Felice Picano's *The Lure.* These novelists reflected aspects of the same new gay world depicted in the photographs of Mapplethope and Tress. They, too, redefined gay sexuality and elaborated a new iconography of sensual bodies and erotic sites. Indeed, photographic shows became cultural events

where photographers, painters, novelists, poets and others could meet and learn of each other's works.

This was true. We were all regularly and maliciously attacked by straight writers and reviewers, and sometimes even more malevolently from within the gay community. At the 1994 book party and photographic show at New York's Seagram Building for Mark Thompson's book *The Long Journey: Thirty Years of The Advocate,* for which I wrote one chapter's introductory essay, I met a fellow who'd been a cofounder of and cohort at Boston's *Gay Community News.* When I told him I'd just come back from a ten-city book tour of Germany for the thirteenth anniversary there of my novel, *The Lure,* he said, "We did everything in our power to destroy you and that book."

I replied, "Yes, and look where we are now. *The Lure* has sold millions of copies in a half dozen languages and is the most popular gay book ever in the German language—and your newspaper is defunct."

The Violet Quill Club was unconditionally present at the Robert Samuel Gallery when it opened, as well as at Leslie Lohmann and other galleries, and we attended most of their bigger events in force. There we became acquainted with a variety of artists, among them a young, talented, still unknown yet very ambitious photographer, Robert Mapplethorpe, and his older lover, Sam Wagstaff, who hosted the first post-Stonewall exhibits of American homoerotic photos, featuring the work of Mapplethorpe, Arthur Tress, Georges Dureau, Joel-Peter Witkin, and several others. Co-owners and daily operators of the gallery were Sam Hardison, Calvin Selfridge, and Steven Miller Myrick. When Wagstaff died, New York's Museum of Modern Art acquired his enormous personal collection—which its famous director, Thomas Hoving, publicly called the foundation of the museum's photo collection.

Mapplethorpe was already doing the range of work for which he became first infamous and then world famous: nude figures of men, children, and women—commissioned formal portraits he began with friends and acquaintances before branching out to corporation executives, the classic flowers and other still lifes, and, of course, those carefully posed and costumed photos of himself and those men around him in sadomasochistic, bondage, and other outré sexual positions and milieus.

The photo I would end up using, and that I believe was the first Mapplethorpe photo to appear on a book cover, was completely different than any of those. It was a half body shot he'd done of his younger brother, Raymond, then just seventeen, fully clothed, with a leather jacket thrown over one shoulder, as though he was about to step outside or had just stepped inside. Raymond looked clean-cut yet seductive, since Mapplethorpe seemed intrinsically incapable of not locating and provoking the particular individual sexual identity and force of anyone he shot, from infants to elderly people.

Author Brad Gooch told me of this particular photo's existence after I'd accepted his book, *Jailbait and Other Stories,* for SeaHorse Press, saying he thought the shot would work well on the book's cover. I asked if Mapplethorpe would allow us to purchase visual rights for the book. Brad said he thought so, as he'd already broached the subject.

I had met Robert a dozen times by then, and my on and off boyfriend of the midseventies, Scott Façon, had worked as Mapplethorpe's assistant for several months at his studio on Bond Street, and had become his protégé. So I phoned one day and spoke to Robert about Brad's book. Typical of Mapplethorpe, he was businesslike, and we discussed all the needed elements involved, payment, how I intended to use the photo, how all rights reverted to him after use, how I needed only a copy, not anything like an original, how I'd credit him wherever the photo or book cover appeared in print. It was all cut and dry and professional. End of subject.

Later that day, he phoned me. It was around midnight and I'd just gone to bed and was reading. This time he was anything but businesslike. He wanted to talk about Brad Gooch, who was as handsome a young man as any in the city, a fashion model, and to my knowledge hooked up with another really cute and talented man, Howard Brookner, a filmmaker, whom I thought had one of the best male asses in New York City.

Robert wanted to talk about Brad and Howard. He mentioned several bizarre rumors about them I'd also heard and that I said I believed to be totally untrue, always with the proviso that one never really knew what any two people actually did when they were together. That subject exhausted, Robert then went on to talk about the person more or less between us, Scott Façon, who was as handsome as Brad and probably slept around far more widely in Manhattan, and so I assumed had also had sex with Robert. Among other attributes, Scott—with his dark hair and close-cut moustache and beard—had one of the best profiles of that era. It was an absolutely typical perversity of Mapplethorpe's that he would photograph that terrific profile close up, then cover it with a jockstrap so you could hardly make it out.

I mentioned this to Robert, and he got more enthused, talking about other ways he wanted to shoot Scott—things as far-out as those in the photos Jesse Helms would later denounce on the floor of the U.S. Senate, all of which I was certain that I'll-try-anything-once Scott would go along with.

Even more excited, Robert then began talking about what Scott had said about the sex Scott and I had had, and more specifically, about my genitals. I'd already seen Robert's famous photos of black men with huge dicks, and told him to calm down, that mine wasn't anything like that.

"Maybe not, but Scott described it in great detail and he said that it was classically proportioned and really nice, and I just know I've got to photograph it here in my studio."

So despite the hour and me having to get dressed again I ended up being persuaded to get in a taxi at 12:45 AM and go to the Lower East Side for an impromptu photo with blow job session—because Robert was definitely sweetening the pill.

As I was leaving his studio an hour later, he showed me a file cabinet drawer he said was filled with photos of men's genitalia he'd taken over the past decade while having sex with them—among which I wasn't too surprised to recognize a few dicks I'd seen and had myself. He had hundreds of such photos he said, and he was premeditating a huge exhibit of them all once he was better known and, crucially, once he'd reached the magic number of one thousand. He'd then add his own cock, Robert said, and call it "One Thousand and One Nights."

Increasingly, however, he was getting more picky about the guys he would include. While he assured me that mine would go into the show, he told me a few recent ones he'd done were only so-so. He needed fresh blood and had been told that Brazil, Germany, and the Baltic States had many handsome penises. He was thinking of going to those countries to reach the magic number. He also handed me a copy of the formal photo of his brother Raymond I was to use on the book cover, which I never mentioned receiving to Brad, who also gave me a copy some weeks later.

When I was art directing *Jailbait* several months after our impromptu photo session, I phoned Robert again to inquire about cropping the photo and wrapping it around the spine of the book. Because it would deform the photo, I wouldn't do it without the artist's express permission. I explained what I wanted to do in great detail and Mapplethorpe approved. He didn't even need to see what I was doing beforehand, as I had offered. The phone call was once again all business.

A few days later I saw him at some big gay cultural event we both attended, and I couldn't help but notice that whenever he met a man, his eyes immediately dropped to his crotch, checking out his basket even before looking at his face. Noticing what I was noticing, a friend of mine said bitchily, "He's really cock crazed," and sailed off into the crowd.

I thought, *If he only knew how much!*

I recalled all this a decade and a half later, after Robert and that bitchy pal were dead, when I began to read Patricia Morrisroe's deluded biography of Mapplethorpe. Not only wasn't Robert in any way interested in women sexually, as Morrisroe tried to persuade readers (we used to kid him mercilessly about Lisa Lyons, the woman bodybuilder he photographed so often, and whom he shot because Robert said she looked like a guy), but because Robert was, as were many other gay men I knew in the seventies—and as my pal had so succinctly put it that night—truly cock crazed.

I think Robert did make it to Germany and Brazil, if not to Estonia, Latvia, and Lithuania, but I have no idea if he reached the magic number of photos he was aiming for. After he died, a foundation quickly and tightly formed to exploit his work, which they have done very methodically, extremely professionally, and for great profit.

Today you can go into any art museum store and get books large and small, as well as booklets, boxed greeting cards, postcards, and all sizes of reproductions of Robert Mapplethorpe flowers, Robert Mapplethorpe rooms, Robert Mapplethorpe cats, and even a very, very tasteful collection of Robert Mapplethorpe nudes. But there isn't a single "Robert Mapplethorpe dicks" among them. I even wonder if the foundation would admit to the existence of those many hundreds of tongue-licked-to-a-bright-shine penis photos in the collection. Hypocritical and sanitized as it's all become, I somehow doubt it.

———

Not one of the other photographers SeaHorse Press or GPNy used for cover art—Arthur Tress, Roy Blakey, or Bill Rice, for example—were then as famous as Robert (although Tress is certainly well regarded today). But some of their art was definitely as good. Tress's photo of two boys peeling the Band-Aid off one of their legs, which I put on the cover of Kevin Esser's man-boy love novel *Streetboy Dreams,* addressed the issues inside the book right up front with its sexiness, its vulnerability, and especially by showing how easily hurt youth can be. The photo, shot from above looking down, titled "First Aid," came to my attention while leafing through a collection of Tress's work that was published in 1979.

Tress was a New Yorker, the son of a working-class mother and well-to-do father who divorced when he was a child, providing him with experience and insight into both worlds and yet membership in neither. He'd gotten a camera when he was twelve years old, and being a shy, gentle, and self-effacing youth, he had used the lens both as protection and as a way to get deeper into life and into other people's lives.

All this I learned from Tress during the two afternoons we spent together after I asked to use "First Aid" on a SeaHorse press book jacket. He lived on Riverside Drive on the Upper West Side, but both times we met in the park across the street from his building, possibly because he didn't want me to be influenced by his (I supposed quite affluent) living conditions. We hung out for several hours, getting to know each other. I believe I'd given him the manuscript of the book I wanted his photo to illustrate. Again, I have no idea if he ever read it. I did tell him the story of the book. And I think even more importantly, during those two afternoon forays along the Hudson River, one uptown in his neighborhood and one down in mine, Arthur came to know me well enough to trust that I would use his art well.

Books like *Streetboy Dreams* about man-boy love are quite rare today, after a decade-and-a-half-long campaign against the practice, so it may be worth explaining a bit about its past. Novels about man-boy love had been published since before the Stonewall Riots in a quantity and with an openness difficult to believe today. One of the first I came across, *The Asbestos Diary* (1963), was so well written that when it came out, literary friends of Vladimir Nabokov opined that he was the real author behind what they considered a transparent pseudonym, Casimir Dukahz, and that this book was his male version of *Lolita*. The first novel published by Winston Leyland's Gay Sunshine Press was a man-boy love story, *O Bom-Crioulo: The Black Man and the Cabin Boy* (1982), an English translation of author Adolfo Caminha's maritime adventure story in which a cabin boy becomes lovers with a first mate.

The Asbestos Diary (the contents were too "hot" to handle, so it needed "protective" covers) was serious yet humorous, a delightful, witty, episodic book about how men and boys came together in a variety of erotic encounters and sites, each tale independent yet linked, à la Scheherazade. It was clear-eyed, objective, and unsentimental. It's a classic that went into multiple printings through its underground publisher and has remained in print ever since. An online site says of the book and its sequels, "These rollicking accounts of amorous encounters with a bevy of teenage charmers are full of puns and double entendres, filled with situations recalling French farce and slapstick comedy. Seldom is erotic writing so humorous."

The manuscript I received from Kevin Esser over the transom at SeaHorse Press, was something different. *Streetboy Dreams,* like another book SeaHorse Press put out the following year, Pete Fisher's *Dreamlovers,* was clearly a book about gay romantic and sexual fantasies. Fisher's book told two stories—one about a special ed teacher and his erotic yet completely hands-off encounter with a teenage student; the second an adult-on-adult erotic inhabiting the insular fictional world of the television serial *Star Trek,* something common today, a fanzine novel, years ahead of its time

While Esser's novel was about a boy lover, the two boys in the book were fully developed characters way beyond mere erotic fantasies; it was their very depth as people, no matter their age, that made for the plot's complications and its insight. A further complication arose from what many would reflexively call its "colonialism," because one of the boys was of Hispanic heritage. Despite all these potential traps, Esser's novel is nimble, true, readable, and quite good. It resonates and it teaches.

Kevin went on to publish five more books, two of them on a similar theme, that SeaHorse wouldn't be around to publish. *Something Like Happiness* (1993) and *One Last Love* both found publishers abroad and international readerships. His sci-fi novel, *Dance of the Warriors* (1998), was about a mid-twenty-first-century America run by the church, opposed by rebellious gangs of teenage boys. That book was good enough to make a best gay novel list. Esser's second book for GPNy, two years after the first, was of a completely different stripe. *Mad to Be Saved* (1985) was a splendidly written, ecstatic, neo-Scott Fitzgerald romp through the many absurdities and wonders of being eighteen, at school, and on your own for the first time in your life.

Anyone who has ever seen my lovers, boyfriends, or life partner knows I'm anything but a boy lover—give me big, muscled men over thirty, thank you, and if they're twice my size, I can handle them just fine. Despite this, I was approached twelve years ago to write for *Gayme,* the newsletter of the North American Man Boy Love Association (NAMBLA), about the many attacks on their group. I did so in an essay titled "Effacing the Boy," which pointed out that any ban against man-boy love is as much against children having sex as it is against so-called predators. I wrote that this kind of ban is sanctioned in our society only because so many otherwise powerless adults have a deep compulsion to completely manipulate and control their children; it has less to do with protecting them than we think. In the essay, I described my own brief "romance" at age ten with a man in his twenties. I had one and a half times his IQ, and I talked him into the relationship, and while it lasted I did whatever I had to to keep him with me. If I'd known about sex, I would have unquestionably used that, too, to keep him interested. The only thing out of my power was his ending it. He fled me, fled town, left his marriage, and reenlisted in the navy—where I hope he had lots of gay sex.

NAMBLA, and then when they voiced support for it, ACT UP and the Lesbian Avengers, were banned from joining the nationally organized march through Manhattan on the twenty-fifth anniversary of the Stonewall Riots in 1994, a shameful and cowardly deed for which I raked organizer Morris Kight over the coals. Those three spurned groups decided to march separately, without official sanction or parade permits, and they invited me, scholar Camille Paglia, and poet Allen Ginsberg to be grand marshals to lead their parade. We all showed up, along with a New York City Police Department estimate of ten thousand other "gay renegades" (although Ginsberg was ill and only marched a short distance) and we were not in the least bit sorry to be there—and not at the official parade.

———

The photograph on the cover of Gavin Dillard's first SeaHorse Press book of poetry, *Notes from a Marriage,* reveals a little-known side of the multitalented John Preston, best known for his many anthologies and for his S/M novel *Mister Benson.* Yes, John did that sweet and tender photo, which I believe— along with the poems and the pistachio ice cream green background—helped that book sell over seven thousand copies.

I didn't know John that well, as we pretty much ran in different circles. But we had many friends in common, among them Andrew Holleran. For years I wondered why it was that I was the only well-known American gay author never asked be part of Preston's anthologies. I even asked Preston about it in person once on a ferry boat party in San Francisco connected to the OutWrite Conference. He said he wasn't angry or upset with me, so I had to assume he just didn't like my work. Fine with me.

Several years after all this, however, Dr. Charles Silverstein called and asked if I'd be interested in coauthoring *The New Joy of Gay Sex,* a substantial revision of the 1975 edition he'd written with Edmund White. Charles had contacted Ed to rejoin him. Ed, who was living in Paris, expressed doubts, and told Silverstein that he felt out of touch with American gay life, that he was married, and that he wasn't the right man for the job. Typically generous, Ed then recommended me to Charles, who knew who I was and even remembered me from the Gay Activist Alliance's Saturday night dance parties at the firehouse on Greene Street in the late sixties. Silverstein admitted he'd not read anything of mine in a while and asked me for a book to read. I sent him *Ambidextrous.*

But I also wondered aloud why Charles didn't contact John Preston, who seemed to me to be the natural choice to write on the subject. After all, Preston was a fine feuilletonist, writing easily and well on a variety of topics. Coauthoring *The New Joy of Sex* seemed so appropriate for him.

No, no. Charles assured me, Preston wouldn't do, and there was a sort of incomprehensible gabble of mumbled semi-explanation which I didn't then nor later ever make sense of.

Bad blood between them, I assumed. Then, after I'd begun to meet with Charles to discuss the project in more depth, I was reminded of Charles's partner, the quicksilver, sharp-tongued, ultracritical (especially on literary matters) William Bory, and it dawned on me: *maybe Bory hates Preston.* But then Bory also hated my writing. In fact, Bory pretty much hated everyone's writing after the time of—from what I could figure out in our rare conversations—the Roman poet Virgil.

Even later on, I wondered if some other element wasn't at work in Charles's choosing me: maybe he was nervous about his own writing ability. Whatever was behind it, once we got to writing, the partnership worked in an unexpected manner. I ended up doing most of the purely scientific, technical, and medical pieces, and Charles ended up writing most of the creative and imaginative ones. Partly this was because Bob Lowe had just died and I was so utterly shell-shocked that for a year I probably couldn't have written anything more emotionally demanding than facts. But we had divided the tasks from the beginning, and Charles had pretty much taken on the more creative ones. During the writing process, I did, however, hear from others that Preston was deeply offended that I'd gotten to do *The New Joy of Sex* and not him, and I couldn't blame him.

A few years later I heard that Preston was dying from complications from AIDS when the opportunity to interview him for a major gay magazine came my way. It had to do with the publication of a book of his autobiographical pieces, *Winter Light: Confessions of a Yankee Queer* (1995). I decided to go further than make amends—I would do an in-depth one-on-one with him. The book had moved me greatly, especially its portrait of him as a young boy from the wrong side of the tracks growing up deprived in many ways and trying to compensate with his innate intelligence, his diligence, and his hard work. There's a scene in which young John is turned down by the very WASPy

Athenaeum, a private school that invariably led to the Ivy League and to the concomitant glittering prizes of life. Not only wasn't John admitted, but he was in effect told by a snooty Boston Brahmin that it would be a complete waste of time and money to school him, and that he would never amount to anything.

By this time, I had come to believe that for decades I, too, had been the victim of prejudice, in academic life and in my chosen career. Not very subtle prejudice either and that I'd been shoved away from lucrative posts, ignored for honors and awards, and especially from foundations and grants—first because of my being of Italian American heritage ("Wouldn't you be happier as a barber?" a collegian at Princeton asked when he heard I was interviewing for the Woodrow Wilson Fellowship) and then because of my being openly gay. So naturally, I identified with Preston's portrait of himself.

During the phone interview (he lived in Maine) I brought up the incident he had written of. John was forthcoming until I told him how much I identified with him.

"You?" he replied. "How could you? You're the New York literary establishment! You're everything I've fought against all my life."

And so, to my astonishment, it came out. I don't know if I ever convinced him otherwise. I do know that in the rest of that interview and conversation I felt like we made some steps toward a rapprochement, and maybe we actually did. Because a few years after his death, that piece I'd done, titled "The Last Interview" prefaced and led off the articles and remembrances in an anthology published by his close friends a few years after his death. They had gone out of their way to invite me in.

11

GPNy Fulfills Its Mission

Good timing is probably the most skittishly difficult of all the human arts. When precisely to launch or even when to arrive is often critical to acceptance. When, even more gracefully, to depart is even more crucial; at least to how you will be remembered.

For Larry, Terry, and me, the world produced its signs and wonders aplenty during the 1980s, but individual events during three months of March in the 1980s stand out as most relevant to us and to what we were hoping to achieve with our individual and the combined Gay Presses of New York. During them Harvey Fierstein received a Tony Award for *Torch Song Trilogy,* and the *Writer's Magazine* featured *Slashed to Ribbons in Defense of Love.*

At the farthest end of the decade, on March 21, 1988, longtime *Newsweek* book reviewer Walter Clemons published his article about gay literature and books, "Out of the Closet and onto the Shelves." Clemons wrote of "the revolution that has taken place in literature whereby a recent minority has by dint of their quality and sales and newsworthiness staked out major ground in contemporary American writing."

The irony, of course, in this last case, is that the person who was behind that article, who for months on end wooed and eventually persuaded Clemons to write it, my pal Robert Ferro, would be dead in half a year; his partner, Michael Grumley, in two months. Two other Violet Quillians, Chris Cox and George Whitmore, would be dead inside of another year—all four obituaries putting a grisly death's head emphasis on the post-Stonewall period.

At the time, naturally enough, and despite AIDS, we at GPNy saw the three above-named events not as a caesura, not as signs of closure, but pointing toward an even more hopeful future. And it's true that there would be one more fairly good decade of flourishing American GLBT literature before the inevitable decline and mainstreaming.

———

Around the time of each of those three GPNy occurrences, there would be corresponding high-water marks for myself as an editor and publisher: Renée Vivien's *Woman of the Wolf and Other Stories* and Allen Bowne's play *Forty-Deuce* in 1983, and the novels *Jack the Modernist* by Robert Glück in1985 and *Love In Relief* by Guy Hocquenghem in 1988.

These books stand out from others done by SeaHorse or GPNy because they arrived on my desk fairly unexpectedly and didn't seem to fit into my/our publishing program. In retrospect, they stand out even more because of their importance in GLBT literature, past, present, and, I believe, future; and also because they are so totally, utterly different.

When I'd first begun SeaHorse Press, I'd written to friends about my hopes for the new press to provide "fine and accessible literature." And until Robert Glück's manuscript arrived, I'd gone out of my way to ensure that everything I published easily fit both parameters. With these four books, however, I began aiming for something more, partly in the belief that I'd already fulfilled my mission as an editor and could intuit where various strands of gay and lesbian writing were headed. But also in the belief that gays were strong enough readers, bright, and open enough to be able to take on and absorb more than the usual.

This point of view is of course in total contrast to the current view of a lot of GLBT publishing, based as it appears to be on the assumption that the lowest common denominator is all that gays and lesbians want to, or are capable, of reading. Many lesbians were already complaining that, for the most part, Naiad Press was doing the same for women's books decades earlier, so maybe it's a constant complaint. So, in 1983, putting out challenging writing would be a leap of faith.

Luckily, the first of the four books arrived with credentials already gaily flying like so many lavender pennants. I'd known Karla Jay since the early days of gay liberation. A distinguished professor of English, the director of the women's studies program at Pace University, and a pioneer in the field of lesbian and gay studies, Karla began to focus her interest more closely during the early eighties on a group of pioneering lesbians from turn-of-the-century Paris. Led by American heiress Natalie Clifford Barney (soon known as "the Amazon") and including the authors Colette and Djuna Barnes, and the painter Romaine Brooks, this group of talented, often brilliant women centering around Barney's *maison* on the rue Jacob combined wealth, artistic flair, scandal, and social climbing in strange and pressworthy new combinations and themselves quickly became unquestionable tourist highlights of the City of Lights.

Among their number was an early lover—and, she soon came to believe, victim—of the gallivanting Barney: a beautiful young Anglo-American girl named Pauline Mary Tarn (1877–1909), who fell rather completely under the Amazon's Sapphic spell, and who wasted away once Barney moved on to more entertainingly exotic (and often bisexual) females. Writing only in French and under the Gallic nom de plume Renée Vivien, Tarn completed four books from 1901 to 1905, along with dozens more poems and a handful of short stories, all influenced by the poetic gods of the French late romantic and symbolist era.

Her first slender volume of verse, *Études et Preludes* (1901), was followed by a second, *The Muse of the Violets* (1902), then a third, *Venus at the*

Blind (1903), all three thrown into the shade of her "scandalous" openly proto-feminist and quite Sapphic autobiographical novel, *A Woman Appeared to Me* (1904).

The latter had already been translated and published by Naiad in one of its rare forays into classic lit in 1976, and reissued in 1979. That book formed one of the bases of the lecture and slide show that Karla had begun in class, and added to so well and so thoroughly, with so much research of her own, including her own translations and extensive photos from various archives, that she was soon presenting her "Amazon Show" in women's and gay bookstores around the U.S. and even in France.

It was at one of the former that I was exposed to Renée Vivien, and afterward I spoke with Karla about the possibility of SeaHorse Press doing a book of the poet's work. At first Karla thought it might be an anthology, to display the Franco-American writer's range of styles and genres. But around the middle of 1982, she phoned to say she had a manuscript ready for me to look at and it consisted of Vivien's shorter fiction—seldom translated, unique, strange, symbolist, and about as "early feminist" as short stories came.

Karla titled it *The Women of the Wolf,* after the longest and most violent tale, and as my partners and I were looking for more women's work, we decided to do it through GPNy rather than SeaHorse Press. Even so, I had full editorial and production control of the project, including careful design inside and out, and I used Patrick Merla's wonderful typography, page layout, and typesetting.

Shortly after our agreement was signed, Naiad put out Vivien's *Muse of the Violets,* raising the profile of the fairly unknown writer in the U.S. But the fiction would go where even poetry couldn't, and the publication of *The Woman of the Wolf* in 1983 was both stylish and critically uplifting for the still fairly new Gay Presses of New York (we'd only put out four books at the time). Reviews soon appeared in a variety of gay and mainstream magazines and newspapers and, later on, in academic journals.

While the title was never expected to be a hit, it did sell out its printing of over three thousand and some hundred-odd copies, including the two hundred copies in the handsome burgundy hardcover library edition. It also got GPNy titles into academic and non-gay independent bookstores where we'd not been before and paved the way for the acceptance of GPNy putting out the two lesbian anthologies we ended up rescuing. It could also be said that publishing Vivien opened up more women to the possibility of publishing new work through us.

For Karla, the publication of her translation of *The Woman of the Wolf and Other Stories* was one more brick in the great wall of her achievement as an author and academic. In 1988, Indiana University Press put out *The Amazon and the Page: Natalie Clifford Barney and Renée Vivien,* her study of that group of women, and she went on to edit the anthologies *Lesbian Texts and Contexts: Radical Revisions* with Joanne Glasgow (1990), *Lesbian Erotics* (1995), *Dyke Life: From Growing Up to Growing Old, A Celebration of the Lesbian Experience* (1996), and a revision of her 1978 anthology *Lavender Culture* in 1994.

All this, however, was capped by her terrific and searingly candid "memoir of liberation," *Tales of the Lavender Menace* (1999), one of the few, and one of the best, on-the-line-as-it-happened autobiographies of the early days of gay and women's liberation and the always uneasy relations between them.

For the founders of GPNy, Renée Vivien's book came as a opening confirmation of what I already suspected: that literature—even if it was eighty years old and written by someone we'd never heard of before—would pay the bills and provide different levels of gratification. This lesson would soon be tested as never before.

———

If it seems that I gave up Karla and Vivien's work to my GPNy partnership awfully easily, in one sense it was because, just as we were negotiating the

.ghts to the translations, I got another offer I couldn't refuse. The play-wright's name was Alan Bowne and I'd already seen two of his plays during the seventies, either because I knew someone in the cast or because someone had insisted I see it and had brought me.

A Snake In the Vein and *Sharon and Billy* were unique as anything being done during a period that in retrospect seems like the last totally creative, hal-cyon era of an American theater forever destroyed by AIDS, all its astounding promise left unfulfilled. Decades later one can look back and see the year 1985 as the turning point. Before that, new American dramatic writing was sky-rockets everywhere, dozens of playwrights like Bowne, Jane Chambers, and Robert Chesley, not to mention GLBT directors, actors, producers, stage man-agers, and even box office managers helping elevate it higher and higher. And after 1995, with most of them dead, serious and commercial American theater seems to consist of little but revivals, Tony Kushner, and endless Andrew Lloyd Webber productions.

There was nothing ordinary about Bowne. A Warhol Factory bad boy from the same era as Jean-Michel Basquiat, Keith Haring, Gilbert and George, and the clubs Underground and Tunnel, Bowne had something of the hustler about him almost equal to that of Robert Mapplethorpe, and like Map-plethorpe, he had talent to burn. The authentically seedy background of Bowne's plays were more than simply something to give them color. Bowne knew that life intimately. No wonder Factory-sanctioned director Paul Mor-rissey decided to use Bowne to carve out scripts for films like *Mixed Blood* (1985), *Spike of Bensonhurst* (1988), and the posthumous TV film *Daybreak* (1993), which was based on Bowne's play *Beirut*.

Unlike most of the hangers-on at the Factory, Bowne had actually been exactly where he set his plays: he had lived the life, walked the walk, and talked the talk. And what talk it was! When *Forty-Deuce* landed on my desk and I began reading, I felt like I'd fallen into some gloriously degenerate rabbit hole filled with lowlifes way below Gorky's, speaking a Marlovian language miles beyond what David Mamet had overwritten in *Glengarry Glen Ross*. Bowne's new play, set in real time, two hours, in a crap-filled hotel room used by a trio of male teenage prostitutes above Forty-second Street ("Forty-Deuce" or simply "The Deuce") grabs you by the collar and holds on until its done delineating several picturesque circles of hell. A child hooker is called "the Fetus." People refer to each other endearingly as, "You stupid testicle!" And what goes down plotwise is equally harrowing.

Included along with this incredible script were a dozen stills taken from the movie that Bowne and Morrissey had independently made out of it, starring the young and half-nude-most-of-the-time Kevin Bacon as the main operator, corruptor, and eventual victim—with a brilliant Orson Bean as the middle-age suburban john they're trying to frame for murder and shake down for money. The reason I wrote stills was because, as Bowne wrote me in his cover letter, the film was already edited, cut, in the can, and waiting for release.

Well, it never was released that I am aware of. Bacon was cast as the male ingenue in the film *Footloose* and someone at the studio must have made sure *Forty-Deuce* wouldn't get out and jeopardize his career. As dozens of flicks and memorable roles from *Diner* to *Invisible Man* have proven, said producer was totally out of his gourd. Sexy as he is, Kevin Bacon is not a male ingenue—he's an extraordinary character actor.

However, we had the photos for the book, and the author said sure, go ahead and use them in the art, on the cover, splash them everywhere. Who knew? Maybe doing so would force someone's hand to release the picture.

The SeaHorse Press edition of *Forty-Deuce* came out in late 1983, and even though I tried like mad to get the author away from his hippie haven in Marin county, where he assured me he'd gone to "dry out once and for all from all of it," we had to have a book party without him at Drama Books in midtown Manhattan. It was a ragtag if fun group, with Factory and off-off-Broadway theater folk stumbling in at all hours. But neither Bowne nor Bacon (who *was* in town) showed up.

The book sold well, mostly through theater bookstores and mail order. Neither Kevin Bacon nor his high-powered agency ever did a thing to stop the

₀ok, despite our widespread use of the actor's face and figure on and inside the book, and in advertising—a little provocatively, too, I fully admit, as I would have welcomed the publicity that might accrue had they sued.

Two years later, Bowne hit the big time. *Beirut,* his fourth produced play, at the West Side Arts Theater in New York, was about a future world in which AIDS was so pervasive that entire cities like New York were turned into "infected zones" like concentration camps. In the play, a typically Alan Bowne nasty, brutish, and short send-up of *Romeo and Juliet,* a pair of straight young lovers are reunited for one night, when the HIV negative girlfriend breaks into the hot zone to see her positive guy.

The play was a sensation and brought Alan fame, some money, and new productions for his previous plays. It also got several of his film collaborations with Morrissey filmed and others released—but not *Forty-Deuce.* And when he and I spoke on the phone a few days after the premiere, I found a way to ask him when he had seroconverted. Knowing that I'd guessed his status from seeing his newest play, Alan told me he'd gotten the bad news on the publication day of our *Forty-Deuce.*

After *Forty-Deuce,* I would be involved in publishing two more collections of plays. For Calamus Press, I art directed the cover and interior of Victor Bumbalo's first book, *Niagara Falls and Other Plays* (1984). Larry Mitchell was the publisher, but I'd known Victor for years, as a playwright whose works I'd seen staged, as well as a close friend of George Whitmore. I can't remember which one of the two contacted me about the book, but neither one had any idea how to make it stand out visually.

As Victor's strongest plays of the time (*Niagara Falls, Kitchen Duty,* and *After Eleven*) dealt with Italian-American life in Buffalo, New York, I decided it would be fun to "telegraph" this fact visually by literally making the cover into two flags. An American one, of course, with it's little box of white stars in the upper left, and florid red and white stripes. But instead of being against blue, the stars would be in a field of green, i.e. repeating the colors of the Italian flag; in effect showing how woven together the two were—that usually being the "problem" of Bumbalo's early plays. The type on the cover would also be in those same three colors.

The next drama book I helped publish through GPNy *Best Plays of Albert Innaurato* (1987), came via Terry Helbing, by then unable to do it himself because of his accident. Innaurato's *The Transfiguration of Benno Blimpie* and *Urlicht* had made him one of off-Broadway's leading lights. Then in 1976, his comedy *Gemini* hit, and hit hard. A year after it had moved to Broadway it was being advertised on local television every night. Albert, a modest, funny, and by his own admission "overweight opera queen" (check out his terrific 1988 play about opera divas, *Magda and Callas*) didn't let success change his lifestyle one bit. He remained living in his Midtown "Dance Belt" basement, and kept all his old friends. But he *was* surprised when no one picked up his plays for publication. Larry and I had seen his newest comedy, *Coming of Age in SoHo* (1984), and thought it his strongest work, and that, *Gemini,* and *Benno Blimpie* became the three we opted to publish in a single volume.

As with all plays, there were minor hassles: getting a still from the latest play in color on the book's cover took several days, and included injunctions on its use tougher than the CIA might specify. And with my attention so divided by this point by people sick, dying, and dead all around me, increasingly requiring me to take on others' workloads, I was seriously overburdened. No wonder then that a half page of Innaurato's intro to the book was repeated verbatim, and I never caught the layout error when proofing it. Although the book came out and looked great, I don't think Albert ever forgave me for this startling, horrible, inexcusable blooper.

Shortly thereafter, in 1989, Alan Bowne died in Petaluma, California, at the age of forty-five. What would he have written if he'd lived another two decades? As with Chambers, Chesley, and so many others, we'll never know.

———

I'd been hearing about the new narrative and language writing through some of the younger writers around at the time, especially Tim Dlugos and Chris Cox. I'd enjoyed Robert Glück's updated translations of Jean de La Fontaine's sixteenth-century *fabilaux* (*La Fontaine*, 1980) and while out West I'd even somehow happened upon copy of Glück's book of stories, *Elements of a Coffee Service* (1983), although I didn't fully appreciate it at that time. So when Chris Cox mentioned that he heard Glück was writing a novel that would be "*the* new narrative" novel, I told him to have Robert contact me when he was done. But before I'd heard from Glück, I read an early chapter in a quarterly magazine and found it both playful, referentially amusing, and intriguing. So we contacted each other at around the same time.

Robert had just ended a three-pronged love affair and gotten a job teaching fiction writing at San Francisco Community College. He decided he needed to get the book done and out. "If you like it," he said of the manuscript, "you can publish it."

He sent it, I read it, and I liked it.

Set in the early 1980s, *Jack the Modernist,* has since become a classic of postmodern gay fiction. The "plot" is simple. Bob is excited and lonely. He meets and pursues the elusive Jack, a director who claims to be able "to transform others without altering himself." Bob goes to the baths, gossips on the phone, goes to a bar, and thinks about werewolves, Japanese foxes, pornography—among other topics he touches upon. A paean to love and obsession, Glück's novel explores the daily in love and life in a new way. Robert Glück himself has written of it:

> My work can be seen as an elaboration of the old feminist maxim, "the personal is political," with a great deal of pressure applied to both terms, so that the equal sign between them breaks down. On the one hand my work explores how we exist in language, in our bodies, and in our societies, and on the other hand it explores moral life and the ways we assign meanings to experience, from gossip to the largest

political structures. I am an autobiographer, and I think that any life, intensely examined, can reveal a whole society, in the same way that a dinosaur femur, properly studied, can suggest the whole animal.

After I'd accepted the book and we agreed on a contract, that's when the real negotiations began. Like Clark Henley and Howard Cruse, Robert kept close control over his work. He wasn't nitpicky or obsessive like the latter, nor vague and obstructionist like the former—instead Glück definitely knew what he wanted and tried to ensure that his first novel was published exactly as he'd envisioned it.

He brought me the cover art, which I liked, and since I had no ideas of my own for a cover, I accepted his suggestion. Meanwhile, he accepted my choice of cover design and type around that art. But *Jack* also came with its own set of artistic and visual clues that had to be included *inside,* and these proved to be more troublesome.

At first Robert wanted color photos. (In a paperback! From a small press!) He settled for black and whites, but he wanted them placed precisely in the text. That couldn't always work out, because until the book was actually typeset and laid out, there was no saying *where* on the page any particular illustration or photo done at the precise size he wished would or could fit. What if the reference happened at the end of the page with two lines left? What then? We couldn't fit a four-inch-high illustration into two lines, could we? And since the text was continuous, it would have looked terrible to leave a space.

This series of potential nightmares was defused early on, when I went ahead with as early typesetting and page layout dates as was financially feasible so we could work out those pesky art problems. This took weeks, many phone calls, and compromises on both sides. Once that was done, and the book met both our satisfaction, another problem surfaced. One of the pictures Glück wanted in the book was a photo of a naked young man with a substantial erection. All the rest of the illustrations were art: Japanese woodcuts, old masters from famous museums, a few movie stills. Even so, my printer's representative, Alvin Greenberg, was adamant: we couldn't possibly take the book to our regular printer and bindery. It would have to go to another one, one that didn't care if a nine-inch boner graced the pages of the books it produced. But that meant a higher per-unit cost for me.

At long last the book was done and sent off. Then we began butting heads on the matter of reviews.

The situation in a nutshell was as follows: Glück was already a literary star in the Bay Area. He also knew how remarkable this novel was—so he naturally enough wanted to ensure that it would be sent to important people on the East Coast. Fair enough. So I called in virtually all the literary favors owed to me and stretched barely existing relationships with people I barely knew at places like the *New York Times,* the *New Yorker,* and worst of all, the *Village Voice.*

Nevertheless, Robert was nervous to the point of panic. Did so-and-so get a copy? he called to find out. Did so-and-so? In fact, in order to keep Robert from calling yet again, begging and despairing, I hand-delivered, during a snowstorm, a copy of *Jack* to the office of the *Village Voice.* This was a blizzard so intense that traffic soon stopped, all taxis, it should go without saying, this being New York City, vanished into thin air, and all subways and buses stopped and the editor and staff—no fools—had already gone home long before. I had to walk back home, across all of lower Manhattan, in said blizzard, and ended up in bed sick for a week afterward.

Sadly, not one of those places ever reviewed the novel. On the other hand, it was reviewed by every paper, magazine, and bar rag in the Bay Area and its environs. After a good two-year sell-through, I could with no trouble at all inform the author that some 73 percent of his book had sold within fifty miles of his home on Clipper Street. Glück, of course, was deeply frustrated by this news. And who could blame him?

Jack was reprinted by Serpent's Tail, which two years later also put out his new novel, the far stranger *Margery Kempe,* based on the life of a fifteenth-century German mystic. Glück is a slow writer and it was a decade between that book and his latest, *The Denny Smith Stories* (2004), which includes some of his best writing ever. But as with other language writers of fiction—especially Sam D'Allesandro, Dodie Bellamy, and Kevin Killian, all of whom I consider to be wonderfully talented, the new narrative is an acquired taste. They're equal in intelligence and originality to authors like Dennis Cooper and Kathy Acker, without their titillation or ferocity factor, and in the end, far more satisfying. I recommend *The Wild Creatures* (2005) a recently issued collection of D'Allesandro's stories edited by Killian, Bellamy's *The Letters of Mina Harker* (2004), and Killian's *Shy* (1989) and *Little Men* (1996)—and of course, Glück's *Jack the Modernist*.

———

Several years after we had worked with Karla Jay, another translator brought me another French author. Michael Whistler was tall and slender, soft spoken with a rumpled-angel mien. He was about my age and had lived in the suburbs of Paris for a decade. He then moved to Bloomington, Indiana, where he'd been working for the Kinsey Institute, still continuing its liberating mission even though the good doctor was now dead.

I don't know exactly how Whistler got in touch with me. He may have looked me up in the phone book. Or Edmund White may have been involved. A year earlier I had dinner with Edmund and his very handsome French boy friend named Gilles Barbedette. Gilles had appeared on the intellectual TV talk show *Apostrophes* and hobnobbed with trendy French *philosophes* like Michel Foucault and Jacques Derrida, and—more importantly to me because we subsequently had a brief, admiration-society correspondence—with gay French novelist Michel Tournier. And of course, Guy Hocquenghem.

In 1972, high-toned Parisian publisher Albin Michel put out a book titled *Homosexual Desire*. It's opening line was "The problem is not homosexuality. It is homosexual desire in others." The book went on to outline, then to detail, this astounding and controversial topic. The author was a young Frenchman named Guy Hocquenghem. It was Australian activist/writer Dennis Altman, I believe, who first brought the book to my attention, and I was slogging through the French when a translation came out in 1980. It was outrageous. It was delicious. It was above all, an unerringly on-target examination of how heterosexuals dealing with their own occasional, utterly unexpected, homosexual desires, had come to categorize homosexuality and then declare it a disease.

Guy was of that generation of French intellectuals who'd come to the fore after the *manifestations* of 1968, the student riots in Paris that had torn up the cobblestones of the *rive gauche* and soon after, the entrenched institutions of France, especially within academia. Along with feminist Monique Wittig, Roland Barthes, Foucault, and others, Guy had galvanized a loose coalition of students around what the French adore as much as food and wine: philosophy.

Hocquenghem put out amazing articles in the most distinguished journals of psychology and philosophy on any number of subjects—not one of which he couldn't find a radical, sometimes truly outré point of view to defend. By 1977, Guy was an openly gay—and rather glamorous—star of the French Left, when he released his documentary film, *Le Race d'Ep!*, which would later be released in the U.S. as *100 Years of Homosexual Imagery in Film*. In doing the film, he joined the ranks of other openly gay directors of the time, such as Germany's Rosa von Praunheim and Rainer Werner Fassbinder, in the process tripling his own glamour quotient, at least in Europe.

But Hocquenghem was also writing novels. And because they were informed by his wide ranging intelligence and his innate talent, they too were good. Albin Michel published *L'Amour en Relief* in 1980. It tells the story of a blind North African boy of great beauty, Amar, who is brought to Paris by tourists. Amar is taken to southern California by a brilliant American who is slowly going mad and who uses the young man in a variety of increasingly bizarre experiments, ending in Amar not only become all-seeing, but also quite literally a "transmitter" of images to millions of others.

SeaHorse being a small press, I was limited in what I could offer to Guy and his translator. But clever Whistler (note this, you aspiring translators) made the latter easy for me. He'd already begun the translation on his own, and told me that he and SeaHorse Press could apply to the appropriate bureau in the French government, and the press would be able to recoup half of the translator's fee—in other words, make it worth Michael's while. It sounded like a good plan, and soon four-way contracts (with Guy, Michel Albin, Michael Whistler, and me) were mailed out.

Whistler had just had to stop work on the book and concentrate on earning money when the French *cheque* arrived. It was sent off to him in Bloomington, and his work went on.

When I received the manuscript, I'd just gotten an autographed copy of the original from Guy himself. I began to read and found myself increasingly forced to read both texts, one against the other. Hocquenghem's language in his nonfiction can be quite technical, even jargonesque, close, dense, and detailed. For someone with only college and newspaper French reading experience, like myself, it's really too much work. The language of his novel, on the other hand, was clean, clear, and fairly unambiguous. So after perusing several chapters of both original and translation it became evident to me that faithful Whistler had translated *from* the French, but not completely *into* the English. Or at least not into *American* English.

I girded my editorial loins and phoned Guy in Paris. I told him the situation. He spoke English well, and we only fell into French once or twice during our talks and then usually only for clarification. He understood the problem I outlined and he gave me carte-blanche, in fact he sort of urged me to "translate over" Michael's work wherever needed so that it sounded as clear as the Voltairean original text—especially, he enjoined me, in the American sections of the book, where the language became almost translucent.

When I mentioned that some of Whistler's terminology was British, not

American, Guy was clear. "Use *subway,* not *metro* or *underground.* Make it as American as possible."

Naturally, my conversation on this matter with Whistler was a lot more circumspect. But what Guy wanted he wanted too, I'll grant Whistler that.

There were also a few factual bloopers in the original that needed correcting. Guy had been to California once, a decade earlier, he said, and he told me that he'd received "a kaleidoscope of impressions." But several facts were downright off. For example, he had his protagonist, Amar, commuting from West Hollywood to Sea World in San Diego daily—by hitchhiking. I pointed out there was no way Amar could make that two-and-a-half-hour trip daily, especially when hitching would double the time.

"Then fix it," Guy said.

I suggested the Long Beach Aquarium instead of Sea World, only forty-five minutes away.

"Good! Use Long Beach instead!"

In the end, the translation was a three-way collaboration. Guy wrote it. Whistler did the translation. I Americanized that and filled in all the gaps.

The result was not the concrete elephant that usually comes out when a committee attempts to make art, but instead a beautiful and unique novel in English. *Love in Relief* was published by SeaHorse Press in the spring of 1988. I airmailed copies—with its mysterious, dark, eye-catching cover art—to Guy, and he was thrilled.

By 1989, I'd been a publisher twelve years and so *Publishers Weekly,* which prides itself on being the book industry's journal, and which had ignored most SeaHorse Press titles, and stinted on those few GPNy titles it reviewed, did come around for Guy's books. With the following result:

Hocquenghem attempts to incorporate eroticism, adventure, science fiction and symbolism into a book about the prejudices and false values of contemporary society. However, the attempt fails, perhaps because the goal is so lofty, but also because the reader fails to feel compassion for the protagonist, Amar, the excruciatingly handsome and blind Arab boy, and the only character able to "see" beyond superficialities. Thus it is difficult to sympathize with him as he prostitutes himself, surfs and dances professionally, prostitutes himself some more, smuggles heroin, goes to prison and becomes a guinea pig in an experiment that transforms him into a human radio receiver able to pick up Soviet signals. Amar's symbolic demise, crucifixion on a radio antenna, serves as the only relief in this story.

Most reviewers felt differently; they identified with Amar and his strange history. The book got mostly good reviews and sold solidly. Hocquenghem published three more novels, and he sent me *La colère de l'agneau* (1986), *Eve* (1987), and *Les voyages et aventures extraordinaires du frère Angelo* (1988). These are strong, often delightful books. But by then, I was too much at war with AIDS among those closest to myself to be able to offer to publish English translations, and no one else has, either—a pity.

12

Epilogue in California

The month of March had always been significant for GPNy and 1994 was no different. On March 8 of that year, Terry Helbing died.

The last three years of his life had been extremely difficult. Terry had gone from healthy one day to a fall victim the next, although we never knew the details of how he'd fallen. As the person who held his health insurance, I was welcomed into the intensive care ward. He lay in a coma for months. A support group formed around him, with Rachel Green at its head. Once Terry came out of the coma, his recovery took years. He had to relearn how to speak, how to walk—almost everything. He had speech and vision problems until the end of his life. One of the surprises I'd gotten when locating him at St. Vincent's hospital was that he also had the AIDS virus. No sooner was Terry on his feet again, acting in plays and beginning to work in other ways, then HIV-related opportunistic disease symptoms began. He lasted another two years. I was involved in his recovery, illness, and last months. It is an amazing story, especially how valuable his—mostly women—friends were to him. He was very beloved.

Following his memorial service, Terry's college friend and longtime helpmate, and Rachel Green, his executor, informed me that I was one of his six heirs. A few minutes later, Francine Trevens approached me. She had worked with

Terry at Meridian Gay Theater, directing the production of my play, *One O'clock Jump,* when it was paired there with *Killer Bangs.* Francine already knew from Rachel that I had inherited JH Press from Terry. She didn't know what my plans were for it. If, however, I didn't want to continue to operate it, she was interested in obtaining rights for most of the plays already published. She and a friend were beginning a GLBT play production/publication company. She was especially anxious to obtain Jane Chambers's and Doric Wilson's works.

It turned out I inherited not only JH Press, but also a small sum of cash. I did sell Francine the plays and rights she wanted, for not much money, and in addition, the rights to the Doric Wilson plays SeaHorse owned. It had been three years since SeaHorse Press had put out a book. We had fewer than one hundred copies of most of our titles—in some cases, we were down to a dozen. My other partner, Larry Mitchell, was now legally blind. He'd stopped writing. He'd even stopped talking about his Calamus Press putting out his friend Jeff Weiss's trilogy of plays, an ongoing dream for a decade. It wasn't too difficult to see the writing on the wall.

Within days, I decided to close down SeaHorse Press as well. Coolly enough, I wrote official letters to any author who still had titles with SeaHorse Press, ceding back their publication rights to them. I offered to sell them whatever copies were still in the warehouse at a very deep discount. I then began a book tour of Germany for the twelfth anniversary of *The Lure* there, out in a brand new translation. When I returned a few weeks later, I wrote the same letter to GPNy authors, reverting rights back to them. I then moved to Berlin, Germany, for the summer of 1994.

My days as a publisher were over. Among GPNy authors and friends, so many were dead: Jane Chambers, Terry Helbing, Bob Chesley, Alan Bowne, Clark Henley, David Martin, George Stavrinos, George Stambolian, Robert Mapplethorpe, Terry Miller, Mark Ameen, Greg Kolovakos, and Violet Quill Club members Christopher Cox, Robert Ferro, Michael Grumley, and George Whitmore, just to mention those I'd worked with at the presses. There were scores more among my social group, and more were dying daily.

In the years to come, I did not look back, I did not think about it, I did not contemplate what it had been, nor what it could have become. Not once.

I'd been living in California for more than three years when the idea of reviving the last, never-finished GPNy project once more arose.

Sasha Alyson had sold his Alyson Press to Liberation Publications Inc., publishers of *The Advocate* and *Advocate Men,* it's glossy semiporn magazine. Only Sasha and those around him could say if he received the million dollars he'd earlier asked of Bill Shinker, then publisher of HarperCollins Books. But at least he received *something,* compared to Gay Presses of New York, which received little more than complaints from authors ("What do I do with this book now?")—and an equal number of thank-yous from all its vendors and printers, whom I'd managed to pay off when I closed the doors.

With one major vendor, the Distributors Inc. of West Haven, Connecticut, going down the tubes fast, we found ourselves out another $8,000. By now I could see the writing before it was on the wall, and had begun demanding returns of quantities of books from everyone whenever unpaid statements began to reach the ninety-day unpaid mark. So we did manage to get some of those unsold books back. We donated more than one hundred books to the new Pat Parker/Vito Russo Center Library at the New York Gay and Lesbian Community Center. The Center sold many to raise money for the library. Some of the books we still had out in stores continued to sell, and cash continued to dribble into GPNy's bank account in small amounts long after we disbanded. Until, that is, the IRS decided to put a stop to that minuscule income.

Through the new accountant Terry had brought in, I had filed the final year of taxes for SeaHorse Press, and GPNy, and then as heir to Terry's JH Press, for that company, too. I'd paid all the necessary federal taxes—a basic corporation tax fee of about $1,000 a year for GPNy—and then filed the official disincorporation papers for GPNy which Larry and I, as the remaining partners, needed to sign.

I kept the GPNy post office box open only to collect the money still filtering in; small checks would come in from stores paying late and those distributors still handling our titles. That was the situation a year after I officially disincorporated, when I received a tax notice saying GPNy owed some astronomical tax figure based on someone's fantasy for the recent year, based on who knew what drug-fueled idea—during which, please recall, the company had been closed. I enclosed another photocopy of the disincorporation papers and the final tax year's filing papers and figured that would be that.

Alas not. Six months later, just before I closed the post office box forever as well as the storage space where we held remaining inventory, I received the same exact ridiculous tax notice for GPNy. This one I sent back marked "addressee unknown." I permanently closed the post office box, in effect totally shutting down the presses forever.

Several years later, while speaking on the phone with Larry Mitchell, he told me that the IRS had continued to hound our previous accountant, whom Larry still used personally and for Calamus Press, and that it had somehow decided to garnish whatever money trickled in to GPNy. I had written it off, simply reassigning it to Larry to collect. As it couldn't have amounted to more than a few hundred dollars, Larry let them have it. Getting *all that money* must have made some jerk IRS investigator happy: he'd managed to illegally get his hands on what was owed to us, and not to the federal government. Larry and I laughed over the assholism of this maneuver, which had confirmed both of our long-held beliefs in the basic stupidity, greed, and fundamental evilness of the U.S. government and those who have sold their souls to work for it.

Liberation Publications soon discovered the purchase of Alyson Press came with a very small backlist. When Bill Shinker had gotten the call from Sasha previously, he'd asked me what their backlist was worth. When I mentioned the few books I thought might be steady sellers, Bill kept saying, "I don't know that book."

So there was the new Alyson Press, with Aaron Fricke's good if dated *Reflections of A Rock Lobster* and Stuart Timmons's evergreen biography of gay rights pioneer Harry Hay, *The Trouble with Harry,* and not a lot else that stood out.

This explains why, when Scott Brassart was hired as West Coast editor in chief, he was looking for new work, and approached me for a book. The one title that came to mind was my unpublished novella, *Looking Glass Lives.* The third time he asked I decided to tell him about the projected final GPNy title, with its substantial artwork—already paid for by me and GPNy. Scott loved Ron Fowler's artwork, Veloxes of which I brought in for him to look at. He agreed to read the manuscript, which was a photocopy of the original typescript first written on my Smith Corona Coronet electric typewriter during three and half weeks of September 1976 at my little rented cottage, 484 Tarpon Walk in Fire Island Pines. I had typed it at one end of the dining room table while Andrew Holleran typed his second novel, *Nights in Aruba,* on his manual Remington manual at the other end.

I'd revised the short novel three years later, a few weeks before I launched *The Lure* with a book tour. Earlier in 1979, I'd completed a second novella, *An Asian Minor,* but *Looking Glass Lives* was actually supposed to join two other planned novellas as part of a proposed trilogy to be titled something casual like *Love, Love is Strange* (after the hit song by Mickey and Sylvia).

I knew I wanted to write two more novellas: one about two guys falling in love when one is a grown man and the other a beautiful infant and how it is only fulfilled decades later (that became *And Baby Makes Three*) and a third story about a gay man and a young woman who fall in love and have a brief affair.

The last, *Late in the Season,* was originally titled *Summer's Lease,* from the line in Shakespeare's sonnet, "Shall I Compare Thee to a Summer's Day." I wrote it very quickly the following summer, and it was published as a separate work by Delacorte Press in June 1981. It's gone on to be one of my longest-lasting and most popular books, also published as a mass-market

Dell paperback here and in England and Germany, where it was titled *Herbst-stürme* (Autumn storm). When its mass-market version went out of print in the U.S., my partners at GPNy republished it as a trade paperback reprint of the hardcover, with artwork by George Stavrinos on the cover, and it sold another six thousand copies for us. In 1997, St. Martin's Press's Stonewall Classics reprinted *Late in the Season* again, and I penned a new afterword. It sold even better than the second time; I still get small royalty checks for it.

Baby Makes Three was the shortest of the three novellas, and it was published in my much-praised GPNy collection of short stories *Slashed to Ribbons in Defense of Love* in hardcover and trade paperback in September 1983 and later, in Alyson Press's edition of *The New York Years,* in 2000.

So there was my favorite of the three shorter books, *Looking Glass Lives,* hung out to dry without any of its companions while they were all out and being read. When I'd first written it, I naturally enough gave it to my agent, Jane Rotrosen, thinking it might be a good follow-up to *The Lure.* But Jane thought a plot fueled by the conceit of reincarnation was too far-out, too philosophical, and too new age, and much too intellectually challenging to be marketed well—by which she meant, I later assumed, it was too intellectually challenging for her to sell for a large amount of money to a publisher like Delacorte/Dell.

At the time I reluctantly acquiesced, not recognizing that this was the beginning of a crucial creative division between Jane and me that would only come to a head more than a decade later. In 1994, she found she couldn't even read *Dryland's End* and she didn't "get" *Like People In History* at all, books many readers consider to be fiction masterpieces. She was subsequently amazed when the latter turned into a best seller for Viking/Penguin here and even more so for Little, Brown/Abacus in England. I naturally felt that I knew how good both of those books were and even more important, how crucial they were to my *oeuvre* (sounds pretentious, yet is true) and eventually to my reputation. And so in the early nineties I felt forced to leave Jane's agency and take those two books elsewhere. But back in 1979, I still had plenty of other things going on and I still believed that Jane and I were in sync about my writing career, so I simply put *Looking Glass Lives* in a drawer and pretty much forgot about it.

In the years in between, I'd not completely forgotten *Looking Glass Lives;* after all, I had mentioned it to David Martin as a possible second illustrated book project. In 1988, while rummaging through my papers, I came across it again, read it in two sittings, and decided that it held up well. I gave it to Larry Mitchell to read.

He agreed it was well written, and philosophically interesting, too, with its theme of a contemporary reincarnated love triangle begun during the Civil War era. Who knows which—Larry or Jane—might have been right at the time. Almost twenty years after I'd first written the book, no one had any problem with it's allegedly challenging ideas, or far-out philosophies. And while some readers were surprised—mostly because the book wasn't particularly gay-themed—the reviews were quite good, in some cases excellent, even if they didn't really stretch much past the GLBT media.

That reading from Larry set in motion *Looking Glass Lives*'s first publication process—it would take several years for Ron Fowler to eventually illustrate the stories. They remain probably the best sustained set of his pen-and-ink work he ever did, and among the best drawn for any book of mine. Oddly enough, he didn't finish illustrating the book until we were out of business.

I was comfortable with Ron Fowler long before I approached him to begin the project. I ended up signing him up for six single-page drawings, four double pages, a full-cover color and, at his request, ceding to him the complete interior design of the book, including typeface and any ornamental art. The project was initiated through SeaHorse Press, but I eventually laid out about $2,500 for the art over the years, less than half of which was being paid back by GPNy (partly because of the new financial hassles due to Terry Helbing's accident and recovery). I approved the art as it slowly came in, sometimes very slowly, with each single drawing or double-spread that arrived from Ron's studio a revelation.

Once Ron had done the cover art—an astounding rainbow-colored snake biting its own tail—he and I agreed that symbol should become the sigil of the book. It appeared in every redone drawing—subtly, as a knot in the background woodwork, as carriage tracks in the snow, or as a new shadow over the face of a just-seduced woman. But at other times it stood out, like when it was carved into a sepulcher or appeared as a distorted tree branch.

———

Ron Fowler's book cover for *Looking Glass Lives* (full size in its original painted version), never used on the Alyson reprint, along with all the various pieces of artwork, from the page proofs to the single and double Veloxes used to reprint the book, appeared at last—in a blaze of glory—in an exhibition titled "Early Gay Presses of New York." I put it together in the fall of 2001 for the opening of the new art gallery at ONE, the National Gay Archives, on the University of Southern California's campus in downtown Los Angeles.

This came about through a man named Michael Magedman. He was visiting from San Diego, staying in my in my loft bed in my little house high in the Hollywood Hills, and thus went to sleep and awakened surrounded by various posters from SeaHorse Press and GPNy that I'd put up there. Although I'd lived in Los Angeles for three years, it wasn't until I got to the North Crescent Heights house that I finally had room to open up some of the many boxes of stuff I'd driven cross-country in a twenty-two-foot U-Haul in 1997, much of which I'd not seen in several years, most of which had remained in Susan Moldow and Bill Shinker's basement in their summer place in Guildford. Among the books, LPs, and other stuff, I found dead snakes and huge, dried-out spiders.

Magedman was a librarian and budding archivist and it was he who told me that I had a historical archive of some importance in hand and that I had a responsibility to get it exhibited and archived where interested parties might access it. If Magedman was the first, old pals and colleagues Mark Thompson and Stuart Timmons were instrumental in getting the work to ONE and helped me get it up on the walls. They also suggested that I come speak about it.

That show and the history of our presses that the exhibit told was so successful it was picked up by the San Francisco Public Library's James C. Hormel Gay and Lesbian Center, where it was shown the following spring. It had even larger show at the Elmer L. Andersen Library at the University of Minnesota, sponsored by the Tretter Collection in GLBT Studies, in the fall of 2003.

At each of the three venues, the exhibit consisted of manuscripts, letters, contracts, and many different kinds of artwork, including interior illustrations, book covers, photos, collages, and posters—and other memorabilia that I'd collected over the years from and about the presses. At each venue, I attended the opening of the exhibit and gave a talk. What began at ONE with an informal if highly informative walk through the gallery developed by the second show into a formal lecture, delivered in front of a seated audience.

Those lectures and talks and the exhibits evoked many questions from reporters, scholars, writers, readers, and viewers. They had many more—and more detailed—questions than I could really answer without giving day-long elaborations.

I wrote this book to answer them, to set the record straight, and to tell what my long and generally excellent memory holds. I also found that I had to do research. In doing so, I once again contacted people from that era who were still alive, and interviewed them. They are thanked on an earlier page. I also began doing research into people I'd worked with, from those I thought I knew well, like Terry Helbing, to those I met once, like Alan Bowne. In that process, I realized I knew far less about any of them than I'd thought. Some are very well represented on the Internet; others, far less so.

I had no idea when I began writing what I expected to come up with. I'd put SeaHorse and GPNy out of my mind because it was connected to that terrible time of the deaths of so many friends, my family, and my soul mate. After having only once heard Gwyn Thomas's quote about World War I, I've never forgotten it, it proved so relevant to my life: "We have walked through the corridors of death and have arrived at an almost unwanted survival," he wrote, and added. "We are betrayed by destinations." Like Thomas I'd stopped looking for destinations—or anything else solid in my life, already long-betrayed by all and everything.

So I was surprised by what and how much I did discover during the process of researching and writing this book. I found myself missing some of the people I wrote about terribly, even crying over their loss. But with others, I didn't.

Today, what stands out above all is how well my partners and I succeeded in our goal: we produced fine and accessible literature for gays and lesbians, as we'd intended, becoming totally embedded in that time and culture in the process. We also produced several literary gems. We launched a score of careers still going strong, and others that went as far as they could, or that ended prematurely in death.

Those years of the SeaHorse Press and the Gay Presses of New York turned out to be a foundational time in GLBT history, and in retrospect, now that so very many people connected with our work are dead, an astonishingly rich time in terms of books, plays, poetry, and of course, personalities. Because of who I was and when and where I "flourished," as academics write, I was privileged to come into contact with a previous generation of gay writers— Williams, Capote, Vidal, Auden, Isherwood; those of my own generation— White, Holleran, Larry Kramer, Armistead Maupin, et al.; and then several future generations, too. My phone book reads like a gay who's who.

I think that all artists believe that they are at the very center of "what is happening." But it turned out that we were truly in the middle of what can now be seen as an iridescently brilliant and lightning-brief period, a modern Renaissance of new gay and lesbian poetry, fiction, nonfiction, art, film, theater, photography, and theater: a landmark period in our GLBT cultural history.

In his introductory essay to *Loss within Loss,* the marvelous, unsung anthology he edited, Edmund White writes:

The history of the gay arts scene in New York and San Francisco during the seventies and eighties has yet to be written, though any history must now take into account the following essays. It was a period and a movement as vital and influential as any other artistic moment in postwar America and one of the few that was both a social and artistic phenomenon. It was a time of interlocking love affairs and friendships, of a slowly emerging sexual identity, a time when gay bookshops were thriving community centers (instead of declining and disappearing porn dispensers as they are at the dawn of the twenty-first century). It was a time when intellect and accomplishment were almost as prized as physical beauty, when certain hot writers, painters, and filmmakers would cause a stir when they entered a bar or gay restaurant, when gay writers didn't yet teach on remote campuses (no university wanted them), when they lived in Manhattan where they supported themselves as advertising copywriters, as gallery employees, as magazine and book editors (even editors of porn magazines), as fashion models or actors—or with welfare and unemployment benefits they'd somehow scammed. They seldom came from artistic or intellectual backgrounds but these gay artists were sophisticated men with their ears to the ground, alert to signal events in all the arts.

I hope that what I've written has added a bit more to this aching gap in our history. I feel greatly privileged to have been a part of it all.